My Daily
Scriptures

A Day by Day Bible Reading Guide

Anthony Ordille

My Daily Scriptures: A Day by Day Bible Reading Guide
Copyright © 2021 by Anthony Ordille. All rights reserved.

www.anthonyordille.com

Cover background provided by Sky Background 2724061 © Anatoliy Terebenin Dreamstime.com
Author photography by Sam Jackson
Book Layout © 2017 BookDesignTemplates.com

Published in the United States of America

ISBN: 978-0-99962-777-8 (Paperback)
ISBN: 978-0-99962-778-5 (eBook)

Religion / Christian Ministry/Devotionals
Christian Books & Bibles/Bible Study & Reference/Guides

CONTENTS

Short History of the Bible

The Christian Bible comprises 66 books: 39 Old Testament and 27 New Testament. The Roman Catholic Bibles have 73 books: 46 Old Testament and 27 New Testament.[1] The Jewish Bible comprises 24 books because they combine Samuel, Kings, Chronicles, Ezra with Nehemiah, and the minor prophets in one book called "The Twelve." Even though they are numbered differently, they are the same Scriptures.[2]

In the Christian Bible, there are 1,189 chapters and 31,102 verses. However, the number of verses will vary with the different Bible editions, religious beliefs, and word count. The longest chapter is Psalms 119. The shortest chapter is Psalms 117. The middle verse is Psalms 118:8. And the shortest verse is John 11:35.

The Bible is a collection of books that make up one story, pointing to Jesus Christ, the Messiah. The Bible takes its name from the Latin word *Biblia ('book' or 'books')*, which comes from the Greek *Ta Biblia* ('the books') traced to the Phoenician port city of Gebal, known as Byblos to the Greeks.[3] Approximately 40 authors on three continents and from three languages over 1600 years, 1450 BC to 95 AD, make up this major love story.

It is divided into two sections: Old Testament (OT) and New Testament (NT). Both point to the prophecy of Jesus, the Life of Jesus, and direction for all mankind. The Jewish Bible is only the Old Testament because they are still waiting for the Messiah to come. There are 400 years between Malachi (OT) and Matthew (NT).

It is imperative to understand that even though individuals wrote the Bible, the coalition of the books was chosen by the Divine Spirit of God.

The Bible translated languages mainly from Hebrew to Greek, and Catholic Church translated it to Latin. John Wycliffe translated it into English in about 1382 AD, and King James translated his New King James (NKJ) version in 1611. Currently, there are over 50 English versions of the Bible.

The Hebrew Bible, Old Testament, is called Tanakh. It is three sections, Torah, Nevi'im, and Ketuvim.[4]

1) *Torah* is the first five books that are instructions/ teachings. Also, the Book is known as the "Law of Moses" or "Five Books of Moses."

2) *Nevi'im* is the "Prophets," which comprises eight books that describe the history of Judaism after the death of Moses, also known as prophecy books. Split into two, the Major Prophets and Minor Prophets.

    a. *Major Prophets:*

        i. *The former Prophets,* Joshua, Judges, Samuel, and Kings

        ii. *The latter Prophets,* Isaiah, Jeremiah, Ezekiel, and Daniel

    b. *Minor Prophets:* ('The Twelve")

        i. Hosea, Joel, Amos, Obadiah, Jonah, Micah, Nahum, Habakkuk, Zephaniah, Haggai, Zechariah, Malachi

3) *Ketuvim,* known as "Writings," comprise eleven books.

    a. Short historical story: Ruth

    b. Poetries: Psalms, Lamentations, Job, Ecclesiastes, Song of Solomon, Proverbs *c.* Historical Works: Chronicles, Ezra, Nehemiah

     d. Romantic historical tale: Esther

Song of Solomon is also referenced as "Song of Songs" or "Canticle of Canticles." Suggesting that it is the most incredible collection of songs. Song of Solomon's title indicates that King Solomon wrote them, but his name was most likely added at a later date by editors. Some scholars have unknown authors. It is focused on a courtship between a young bride and her groom.

Some authors of the Bible are disputable by today's scholars worldwide. I have researched the following to be agreeable by mostly everyone.

➢ Old Testament:

➢ The first five books of the Old Testament are Moses

➢ Joshua, Judges, Ruth, 1 Samuel, 2 Samuel, 1 Kings, and 2 Kings are unknown

➢ 1 Chronicles, 2 Chronicles, and Ezra are Ezra

➢ Nehemiah is Nehemiah

➢ Esther and Job are unknown

➢ Psalms various

➢ Proverbs, Ecclesiastes, and Song of Solomon are Solomon

➢ Isaiah is Isaiah

➢ Jeremiah and Lamentations are Jeremiah

➢ Ezekiel, Daniel, Hosea, Joel, Amos, Obadiah, Jonah, Micah, Nahum, Habakkuk, Zephaniah, Haggai, Zechariah, and Malachi by their title

➢ New Testament:

➢ Mathew, Mark, Luke, and John are known as the Gospels and are by their name

➤ Acts is a history book by Luke
➤ Romans, 1 Corinthians, 2 Corinthians, Galatians, Ephesians, Philippians, Colossians, 1 Thessalonians, 2 Thessalonians, 1 Timothy, 2 Timothy, Titus, and Philemon are letters by Apostle Paul
➤ The Book of Hebrews is a letter accredited to Paul
➤ James, Peter, 1 John, 2 John, 3 John, and Jude are letters and are by the name of each book
➤ Revelation is a Prophecy by Apostle John

As you can see, Apostle Paul is the single most author of the New Testament with 14 books.

Apostle Paul's Epistles (Letter) and Journeys

Epistles (Letters):

➤ *First* and *Second Thessalonians*—51 AD from Corinth during second missionary journey
➤ *Galatians*—53-57 AD, maybe after the second journey or in the third journey
➤ *First Corinthians*—55 AD from Ephesus during the third journey
➤ *Second Corinthians*—55 AD from Macedonia, a few months after the first letter
➤ *Romans*—57 AD from Philippi during the end of the third journey
➤ *Ephesians, Colossians, and Philemon*—60 AD from Rome during two-year imprisonment in a rented home
➤ *Philippians*—61 AD, shortly after writing Ephesians, Colossians, and Philemon from Rome during two-year imprisonment in a rented home
➤ *Hebrews*—64-65 AD from Italy while in prison

> *Titus* and *First Timothy*—63-65 AD possible from Macedonia after the first imprisonment in Rome, but not in prison
> *Second Timothy*—66-67 AD from the second imprisonment in Rome just before he dies

Missionary **Journey/Imprisonment:** (Martyred 68 AD)
> Paul at Damascus—37-40 AD
> First Missionary Journey—46-49 AD
> Second Missionary Journey—50-52 AD
> First arrested in Philippi—51 AD
> Third Missionary Journey—53-58 AD
> Second arrest, Imprisonment in Caesarea—57-59 AD
> Voyage to Rome—59-60 AD
> First Imprisonment in Rome—60-62 AD
> Second Imprisonment Journeys—66-68 AD

Deuterocanonical books
Additional Books (familiar to Catholics and Orthodox)
> Tobit, Judith, 1 Maccabees, 2 Maccabees, Book of Wisdom, Sirach, Baruch, Letter of Jeremiah, Additions to Daniel, Additions to Esther

Greek & Slavonic Orthodox
> 1 Esdras, 3 Maccabees, Psalm 151, Prayer of Manasseh

Georgian Orthodox
> 2 Esdras, 4 Maccabees

Deuterocanonical books mean "Second Canon" in Greek. It usually means the parts of the Bible that are only used by some Christian Churches (primarily Roman Catholic and

Orthodox). The books were initially written in the Greek language between 250 and 50 BC.

The books are not part of the Hebrew Bible (also called the Jewish Tanakh) since their original language is Greek.

The Book of Daniel and the Book of Esther are longer in the Catholic Bibles than the Protestant Bibles because they have more stories.

Most Protestant Christian Churches do not think that God inspired the deuterocanonical books. They call these books Apocrypha. Martin Luther considered these books good to read, while John Calvin read and studied them but did not think they should be part of the Bible.[5]

What do different date abbreviations mean?
In the centuries of tradition, the terms "BC" and "AD" are to be replaced with a system known as the "Common Era." The Latin term Anno Domini, meaning "In the Year of Our Lord," becomes Common Era or CE, and "Before Christ" becomes Before the Common Era, or BCE. Another example of human time-tracking means precisely the same thing as AD and BC

BCE—Before the Common Era—is a secular version of BC
CE—Common Era
BC—Before Christ
AD—Anno Domini, Latin for "In the year of our Lord," also known as "After the Death of Christ"[6]

Order of Disciples/Apostles:

1. Simon, later known as Apostle Peter—Fisherman
2. Andrew, Peters brother—also a fisherman
3. James, son of Zebedee—also a fisherman
4. John, James' brother—also a fisherman
5. Philip—most likely a fisherman because he was at the Sea of Galilee
6. Nathanael—known as Bartholomew, son of Tolmai, and introduced by Philip
7. Matthew—known as Levi in the books of Mark and Luke—was a tax collector and son of Alphaeus
8. Thomas—also known as Doubting Thomas
9. James—son of Alphaeus and could be a brother to Matthew
10. Judas Thaddaeus, not Iscariot—also known as Lebbaeus
11. Simon the Zealot—not Peter
12. Judas Iscariot—replaced by Matthias

Inner circle apostles were Peter, James, and John

Priest Garments

Tunic—An undergarment that covered the priest's body from the neck to the feet, with sleeves reaching to the wrists.

Turban—Head covering, mainly white with a gold plate by the forehead, with the words "Holy to the Lord" engraved.

Ephod—A shawl or wrap made of linen in blue, purple, and scarlet, with golden threads woven into it. It was made in two pieces and joined together at the shoulders with golden clasps, each with an onyx stone.

Sash/Girdle—Wrapped around the pod and tied about the priest's waist. Also, blue, purple, and scarlet linen are intertwined with golden threads.

Breastplate—A pouch about 22 centimeters square made of the same materials as the pod that went over the pod. On the front were fastened twelve precious stones in four rows of three. Each stone had engraved the name of a tribe of Israel.[7]

Genealogy of Jesus

1-Adam—Approximately 4000 BC
 2-Seth
  3-Enosh
   4-Caiman
    5-Mahalalel
     6-Jared
      7-Enoch
       8-Methuselah
       9-Lamech
        10-Noah———-[3000 BC]
         11-Shem
          12-Arphaxad
          13-Salah
          14-Eber
          15-Peleg
          16-Rev
          17-Serus
          18-Nahor
          19-Terah
          20-Abraham———-[2000 BC]
           21-Isaac
           22-Jacob/renamed to Israel

Jacob Wives:
     Leah—who had Ruben, Simeon, Levi*, Judah*, Issachar, Zebulun
         *Levi is the Ancestor of the Levites
     Zilpah—who had Gad and Asher
     Bilhah—who had Dan and Naptali
     Rachel—who had Joseph* and Benjamin

*This is the Joseph from Egypt; his sons are Manasseh and Ephraim

*God chose the line of Judah to rule Israel.

23-Judah
  24-Perez
   25-Hezrow
    26-Ram
     27-Amminadab
      28-Nahshon
       29-Salmon
        30-Boaz
         31-Obed
          32-Jesse
           33-David———-[1000 BC]

Note: Jesus's stepfather, Joseph, the husband of Mary, and mother of Jesus, is a descendant of David's eighth son, Nathan, not under Solomon. Mary's father, Joseph, is under Solomon's line.

❖ 14 Generations from Abraham to David
❖ 14 Generations from David until the captivity in Babylon
❖ 14 generations from captivity to Jesus
David
  34-Solomon
   35-Rehoboam
    36-Abijah
     37-Asa
      38-Jehoshaphat
       39-Joram
        40-Uzziah
         41-Jotham

42-Ahaz
43-Hezekiah
44-Manasseh
45-Amon
46-Josiah
47-Jeconiah
48-Jeconiah
49-Shealtiel
50-Zerubbabel
51-Abihud
52-Eliakim
53-Azor
54-Zodok
55-Achim
56-Eliud
57-Eleazar
58-Matthan
59-Jacob
60-Joseph*
61-Mary
62-Jesus

*This Joseph is Jesus's Grandfather, Mary's dad.

Kings of Israel and Judah

All northern kings and thirteen, marked by "*" of southern kings, were wicked in God's eyes.

Israel as One Kingdom:
*Saul—Anointed King 1043 BCE
Reigned 1020-1000 BCE (Around forty years old)
*Ish-bosheth—1000-998 BCE, Coregency
David—40 years, 1010-967 BCE
(Made Jerusalem capital of Israel)
Adonijah—pretender 970 BCE
Solomon—40 years, 970-931 BCE
*Rehoboam—931-913 BCE (3 years into reign kingdom split, became 1st king of Judah)

Judah – Southern Land
2nd—*Abijah—3 years, 913-911 BCE
3rd—Asa—41 years, 911-870 BCE
4th—Jehoshaphat—25 years, 873-848 BCE
5th—*Jehoram—8 years, 853-841 BCE Coregency
6th—*Ahaziah—1 year, 841 BCE Coregency Killed by Jehu
7th— [Ahaziah's mother] *Athaliah—6 years, 841-835 BCE
House of David restored, Army kills Athaliah
8th—Jehoash—40 years, 835-796 BCE
Also, known as Joash, the youngest king at 7, Killed by servants
9th—Amaziah—29 years, 796-767 BCE Coregency
10th—Azariah, Also known as Uzziah—52 years, 792-740 BCE
11th—Jotham—16 years, 750-732 BCE Coregency
12th—*Ahaz—16 years, 735-716 BCE Coregency
13th—Hezekiah—29 years, 729/716-697/687 BCE Coregency
14th—*Manasseh—55 years, 697/687-643 BCE worst and longest king
15th—*Amon—2 years, 643-641 BCE Killed by servants
16th—Josiah—31 years, 641-609 BCE, Killed by Pharaoh Necho
17th—*Jehoahaz—3 months, 609-BCE Deposed to Egypt
18th—*Jehoiakim—11 years, 609-598 BCE

19th—*Jeconiah—3 months, 598-597 BCE Deposed to Babylon
20th—*Zedekiah—11 years, 597-586 BCE
Babylon Captivity—70 years, 608-538 BCE
Hasmonean Dynasty—140 BCE
21st—Aristobulus I—104-103 BCE
22nd—Alexander Jannaeus—103-76 BCE
23rd—Salome Alexandra—76-67 BCE
24th—Aristobulus II—67-63 BCE
25th—Hyrcanus II—63-40 BCE
26th—Antigonus II Mattathias—40-37 BCE
27th—*Herod the Great—37-4 BCE
28th—*Herod Agrippa—41-44 AD

*Israel – Northern Land

1st—Jeroboam—22 years, 931-910 BCE
2nd—Nadab—2 years, 910-909 BCE, Killed by Baasha
3rd—Baasha—24 years, 909-886 BCE
4th—Elah—2 years, 886-885 BCE, Killed by Zimri
5th—Zimri—7 days/Suicide because of Treason, 885 BCE
6th—Tibni pretender / Omri—12 years, 885-874 BCE
7th—Ahab—22 years, 874-853 BCE
8th—Ahaziah—2 years, 853-852 BCE, Accident
9th—Jehoram—12 years, 852-841 BCE, Killed by Jehu
10th—Jehu—28 years, 841-814 BCE
11th—Jehoahaz—17 years, 814-798 BCE
12th—Jehoash—16 years, 798-782 BCE—Coregency
13th—Jeroboam II—41 years, 793-753 BCE
14th—Zechariah—6 months, 753-752 BCE, Killed by Shallum
15th—Shallum—1 month, 752 BCE, Killed by Menahem
16th—Menahem—10 years, 752-742 BCE, Coregency
17th—Pekahiah-2 years, 742-740 BCE, Killed by Pekah, Coregency
18th—Pekah—20 years, 752-731 BCE, Killed by Hoshea
19th—Hoshea—9 years, 731-722 BCE, Deposed to Assyria

Israel was conquered by the Neo-Assyrian Empire and Destroyed in 722 BCE

Israel's Journeys In The Wilderness

These are the camps of Israel in their journey from Egypt to the Promised Land as listed in Numbers 33. Even though they were wandering for forty years, they did have places of rest.

They started from Rameses, the city they built for Pharaoh, They left Egypt in the first month, on the fifteenth day of the first month, and on the day after the Passover, the Israelites went out of Egypt with a high hand and triumphantly in the sight of all Egyptians.

1. Succoth
2. Etham—on the edge of the wilderness
3. Migdol—Turned back to Pi-Hahiroth, which is east of Baal-Zephon and they camped near Migdol. And they departed from before Pi-Hahiroth and passed over through the midst of the Red Sea into the wilderness, went three days' journey in the Wilderness of Etham, and camped at Marah.
4. Marah
5. Elim—At Elim were twelve springs of water and seventy palm trees
6. By the Red Sea
7. Wilderness of Sin
8. Dophkah
9. Alush
10. Rephidim—this is where there was no water for the people to drink
11. Mount Sinai—this is where the Covenant was made. They stayed eleven months and twenty days in the Wilderness of Sinai and departed on the twentieth day of the second month of the second year.
12. Kibroth-Hattaavah
13. Hazeroth
14. Rithmah in the Wilderness of Paran, at Qadesh—from where the twelve spies were sent

15. Rimmon-Perez
16. Libnah
17. Rissah
18. Kehelathah
19. Mount Shepher
20. Haradah
21. Makheloth
22. Tahath
23. Terah
24. Mithkah
25. Hashmonah
26. Moseroth
27. Bene-Jaakan
28. Hor-Haggidgad
29. Jotbathah
30. Abronah
31. Ezion-Geber

The Fortieth Year

32. Kadesh in the Wilderness of Zin—in the first month
33. Mount Hor—on the boundary of the land of Edom where Aaron the priest died in the fortieth year after Israel had come out of the land of Egypt, on the first day of the fifth month.
34. Zalmonah
35. Punon
36. Oboth
37. Iye-Abarim—on the border of Moab
38. Dibon-Gad
39. Almon-Diblathaim
40. In the mountains of Abarim, before Nebo
41. In the plains of Moab by the Jordan—and they camped by the Jordan from Beth-Jeshimoth as far as the Abel-Shittim in the plains of Moab.

From here they crossed the Jordan River into the land of Canaan, *The Promised Land.*

37 Miracles of Jesus in Chronological Order

#1—Jesus Turns Water into Wine at the Wedding in Cana—John 2:1-11

#2—Jesus Heals an Official's Son at Capernaum in Galilee—John 4:43-54

#3—Jesus Drives Out an Evil Spirit From a Man in Capernaum—Mark 1:21-27, Luke 4:31-36

#4—Jesus Heals Peter's Mother-in-Law Sick With Fever—Matthew 8:14-15, Mark 1:29-31, Luke 4:38-39

#5—Jesus Heals Many Sick and Oppressed at Evening—Matthew 8:16-17, Mark 1:32-34, Luke 4:40-41

#6—First Miraculous Catch of Fish on the Lake of Gennesaret—Luke 5:1-11

#7—Jesus Cleanses a Man With Leprosy—Matthew 8:1-4, Mark 1:40-45, Luke 5:12-14

#8—Jesus Heals a Centurion's Paralyzed Servant in Capernaum—Matthew 8:5-13, Luke 7:1-10

#9—Jesus Heals a Paralytic Who Was Let Down From the Roof—Matthew 9:1-8, Mark 2:1-12, Luke 5:17-26

#10—Jesus Heals a Man's Withered Hand on the Sabbath—Matthew 12:9-14, Mark 3:1-6, Luke 6:6-11

#11—Jesus Raises a Widow's Son From the Dead in Nain—Luke 7:11-17

#12—Jesus Calms a Storm on the Sea—Matthew 8:23-27, Mark 4:35-41, Luke 8:22-25

#13—Jesus Casts Demons into a Herd of Pigs—Matthew 8:28-33, Mark 5:1-20, Luke 8:26-39

#14—Jesus Heals a Woman in the Crowd With an Issue of Blood—Matthew 9:20-22, Mark 5:25-34, Luke 8:42-48

#15—Jesus Raises Jairus' Daughter Back to Life—Matthew 9:18, 23-26, Mark 5:21-24, 35-43 Luke 8:40-42, 49-56

#16—Jesus Heals Two Blind Men—Matthew 9:27-31

#17—Jesus Heals a Man Who Was Unable to Speak—Matthew 9:32-34

#18—Jesus Heals an Invalid at Bethesda—John 5:1-15

#19—Jesus Feeds 5,000 Plus Women and Children—Matthew 14:13-21, Mark 6:30-44, Luke 9:10-17 John 6:1-15

#20—Jesus Walks on Water—Matthew 14:22-33 Mark 6:45-52, John 6:16-21

#21—Jesus Heals Many Sick in Gennesaret as They Touch His Garment—Matthew 14:34-36, Mark 6:53-56

#22—Jesus Heals a Gentile Woman's Demon-Possessed Daughter—Matthew 15:21-28, Mark 7:24-30

#23—Jesus Heals a Deaf and Dumb Man—Mark 7:31-37

#24—Jesus Feeds 4,000 Plus Women and Children—Matthew 15:32-39, Mark 8:1-13

#25—Jesus Heals a Blind Man at Bethsaida—Mark 8:22-26

#26—Jesus Heals a Man Born Blind by Spitting in His Eyes —John 9:1-12

#27—Jesus Heals a Boy With an Unclean Spirit—Matthew 17:14-20 Mark 9:14-29, Luke 9:37-43

#28—Miraculous Temple Tax in a Fish's Mouth—Matthew 17:24-27

#29—Jesus Heals a Blind, Mute Demoniac—Matthew 12:22-23 Luke 11:14-23

#30—Jesus Heals a Woman Who Had Been Crippled for 18 Years—Luke 13:10-17

#31—Jesus Heals a Man With Dropsy on the Sabbath—Luke 14:1-6

#32—Jesus Cleanses Ten Lepers on the Way to Jerusalem—Luke 17:11-19

#33—Jesus Raises Lazarus from the Dead in Bethany—John 11:1-45

#34—Jesus Restores Sight to Bartimaeus in Jericho—Matthew 20:29-34, Mark 10:46-52, Luke 18:35-43

#35—Jesus Withers the Fig Tree on the Road From Bethany —Matthew 21:18:22, Mark 11:12-14

#36—Jesus Heals a Servant's Severed Ear While He Is Being Arrested—Luke 22:50-51

#37—The Second Miraculous Catch of Fish at the Sea of Tiberias—John 21:4

Introduction

How the Day-by-Day Bible Reading Guide Works

I took the Book of Psalms as a daily song and the Book of Proverbs as daily wisdom from the Old Testament to include each as part of the reading plan. Then I took the remaining books of the Old Testament (will be seen as OT}) and divided them into 365 days. Lastly, I took the New Testament (will be seen as NT}) and divided it into 365 days. Some chapters will be read whole, and others will be read over multiple days. You will see scriptures on each day starting from January 1 to December 31 in four parts: Old Testament, Psalms, Proverbs, and New Testament.

Note: The Deuterocanonical books are not part of this reading plan, if you follow them, take the number of scriptures in each book, divide them by 365 to add them to your daily reading.

The time you spend reading each day will depend on what version you are reading from and how much meditation and research you do. Obviously, if you use the amplified version like me, it will take you longer. Also, it will be longer if you use the references found in your Bible to study the word. Typically, it should be 15-30 minutes, plus any time you spend in prayer.

I give a short highlight for each Old Testament and New Testament daily reading. I pray that as you use this guide to aid in reading the Bible, you will receive a renewed passion for God's Word and form a habit of completing the Bible-in-a-year goal. With the passing of each year, your knowledge will grow, and you will also experience hearing Holy Spirit speak the direction for your life. If you commit to this plan as part of your daily life, I promise this will impact you in ways you never even thought.

 If you are using a physical Bible, I suggest getting sticky notes to mark where you left off each day for each part so you do not lose your place. They have small ones that work great, or if you use the larger ones, you can cut them into smaller pieces. I also suggest getting five book markers for each part of the reading and one for this book, four if your Bible has a string marker, so you do not lose your spot. Because the book is so thick, place your Bible on top of the open page, so it does not keep closing.

Some questions you might want to ask yourself every day:
> What lesson did I learn from today's reading?
> What has my faith in Jesus cost me?
> Following Jesus is more important than…
> If Christ asks for my life, what does he get in return?

So, let's get started:
Start each day off with a prayer asking Holy Spirit for his help. I included one for each day, but you can pray however you feel you need to; just start with something.

Day 1—January 1st

Prayer: Teach me oh Lord what you want me to learn today.
Help me Holy Spirit to unfold today's daily scriptures. Amen!
After reading question: What is God saying to me today?

Genesis 1-2
Psalm 1
Proverbs 1:1-3
Matthew 1:1-12

Genesis is a Greek word meaning "B*eginning*." It is the introduction to God's progressive self-revelation to the human race. God created the heavens and the earth in six days. The account in this book shows that our existence is revolutionary, not evolutionary.

The Book of Psalms is a collection of songs from about seven authors; David, Asaph, Sons of Korah, Moses, Heman, and Solomon. Psalms reflect various feelings, emotions, attitudes, and interests. Psalms will be part of your reading plan for the whole year.

In the Book Proverbs, also known as "The Proverbs of Solomon," the stated purpose of this book is to impart skillful and Godly wisdom. Wisdom is one of the names of God.
Proverbs will be part of your reading plan for the whole year.

We start in the New Testament with "The gospel According to Matthew," the first of four Gospels. Each will have a little twist on how it was viewed or understood by the author. But they all still point to the teaching ministry of Jesus.

Day 2—January 2

Prayer: Teach me oh Lord what you want me to learn today. Help me Holy Spirit to unfold today's daily scriptures. Amen!

After reading question: What is God saying to me today?

OT}—Satan comes in the form of a serpent to deceive Eve, who then turns to her husband, Adam, to bring sin into the world. Then the first expression of embarrassment is when God shows up in the garden, and Adam throws his wife under the bus for blame. Until now, life was incredible; everything they needed was handed to them on a silver platter without any effort. Then they ruined it by not keeping God's Word in their heart, and we see the first labor pains. God wants us to believe in his Word and trust what he says, as any parent.

In chapter 4, we see the first offering, first strife expressed, and first murder enter the world—the beginning of the genealogy of Jesus.

Genesis 3-4
Psalm 2:1-6
Proverbs 1:4-6
Matthew 1:13-25

NT}—An angel of the Lord, most likely Gabriel, God's chief messaging angel, appeared to Joseph because when he found out about Mary's pregnancy, he most likely did not believe that she was pregnant by Holy Spirit and needed confirmation from God that it was indeed him, and not that Mary was with another man.

Day 3—January 3

Prayer: Teach me oh Lord what you want me to learn today. Help me Holy Spirit to unfold today's daily scriptures. Amen!

After reading question: What is God saying to me today?

OT}—Today speaks of the generations of the offspring of Adam with an introduction to Noah. God regrets that he made man and is grieved for doing so, so he tells Noah he will destroy mankind and all creatures.

God became disappointed in his creation because the world became degenerate, debased, vicious, and corrupt to him. As much as he wanted to give up on it all, he found hope in one man, a just and righteous man, Noah. With hope, God informs Noah that he needs to build an ark.

Genesis 5-6

Psalm 2:7-12

Proverbs 1:7-9

Matthew 2:1-12

NT}—King Herod hears about the birth of Jesus and becomes jealous, so he sends out wise men (astrologers) to find him. We see the supernatural happening with the star that points the way to Jesus. At this point, Jesus is a young child. Verse 9 and verse 11 confirm by pointing out that they went into the house, not a stable. Then they were warned in a dream from God not to go back to Herod, so they went back to their country by a different route.

Day 4—January 4

<u>Prayer:</u> Teach me oh Lord what you want me to learn today. Help me Holy Spirit to unfold today's daily scriptures. Amen!

<u>After reading question:</u> What is God saying to me today?

OT}—God tells Noah he is pleased and rewards him by allowing him and his household to be saved. This is new beginnings! Noah, his family, and all living creatures spent the following year in the ark until the waters receded, and they could walk on dry land after God shut them in and closed the door, as seen in verse 16.

It is estimated that it took Noah between fifty-five and seventy-five years to build the ark. Noah was 500 years old when he had his third son, Japheth, and 600 years old when the floodwaters came. If we calculate some time for the sons to grow to be able to help, and time to draw out the plans and start to gather materials, and then the time to set up the ark with the animals and all that they needed, it can easily be twenty-five or more years.

Genesis 7-8
Psalm 3
Proverbs 1:10-12
Matthew 2:13-23

NT}—God then appeared to Joseph in a dream to take his family and flee to Egypt because Herod was seeking to kill Jesus by ordering all children two years old and under to be killed. After Herod died, they went to the town of Nazareth.

Day 5—January 5

Prayer: Teach me oh Lord what you want me to learn today. Help me Holy Spirit to unfold today's daily scriptures. Amen!

After reading question: What is God saying to me today?

OT}—God makes a covenant with Noah and his sons. He pledged that he would never flood the earth again with a sign of the rainbow to mark that pledge. Noah lived 950 years, 350 years after he finished the ark. He had three sons, and the whole earth was replenished from them. In Second Peter 2:5, we can see that it was a total of eight people.

Genesis 9-10
Psalm 4
Proverbs 1:13-15
Matthew 3

NT}—Matthew introduces John the Baptist, a cousin to Jesus, who was a forerunner to the ministry of Jesus. John baptized many, and he had a large following. This type of baptism John performed was only through their repentance of sins. It is not the infilling of the Holy Spirit that only comes through Jesus Christ. Therefore, they all had to be baptized a second-time years later.

The first one to be baptized with Holy Spirit was when John baptized Jesus.

Day 6—January 6

<u>Prayer:</u> Teach me oh Lord what you want me to learn today. Help me Holy Spirit to unfold today's daily scriptures. Amen!

<u>After reading question:</u> What is God saying to me today?

OT}—This is where we hear about the Tower of Babel. The Babylonians wanted to make a mighty city and a structure that would reach the heavens. God disrupted it by confusing the language, which at the time was only one, so they could not understand each other. The work was never completed.

We get the genealogy of Shem, Noah's firstborn.

Abram is instructed to leave his country and relatives, and deception appears by the end of the chapter.

Genesis 11-12

Psalm 5:1-6

Proverbs 1:16-18

Matthew 4:1-12

NT}—Satan tempts Jesus in the wilderness. Jesus uses the Word of God to push the enemy away. First, was God's provision, "Man shall not live by bread alone." The second response Jesus gave was protection, "You shall not test the Lord your God." And lastly, is power, "You shall worship the Lord your God."

Day 7—January 7

OT}—Abram tries to keep peace with his nephew by splitting up the land. He even gives Lot the option to pick the land that he wants. Abram knew the blessing God gave him and believed the word God spoke to him for his future. Consequently, to him, it did not matter what land he ended up with; it would flourish.

Then he turns to rescue Lot from Chedorlaomer.

Genesis 13-14
Psalm 5:7-12
Proverbs 1:19-21
Matthew 4:13-25

NT}—Basically, this is where Jesus starts his ministry by assembling the twelve apostles, see the order on page seven, and teaching the gospel by healing every disease and infirmity that is still today.

In verse 17, Jesus makes a powerful statement that many have used over the years, but do people really see what Jesus was saying? The word *"Repent"* is the first word of the sentence from Jesus. He is telling us to change our minds for the better and heartily amend our ways with abhorrence of our past sins. An actual letting go!

Day 8—January 8

<u>Prayer:</u> Teach me oh Lord what you want me to learn today. Help me Holy Spirit to unfold today's daily scriptures. Amen!

<u>After reading question:</u> What is God saying to me today?

OT}—God prophesies to Abram that the Israelites will be enslaved after he tells him his descendants will be countless, and because Abram trusted God, he believed.

Because Sarai was barren, they lost trust and went ahead of God's promise to start a family using Hagar, Sarai's maidservant. Then Sarai despises Hagar and beats her, so she flees. Then God appears to Hagar and tells her to name the child Ishmael (God Hears). Ishmael was Abram's firstborn at the age of eighty-six.

Genesis 15-16
Psalm 6:1-5
Proverbs 1:22-24
Matthew 5:1-16

NT}—Jesus introduces his blessings to the disciples. You may know this as the sermon on the mount. Jesus calls us to be the light of the world, a city set on a hill for all to see.

Who are you?
If you are a child of God, do not put your faith under a bushel where no one can see it. But instead, let everyone know who you are. If the people around you do not know you are a Christian, it is time to remove the bushel.

Day 9—January 9

<u>Prayer:</u> Teach me oh Lord what you want me to learn today. Help me Holy Spirit to unfold today's daily scriptures. Amen!

<u>After reading question:</u> What is God saying to me today?

OT}—God appears to Abram to say that if he would live blameless, whole-hearted, and complete, God would make a covenant with him. Abram immediately falls on his face with admiration, and then God changes Abram's name to Abraham (*father of many nations*) and Sari to Sarah (*princess*) and then tells them they will have a son.

We read about the Circumcision that became a covenant between God and man. And Abraham speaks to God, asking for mercy for Sodom six times for God not to destroy it because of their vile/wicked ways.

Genesis 17-18
Psalm 6:6-10
Proverbs 1:25-27
Matthew 5:17-32

NT}—Jesus announces that he did not come to condemn the Law (Ten Commandments) but to fulfill (complete) them. Jesus starts to break them down for the disciples, first saying that if anyone wants to enter into the kingdom of heaven, they are not to be like the scribes, who were involved in many administrative tasks and knew the law, and Pharisees, who were spiritual and political leaders of the Jewish people who imposed the religious laws, were hypocrites.

Day 10—January 10

Prayer: Teach me oh Lord what you want me to learn today. Help me Holy Spirit to unfold today's daily scriptures. Amen!

After reading question: What is God saying to me today?

OT}—God has mercy on Lot, but because Lot's wife disobeys the angels, she turns into a pillar of salt when she looks back as they leave Sodom. This has been used many times as an example of when God tells us to move forward, not to look back at where we were, but to look at where we are going.
Two Angels appear in human form. And Abraham passes Sarai off as his sister for a second time.

Genesis 19-20
Psalm 7:1-9
Proverbs 1:28-30
Matthew 5:33-48

NT}—Jesus proclaims what turned out to be one of the most quoted commandments, "Love your enemies and pray for those who persecute you." Wherefore, one may ask, how do I direct my heart to love what it should?

1. Die to yourself, Psalm 37:4, shift your thoughts
2. Spend time engaging with God through;
    A. Prayer
    B. Communication
    C. Scripture
    D. Worship
3. Actively listen for direction

Day 11—January 11

Prayer: Teach me oh Lord what you want me to learn today. Help me Holy Spirit to unfold today's daily scriptures. Amen!

After reading question: What is God saying to me today?

OT}—Sarah gives birth to Isaac, which means *"laughter."* Laughter because to them, it was funny that they had a kid at their age. Abraham was a hundred, and Sarah was ninety. After some time passed and Isaac grew, Abraham was tested by God to sacrifice his son Isaac. Because Abraham believed in God's Word that his descendants would be many and that God would provide a lamb, he went through with it. *"Jehovah Jireh"*—the Lord will provide!

Genesis 21-22
Psalm 7:10-17
Proverbs 1:31-33
Matthew 6:1-18

NT}—Jesus continues teaching and gives a lesson on how to pray. We call this the "Lord's Prayer."

We also learn that we should not be boastful in our giving. Giving to others is to be obedient to the Word, not to be a showoff. God is the rewarder of our good deeds, not man, which is why they should be anonymous. It is OK to use our giving as a teaching lesson, or even when we fast, but we must ensure our hearts are set right.

Day 12—January 12

<u>Prayer:</u> Teach me oh Lord what you want me to learn today. Help me Holy Spirit to unfold today's daily scriptures. Amen!

<u>After reading question:</u> What is God saying to me today?

OT}—Sarah dies at the age of 127 in Kiriath-Arba, in the land of Canaan, known as Hebron. She is buried in the cave of the field of Machpelah, to the east of Mamore.

Abraham sends his servant out to find a wife for Isaac and returns with Rebekah, the daughter of Bethuel, the son of Nahor, Abraham's brother.

Genesis 23-24

Psalm 8

Proverbs 2:1-2

Matthew 6:19-34

NT}—We are called to live for another place and time. If we follow Jesus, we are on a mission away from home.

We have two primary ways that the devil uses to attempt to destroy our souls:

1. Eye gate
2. Ear gate

Today we read about the eye gate.

Jesus tells us to stop being anxious and worrying about our life. But to seek his kingdom and righteousness first, all things taken together will be given to us.

Day 13—January 13

Prayer: Teach me oh Lord what you want me to learn today. Help me Holy Spirit to unfold today's daily scriptures. Amen!

After reading question: What is God saying to me today?

OT}—Abraham takes another wife, Keturah, who gives him six sons. He dies at age 175 and is buried with his wife, Sarah.

We learn the history of Abraham's sons.

Genesis 25-26

Psalm 9:1-7

Proverbs 2:3-4

Matthew 7

NT}—Jesus ends the sermon on the mount, and we see another famous scripture; "Ask, and it will be given to you; seek, and you will find; knock, and it will be opened to you" (NKJV). Unfortunately, people have used it as if Jesus is living in a Jeannie jar, and if you rub it long enough, he will give you what you want. This is not how this scripture goes. Back up to the beginning of chapter 7 to line it up:

Ask: If you are lined up with God's will, treat his creation right, and put his kingdom first, God will hear your prayers.

Seek: Seeking his righteousness, his heart, and his will.
Knock: What are you knocking on? Jesus! He is the door to all things.

Day 14—January 14

Prayer: Teach me oh Lord what you want me to learn today. Help me Holy Spirit to unfold today's daily scriptures. Amen!

After reading question: What is God saying to me today?

OT}—Rebekah plots a plan to deceive her husband Isaac so that the younger son, Jacob, would get the blessing that usually would go to the oldest son. But because of what we read in chapter 25:23, she felt she needed to help the Lord. Then the family feud begins. Jacob leaves for Padan-Aran because of the threat from Esau.
Esau becomes defiant of his father's words.

Genesis 27-28
Psalm 9:8-14
Proverbs 2:5-6
Matthew 8:1-17

NT}—Jesus comes down from the mountain and continues his ministry by healing, prophesying, deliverances, and fulfilling what was spoken by the prophet Isaiah in Isaiah 53:4. He healed a Leper, a paralyzed boy, fever, and many demon-possessed with a word given to him by the father.

The paralyzed boy was the son of a centurion who was a Roman soldier. Most likely, he was not saved, and that is why he replied to Jesus, "Lord, I am not worthy or fit to have you come under my roof...." But he understood authority and saw the truth in Jesus through the eyes of faith.

Day 15—January 15

OT}—Jacob meets his mother's brother and family. As soon as he sees Rachel, the youngest daughter, he falls in love. He works for seven years for her hand in marriage, and then the father deceives him. Back then, the youngest daughter could not marry first, so Laban got Jacob drunk and put his firstborn, Leah, in the bedroom in place of Rachel. Thus, Jacob consummated a marriage with the wrong woman and had to work another seven years to get the one he wanted. Then Jacob returns the favor and deceives his father-in-law.

Genesis 29-30
Psalm 9:15-20
Proverbs 2:7-8
Matthew 8:18-34

NT}—Jesus rebuked the winds and the sea, showing those with him in the boat how little their faith was.

Faith is critical to a believer's life!

We also see an example with a well-known story on how spirits know other spirits. We walk around this planet like we are the only ones here because it is easy to live by sight. The Bible is clear that we are not alone in the world.

Day 16—January 16

Prayer: Teach me oh Lord what you want me to learn today. Help me Holy Spirit to unfold today's daily scriptures. Amen!

After reading question: What is God saying to me today?

OT}—After twenty years, fourteen for his wives and six for his flocks, Jacob flees with his family to return home. Then after Laban pursued them, the two built a pillar and monument of stone to symbolize an oath between them.

Today we also read about Jacob wrestling with a man all night. Many scholars believe that this man was Jesus himself. This is when the Lord changes the name of Jacob to Israel (*contender with God*).

Genesis 31-32

Psalm 10:1-6

Proverbs 2:9-10

Matthew 9:1-19

NT}—Jesus confronts some of the scribes about why he heals with the prerogatives of God and in the name of God.

Matthew joins the team as the seventh disciple. What is so remarkable is that Matthew, a publican, and a tax collector for the Roman Empire, did not even question Jesus's invitation! Because Jesus chose to associate himself with wicked sinners, the Pharisees got upset, but Jesus put them in their right place.

Day 17—January 17

Prayer: Teach me oh Lord what you want me to learn today. Help me Holy Spirit to unfold today's daily scriptures. Amen!

After reading question: What is God saying to me today?

OT}—Jacob is reunited with his brother, even though he fears Esau might kill him. Jacob trusted God's Word about having a multitude of descendants and believed that God would deliver him out of his brother's hand. And he was right. When Esau saw his brother, he ran to meet him, embracing him, falling on his neck, and kissing him.

Can you imagine a world like that today?

Genesis 33-34
Psalm 10:7-12
Proverbs 2:11-12
Matthew 9:20-38

NT}—Today, a woman with an issue of blood is healed because of the power of faith and believing in the work of Jesus. This woman understood Jesus's authority through all the healing she heard he had done. She was not looking for anything fancy or a sideshow that we may see in some churches today, just a touch.

I see from this story that God can heal me right where I am; I just need to believe he will at any time.

Day 18—January 18

Prayer: Teach me oh Lord what you want me to learn today. Help me Holy Spirit to unfold today's daily scriptures. Amen!

After reading question: What is God saying to me today?

OT}—After Jacob fled from his brother, Esau, God told him to go to Bethel to live. He then builds an altar and calls it El-Bethal, "God of Bethel," to make a sacrifice of all the images of strange gods.

God needs to remind Jacob that his name is Israel (*Contender with God*).

Today Rachel and Isaac died. Isaac was 180 years old, and Rachel was around 36. I believe it was because she stole the idols from her father that it put a curse on her life, mainly because she lied about taking them when her father asked Jacob the day Laban caught up to them after they fled.

Genesis 35-36
Psalm 10:13-18
Proverbs 2:13-14
Matthew 10:1-23

NT}—Jesus commissions the twelve apostles to go to the house of Israel and not go to the Gentiles, or Samaritans, to preach, cure the sick, raise the dead, cleanse the lepers, and drive out demons. This account is not in the other gospels and lines up with the statement made in the great commission found in chapter 28:16-20, Jews first.

Day 19—January 19

Prayer: Teach me oh Lord what you want me to learn today. Help me Holy Spirit to unfold today's daily scriptures. Amen!

After reading question: What is God saying to me today?

OT}—Joseph, son of Jacob, and the second youngest of twelve sons, has a dream that the older brothers will bow before him. The problem was that Joseph told the dream to his brothers, so Joseph was thrown in a pit at seventeen and then sold. God steps in and uses this for the future of Israel.

Note to self: do not brag about your dream to anyone because it will give the devil time to stop it.

Genesis 37-38
Psalm 11
Proverbs 2:15-16
Matthew 10:24-42

NT}—Jesus warns that anyone who does not take up his cross and follow him is not worthy of Jesus.

To carry your cross behind Jesus means he is in front of you, showing you the path to take and the will of the Father.

Research what it means to take up your cross to understand this statement fully.

Day 20—January 20

<u>Prayer:</u> Teach me oh Lord what you want me to learn today. Help me Holy Spirit to unfold today's daily scriptures. Amen!

<u>After reading question:</u> What is God saying to me today?

OT}—Now, the good part of the story of Joseph begins. God reveals himself throughout Joseph's time in prison to build him up to be the most influential person in all the land. Consequently, for around thirteen years, Joseph tolerated the pain to get to where God needed him to be, never losing faith that God would deliver him. God uses him to interpret three dreams during the course of those brutal years that open doors for him.

Genesis 39-40

Psalm 12

Proverbs 2:17-18

Matthew 11

NT}—Just because Jesus commissioned the apostles does not mean it was time for the teacher to relax. He continues to the Galilean cities.

John the Baptist is now in prison and gets offended at Jesus when he asks for clarity on who Jesus was. Jesus appears to be unkind to John the Baptist but is just using him to focus on how the people viewed him and himself.

Day 21—January 21

Prayer: Teach me oh Lord what you want me to learn today. Help me Holy Spirit to unfold today's daily scriptures. Amen!

After reading question: What is God saying to me today?

OT}—Joseph is called out of prison to interpret Pharaoh's dream because Joseph, through God, is the only one who can. After he did, Pharaoh said to Joseph, "Forasmuch as your God has shown you all this, there is nobody as intelligent, discreet, understanding, and wise as you are." Pharoah then removes his signet ring and puts it on Joseph's finger. He then cloths him in fine linen and parades him around the land as the new person in charge. Setting the stage for his dream he had twenty-three years prior.

Genesis 41-42
Psalm 13
Proverbs 2:19-20
Matthew 12:1-17

NT}—Jesus confronts the Pharisees about the law of the sabbath because they misplaced their belief in the law. They thought the disciples were working on the Sabbath, but they were just hungry.

The Pharisees believed in supernatural angels, demons, heaven, hell, prayer, and the study of God's law, which is why they frequently questioned Jesus.

Day 22—January 22

<u>Prayer:</u> Teach me oh Lord what you want me to learn today. Help me Holy Spirit to unfold today's daily scriptures. Amen!

<u>After reading question:</u> What is God saying to me today?

OT}—During the famine, Joseph sees his brothers for the first time in years. I am thinking about twenty-two to twenty-five years, depending on how long Jacob ran out of food. Joseph was seventeen when he was sold and thirty when he interpreted Pharoah's dream. There were seven years of plenty, putting Joseph at thirty-seven at the beginning of the famine. About two years into the famine, Jacob sends his sons for grain.

Just FYI, Joseph was fifty-six when his dad died.

Genesis 43-44
Psalm 14
Proverbs 2:21-22
Matthew 12:18-33

NT}—Jesus heals the blind and dumb man and starts a ruckus in the community. The Pharisees, who felt they were superior, said that Jesus had to be doing this work with the help of Beelzebub, the prince of demons.

Jesus tells them how he is not doing this work with the help of Satan because a house divided against itself with not stand.

Day 23—January 23

Prayer: Teach me oh Lord what you want me to learn today. Help me Holy Spirit to unfold today's daily scriptures. Amen!

After reading question: What is God saying to me today?

OT}—Joseph reveals himself to his brothers, what a family reunion that must have been, and Joseph tells how God is the one who orchestrated his journey.

Talk about faith, love, and forgiveness! If we could only walk as he walked.

Genesis 45-46

Psalm 15

Proverbs 3:1-3

Matthew 12:34-50

NT}—Here is a part that makes me laugh every time I read it. The scribes and Pharisees asked Jesus for a sign proving he was what he was claiming to be. How many signs or teachings do you think he gave up to this point? A lot!

Jesus takes his past and puts it under the authority of his ministry, the purpose of his life as a man. He is not being cruel or unkind to his mother, sister, or brothers. He groups all mankind as one, "Who is My mother, and who are My brothers?" Verse 50; "For whoever does the will of My Father in heaven is My brother and sister and mother."

Day 24—January 24

Prayer: Teach me oh Lord what you want me to learn today. Help me Holy Spirit to unfold today's daily scriptures. Amen!

After reading question: What is God saying to me today?

OT}—Because the king respected Joseph, Pharaoh gave Jacob and his family the best of the land. Israel dwelt in the land of Egypt, in the country of Goshen, and they gained possessions and multiplied exceedingly.

After getting settled in, he blesses the sons of Joseph.

Genesis 47-48
Psalm 16:1-6
Proverbs 3:4-6
Matthew 13:1-30

NT}—Jesus preaches from a boat with parables. One of them is a very well-known one, the parable of the Sower of Seeds. Jesus explains the parable, "Having the power of seeing, they do not see; and having the power of hearing, they do not hear, nor do they grasp and understand the spirit."

Meaning:
Those that do not see, hear, or understand, are worldly-minded people—but those that do see, hear, and understand are filled with the spirit who reveals all things to them.

Day 25—January 25

Prayer: Teach me oh Lord what you want me to learn today. Help me Holy Spirit to unfold today's daily scriptures. Amen!

After reading question: What is God saying to me today?

OT}—Jacob calls his sons together to give them words of encouragement, blessings, and directions before dying at the age of 147. Joseph reassures his brothers that he will not harm them just because their father died. This is the first-time forgiveness is mentioned in the Bible.

Genesis 49-50
Psalm 16:7-11
Proverbs 3:7-9
Matthew 13:31-58

NT}—Hidden Treasure-"The kingdom of heaven is like a [very precious] treasure hidden in a field, which a man found and hid again; then in his joy, he goes and sells all he has and buys that field [securing the treasure for himself]."

Have you ever seen a mustard seed? It is one of the smallest seeds on earth and usually about one to two millimeters in diameter (1/10 inch), and can grow about five to six feet tall.[8] Jesus uses this seed as an example of what our faith should be like. We are small when we come to him, and we should grow into something powerful for his kingdom, just like the mustard seed will grow into a large tree for the birds to find shelter in its branches.

Day 26—January 26

Prayer: Teach me oh Lord what you want me to learn today. Help me Holy Spirit to unfold today's daily scriptures. Amen!

After reading question: What is God saying to me today?

OT}—Today, we go into the Second Book of Moses, commonly known as Exodus, from *The Septuagint* translations meaning "Exit" or "departure." This is the story of the Israelites after the death of Jacob, and when a new Pharaoh was on the throne and knew nothing about the works of Joseph and what his predecessor promised Joseph. All he saw was the blessings, and how strong Israel became, and in fear of being overthrown, he put them in slavery.

Exodus 1-2

Psalm 17:1-8

Proverbs 3:10-12

Matthew 14

NT}—Herod has a birthday party, and his lust for his stepdaughter orders the head of John the Baptist as a gift, trying to win her heart, even though it was her mother who asked for it. Jesus then hears about it and tries to get alone to mourn, but the people follow him.

Even though he did not have much time alone to mourn, he has deep sympathy for the people, and we see two miracles, the first of two, the feeding of 5,000, and then Jesus walking on water. He releases his plan by helping others with theirs.

Day 27—January 27

Prayer: Teach me oh Lord what you want me to learn today. Help me Holy Spirit to unfold today's daily scriptures. Amen!

After reading question: What is God saying to me today?

OT}—We saw yesterday that Moses was born, and Pharaoh's daughter reared him as her own. When Moses grew, he defended one of his own and ran away to the land of Midian in fear of punishment. Moses takes a wife, starts a family, and is visited by an angel of the Lord after forty years. It is said that this angel was Jesus himself. God commands Moses to return to Egypt and tells Pharaoh to let his people go. Moses has a hard time with it, and God gets mad and tells him to use his brother Aaron as a mouthpiece to speak to the people.

Exodus 3-4

Psalm 17:9-15

Proverbs 3:13-15

Matthew 15:1-20

NT}—Scribes and Pharisees confront Jesus again about traditions. Jesus calls them out on their complaining and how they are all talking but have no action in their heart for the true kingdom.

Verse 11 is used as an example of all their studying of scripture going in, but their mouth is vile.

Day 28—January 28

Prayer: Teach me oh Lord what you want me to learn today. Help me Holy Spirit to unfold today's daily scriptures. Amen!

After reading question: What is God saying to me today?

OT}—Now that Moses is done with his tantrum, he gathers his family to return to Egypt. They speak to Pharaoh without any sound side effects. Take number one ends badly for the Israelites. Then the Lord tells Moses to try again. Therefore, Moses and Aaron repeat the words of God to Pharaoh for a second time.

Exodus 5-6

Psalm 18:1-6

Proverbs 3:16-18

Matthew 15:21-39

NT}—Despite what the scribes and Pharisees are saying, Jesus continues to move forward with his ministry, starting with healing a young girl possessed by a demon. We also see today the second feeding of Jesus's followers with the seven loaves and fishes.

No matter how much was being thrown at Jesus, he always walked it out with pity and sympathy. He did not complain or say at any time that things were unfair. He just keeps giving up his time and whatever resources he has.

Day 29—January 29

OT}—At this point, Moses was eighty years old, and Aaron was eighty-three when they spoke to Pharaoh. They believed in God sincerely and trusted what he said to them, so a second wind blew in their sails for strength. The second talk ends with the first sign of Moses's rod turning into a serpent. They speak to Pharaoh three more times with four more signs.

Exodus 7-8

Psalm 18:7-12

Proverbs 3:19-21

Matthew 16:1-12

NT}—Now, this time, the Sadducees join in on trying to undermine Jesus. Sadducees were high priests, aristocratic families, and merchants. They had a conservative view within Judaism and did not believe in what the Pharisees believed. They asked for a sign from heaven to attest to Jesus's divine authority. Jesus refused to bow down to their foolishness. Knowing the truth about these so-called leaders, Jesus tells the disciples not to trust them because their motives are tainted.

Day 30—January 30

<u>Prayer:</u> Teach me oh Lord what you want me to learn today. Help me Holy Spirit to unfold today's daily scriptures. Amen!

<u>After reading question:</u> What is God saying to me today?

OT}—God speaks to Moses four more times to go to Pharaoh, each time with a different sign. In between, Pharaoh sends for Moses four times. Egypt's livestock died, boils on the Egyptians, hail, locusts, and darkness fell over the land. All are trying to get Pharaoh to let the Israelites go free.

Exodus 9-10
Psalm 18:13-18
Proverbs 3:22-24
Matthew 16:13-28

NT}—Jesus was asking his disciples whom they thought he was. When Peter replies, "You are the Christ, the son of the living God," he confirms that Peter is hearing from God and then prophesies that Peter (*Petra*) is the rock of revelation and that on him, mainly through him, Jesus will build his church. Church: "Calling out people," Greek word, "*ekklesia.*"[9]

In the Bible, the church is not mentioned as a building. If you are a follower of Jesus, you are part of the church.

Until now, Christ has not been added to Jesus's name. And just a side note, Christ is not his last name; it is who he is, The Messiah, The Anointed one.

Day 31—January 31

Prayer: Teach me oh Lord what you want me to learn today. Help me Holy Spirit to unfold today's daily scriptures. Amen!

After reading question: What is God saying to me today?

OT}—With Pharaoh primed and ready, God has one more sign to release, number eleven. This was the big finale. All the firstborns in the land would die. God instructs the Israelites to paint sacrificial blood on their door frames so that no plague shall be upon them when the Spirit of Death passes over. Then Pharaoh calls for Moses and Aaron one last time.

➤ God speaks to Moses and Aaron ten times.
➤ Pharaoh requested them seven times and a total of eleven signs, of which ten were plagues: blood, frogs, lice, flies, livestock pestilence, boils, hail, locusts, darkness, and firstborn death.

The timeline is unknown, but it looks like it could have been within a few months.

Exodus 11-12
Psalm 18:19-24
Proverbs 3:25-27
Matthew 17:1-13

NT}—Today, we see Jesus in full glory for the first time. Three inner circle disciples get a first-hand experience of the glory of God, and even though Peter gets the first-hand visit, he still has earthly thoughts. We see the reference made between John the Baptist and Elijah.

Day 32—February 1

Prayer: Teach me oh Lord what you want me to learn today. Help me Holy Spirit to unfold today's daily scriptures. Amen!

After reading question: What is God saying to me today?

OT}—After the heroic acts of Moses and Aaron, the Israelites are freed from four hundred and thirty years of slavery. They are led towards the promised land by the Lord as a pillar of cloud by day and a pillar of fire by night. They were faced with a no-hope situation that, once again, revealed God's love for them, where their complaints began. Then God opens the Red Sea, about three miles wide and two miles long. It took four hours for them to cross on dry land.

God tells us to keep to the promise and not look back to where we once were, but they could not get that into their hearts.

Exodus 13-14
Psalm 18:25-30
Proverbs 3:28-30
Matthew 17:14-27

NT}—Jesus shows the disciples they still have a lot to learn from not being able to deliver a demon out of a boy. Jesus turns to them and says that not every deliverance is just by words but by prayer and fasting.

This is why we need to have a life of prayer so that we can fulfill God's work when an opportunity arises.

Day 33—February 2

<u>Prayer:</u> Teach me oh Lord what you want me to learn today. Help me Holy Spirit to unfold today's daily scriptures. Amen!

<u>After reading question:</u> What is God saying to me today?

OT}—Pharaoh and his army are destroyed, complaint numbers two and three surfaces, and Moses learns he has his hands full. God provided water and food, and it still was not enough. The food was Manna, being like coriander seed and white in color that tasted like a wafer with honey. Chiefs around the world are still using Manna.

Exodus 15-16

Psalm 18:31-36

Proverbs 3:31-33

Matthew 18

NT}—Jesus speaks on forgiveness and how we are to treat each other and receive him like a little child.

Verse 19 is another quoted scripture I have often heard in prayer gatherings. It is similar to what I mentioned on January 13 from Matthew 7 about people using it for their gain. But back up one verse and meditate on that for a second. Does it reflect what verse 19 said about asking for anything? No, it does not! When two or more agree and ask what has already been done in heaven, it is when God is in the midst and will confirm his will, not ours. This is why it is essential to know his Word and Will.

Day 34—February 3

OT}—Wait for it, here it comes…complaint number four. It was not enough that God gave them water after crossing the Red Sea. They still needed to complain that they needed more or they were going to die. Do you think God did all that he did only to bring them to the wilderness to die? I do not think so either, but I guess they were weak after four hundred and thirty years as enslaved people.
Here we see the first government formed after Moses's father-in-law tells him he needs help judging the people.

Exodus 17-18
Psalm 18:37-42
Proverbs 3:34-35
Matthew 19:1-15

NT}—The Pharisees return with a question about marriage and divorce. We often hear this reference at weddings, one man and one woman united in marriage until death. Does that not sound simple? People today do not take today's reading to heart, whether it is in the church or outside of the church. We lost the depth of our heavenly heritage. I, for one, would love to see every Christian honor this passage to its true meaning because it opens many doors to sin.

Day 35—February 4

<u>Prayer:</u> Teach me oh Lord what you want me to learn today. Help me Holy Spirit to unfold today's daily scriptures. Amen!

<u>After reading question:</u> What is God saying to me today?

OT}—Three months into the wilderness experience, Moses is called up to Mount Sinai. Moses first brought the people to the foot of the mountain, where they met God. God came down, wrapped the mountain in smoke, and descended upon it in a fire. They heard God's voice probably for the first time in their lives. Then the Lord called Moses to the top, where he received the Ten Commandments. When Moses comes off the mountain, the Israelites tell him, out of fear, that they will listen to him speak and for him not to let God talk to them, lest they die.

Also, today God instructs how he wants an altar built.

Exodus 19-20
Psalm 18:43-50
Proverbs 4:1-2
Matthew 19:16-30

NT}—A young rich man approaches Jesus, trying to buy his way into heaven, and Jesus says he cannot buy his way in but live by the law and sell all he has. The young man grieved and ran away.

Day 36—February 5

Prayer: Teach me oh Lord what you want me to learn today. Help me Holy Spirit to unfold today's daily scriptures. Amen!

After reading question: What is God saying to me today?

OT}—God instructs Moses to pass along to the people.

We learn about servants and how they will be treated: a daughter sold as a maidservant or bondswoman, murder, child disobedience, kidnapping, that old phrase; an eye for an eye, tooth for tooth, thievery, borrowing, lending, kindness, and end with being holy.

Thankfully some of these are not followed today!

Exodus 21-22

Psalm 19:1-7

Proverbs 4:3-4

Matthew 20

NT}—Jesus teaches how the first will be last, and the last will be first, "For many are called, but few chosen." The story behind this is that we are not to compare ourselves with others and our reward, or payment, is not by works but by his mercy and his choosing.

Day 37—February 6

OT}—Instructions continue, including keeping three feasts throughout the year:
1. Feast of Unleavened Bread
2. Feast of Harvest (Pentecost)
3. Feast of Ingathering, also known as Booths or Tabernacles

God calls Moses, Aaron and his sons, and seventy elders to worship in the placement of the new government. Aaron and his sons, Nadab and Abihu, are priests, with Aaron as a high priest. Then Moses is called up into the mountain again for the tables with the laws and commandments.

Exodus 23-24
Psalm 19:8-14
Proverbs 4:5-6
Matthew 21-1-22

NT}—Jesus enters Jerusalem on a donkey and her colt with a crowd of people praising him. He then gets mad at the temple, maybe the first time he got angry as a man. Then he teaches us about faith.

Note: Matthew is the only gospel that mentions a donkey and her colt.

Day 38—February 7

Prayer: Teach me oh Lord what you want me to learn today. Help me Holy Spirit to unfold today's daily scriptures. Amen!

After reading question: What is God saying to me today?

OT}—We learn how the Ark of the Testimony (Covenant) was to be constructed. No one knows what items were put in there because it has never been found. We do know from today's reading that the tablets with the Ten Commandments went in. Hebrews 9:4 has the best list that I could find.

Over the next few days of readings, you will hear Moses's conversation with our creator.

Exodus 25-26
Psalm 20
Proverbs 4:7-8
Matthew 21:23-46

NT}—The chief priest and elders approach Jesus about his authority in his teachings. Jesus then rebukes them with a another parable.

I love how Jesus uses parables for comparisons as stories to illustrate what he is trying to say. Not that he is trying to trick them, but to show the simplicity of why he is there if they would open their hearts and minds to who he is.

Day 39—February 8

Prayer: Teach me oh Lord what you want me to learn today. Help me Holy Spirit to unfold today's daily scriptures. Amen!

After reading question: What is God saying to me today?

OT}—Moses gets direction on how to build the Bronze Altar and the Court of the Tabernacle. Also, how the priest will dress from now on; a breastplate, ephod, robe, tunic, turban, and a sash/girdle.

See page eight for a description of each one.

Exodus 27-28
Psalm 21:1-7
Proverbs 4:9-10
Matthew 22:1-22

NT}—Today's parable is about the calling of people back to God. Some say the first part would be the Jews, God's chosen people, being allowed to enter heaven. God gives them a personal invitation to the central feast, but they do not believe it is taken place, so they pay it no mind. Next could be all the prophets and such, dying for the cause. God then extends the invitation out to the Gentiles and the rest of the world, and then the church's deviation comes into play, and that is where we see the different religions, or better said, believers.

Day 40—February 9

Prayer: Teach me oh Lord what you want me to learn today. Help me Holy Spirit to unfold today's daily scriptures. Amen!

After reading question: What is God saying to me today?

OT}—To uphold the holiness of the temple, the consecration of the priests, and the altar of incense, are added to Moses's list of things to do. We also learn the ingredients of anointing oil. Something we do not see too much in our churches today, but helpful in healing according to James 5:14.

Exodus 29-30
Psalm 21:4-13
Proverbs 4:11-12
Matthew 22:23-46

NT}—The Sadducees and then the Pharisees are back on the scene. Sadducees who do not believe in the resurrection ask about the dead—the resurrection of a man and seven brothers who all had the same wife. The Pharisees chime in with the question of the greatest commandment. Man, they are hitting him from all sides.

By the way, the greatest commandment is to love your God with all your heart, mind, and soul. The second is to love your neighbor as you love yourself.

The way that we love God is by valuing other people.

Day 41—February 10

Prayer: Teach me oh Lord what you want me to learn today. Help me Holy Spirit to unfold today's daily scriptures. Amen!

After reading question: What is God saying to me today?

OT}—Israel complains for the fifth time about how long Moses is taking. After Aaron turns against his brother, they build a golden calf to worship, then Moses comes down with the tables written on both sides by the finger of God. Aron then lies about his actions.

Moses's love is, "I would be separated from God if they, other Jews, [Israelites], would be united with God."

Exodus 31-32
Psalm 22:1-7
Proverbs 4:13-14
Matthew 23:1-17

NT}—Here, we see a Bible saying that one might say to their kid, "Do as I say, not as I do." Jesus calls the scribes and Pharisees pretenders, or better said, "Hypocrites," saying they look good on the outside, but the inside spirit is filled with hate, lying, and cheating, and they pretend to follow the law. They love the place of honor of their titles and good works. They are putting themselves up on a pedestal.

It is OK to have a leadership position in the church or a ministry, but remember it is God who is the true leader, Father, Rabbi, Priest…

Day 42—February 11

Prayer: Teach me oh Lord what you want me to learn today. Help me Holy Spirit to unfold today's daily scriptures. Amen!

After reading question: What is God saying to me today?

OT}—After forty days and nights, Moses is released by God to return to his people, mainly because they quickly turned from all that Moses had taught them. As soon as Moses saw the golden calf and all the partying, anger rose, and he threw the two tables from his hands, and they broke. He then melted the calf down to powder and scattered it over the water commanding them to drink it. God tells them to move on, and unlike the first set of tables, Moses has to make two new ones with his own hands.

Exodus 33-34

Psalm 22:8-15

Proverbs 4:15-16

Matthew 23:18-39

NT}—Jesus continues to confront the scribes and Pharisees (hypocrites), and then he prophesies the second coming. In earlier readings, we have seen who the scribes and Pharisees were and why Jesus calls them pretenders. Unfortunately, we still see people like them today reading the Word but do not honestly believe what it says. They read the Word, had Jesus in front of them, and still needed to question him. If future generations do not take hold of this Word, verse 39 will be hard to come to pass.

Day 43—February 12

Prayer: Teach me oh Lord what you want me to learn today. Help me Holy Spirit to unfold today's daily scriptures. Amen!

After reading question: What is God saying to me today?

OT}—Today marks the beginning of the Sabbath, a rest to the Lord. As you will see, God's love was so great for the Israelites that God kept loving them no matter how defiant they were.

Moses constructs the tabernacle, a portable sanctuary, with every detail of craftsmanship according to God's plans to be used for offerings and where the Ark of the Covenant will be placed. The Lord requires an offering from the people to provide for the project. This time when the people bring their jewelry, it is not to build a false god, calf; it is for the true living God.

Exodus 35-36
Psalm 22:16-22
Proverbs 4:17-18
Matthew 24:1-25

NT}—The disciples were curious about the timing of Jesus' return. Then Jesus proclaims what it will look like at that time. But no one, not even Jesus knows the day or hour he will be sent back, only the Father. This is why we are told to be watchful in all matters so that we are not left behind when the time comes.

Day 44—February 13

Prayer: Teach me oh Lord what you want me to learn today. Help me Holy Spirit to unfold today's daily scriptures. Amen!

After reading question: What is God saying to me today?

OT}—The work on the tabernacle continues.

This was a precise plan and had to be followed precisely as God said. God did not trust anyone to fulfill this mission, which is why Moses was in command. Because of the holiness on the tabernacle, the priest were the main ones to do the work under the direction of Ithamar, son of Aaron, the high priest. Also, Bezalel, son of Uri, and Aholiab, son of Ahisamach, an engraver, a skillful craftsman, and an embroiderer in fine linen.

Exodus 37-38
Psalm 22:23-31
Proverbs 4:19-20
Matthew 24:26-51

NT}—Just as the tabernacle was built precisely to God's plan, so was the return of his son. When God feels that the "*Good News*" has been preached to the whole world and every tongue will have the opportunity to confess Jesus as Lord, the end will be at hand.

Day 45—February 14

Prayer: Teach me oh Lord what you want me to learn today. Help me Holy Spirit to unfold today's daily scriptures. Amen!

After reading question: What is God saying to me today?

OT}—The tabernacle is finished. I have heard that in calculations, it might have taken around nine months to construct. Moses was given the plan in the third month of being released from slavery, and the erection of the tent took place in the first month of the following year.

Exodus 39-40
Psalm 23
Proverbs 4:21-22
Matthew 25

NT}—Jesus tries to convey what it will be like at the moment of his return. How wise are we with our talents and our resources? As Christians, do we just sit on the sidelines and do nothing to build ourselves up? No reading the Word, not even going to meetings, or even paying attention when we go to church. How about doing nothing with the talents that God has given us? Are we using them for the sake of the kingdom? God has blessed us with good resources, but do we help others? If the answers to these questions are no, verses 30 and 45 are for us.

I know that I ask myself a lot; will I be ready?

Day 46—February 15

Prayer: Teach me oh Lord what you want me to learn today. Help me Holy Spirit to unfold today's daily scriptures. Amen!

After reading question: What is God saying to me today?

OT}—Today, we start on the Third Book of Moses called "Leviticus." It was given as instructions during Israel's one-year encampment at Mount Sinai. The critical statement of Leviticus is found in chapter 11, verse 45, "You shall be holy, for I am holy." What more can we ask for from our heavenly Father who teaches us how to live? It starts with God calling out to Moses. It is a Hebrew word, *"Vayikra,"* meaning, *"and he called!"*

Leviticus 1-3
Psalm 24:1-5
Proverbs 4:23-24
Matthew 26

NT}—This is a chapter packed with prophecy, truth, love, betrayal for twenty dollars and sixty cents, fellowship, selfishness, denial, abandonment, and lack of respect.

Jesus prepares the disciples for what will happen to him and prepares for the Passover. During the Passover supper, Jesus confronts his betrayer.

We also read today that when Jesus gets arrested, they start his drawn-out trial.

Day 47—February 16

<u>Prayer:</u> Teach me oh Lord what you want me to learn today. Help me Holy Spirit to unfold today's daily scriptures. Amen!

<u>After reading question:</u> What is God saying to me today?

OT}—Leviticus starts with how to offer themselves to God, a ceremony we no longer need to perform because Jesus was the last sacrifice needed. Now we just submit ourselves to him by our worship and living right.

As you read over these chapters about how they were to bring their offerings to make restitution for their sins, notice that God makes available a way for each class of people, rich to poor. God's mercies are fantastic!

Leviticus 4-5
Psalm 24:6-10
Proverbs 4:25-27
Matthew 27

NT}—Judas realizes that he made a mistake, and it breaks his heart. He returns the thirty pieces of silver, which fulfilled Jeremiah's word in Zechariah 11:12-13.

Jesus is taken down the most brutal journey and becomes the ultimate sacrifice to save a broken, fallen world. Because of this journey is why we should be thankful every day for our salvation. Sinners being made righteous is why Jesus walked that path to the cross. Praise God for that kind of love.

Day 48—February 17

<u>Prayer:</u> Teach me oh Lord what you want me to learn today. Help me Holy Spirit to unfold today's daily scriptures. Amen!

<u>After reading question:</u> What is God saying to me today?

OT}—As you will read, this teaching that God provided lines up with the Ten Commandments he gave to Moses. Today speaks about how we deal with our neighbors, not just those who live next door to us. A neighbor is anyone we are in contact with: a co-worker, team member, or even the person we pass on the street or stand in line with at the store. What will you do if the person in front of you pulls their hand out of their pocket and a twenty-dollar bill falls on the floor?

Leviticus 6-7
Psalm 25:1-7
Proverbs 5:1-3
Matthew 28

NT}—Jesus has risen and returned to where he came from. Returns to full glory to be an advocate to Father God.

We are anointed for ministry/discipleship. God has called all of us to change the world. Everyone has been ordained to build and teach. Therefore, prepare for your ministry by;
- ➤ Study
- ➤ Learn to pray
- ➤ Learn how to disciple
- ➤ Seek first the Kingdom of God

Day 49—February 18

Prayer: Teach me oh Lord what you want me to learn today. Help me Holy Spirit to unfold today's daily scriptures. Amen!

After reading question: What is God saying to me today?

OT}—Here, we see how the priest, Aaron and sons, prepared themselves so that they could stand in the gap for the people.

Today we have the authority given to us by Jesus to do the same thing for ourselves. We can prepare our lives daily and go to the father with our sins, asking for forgiveness. Reading your daily scriptures is a great place to start, so keep it up!

Leviticus 8-9
Psalm 25:8-14
Proverbs 5:4-6
Mark 1:1-22

NT}—Today, we begin the Second Book of the Gospels, Mark. It was written during Peter's lifetime or shortly after his death. (A.D. 55-65)

Even though John Mark's name is not mentioned, many scholars believe he is the author. He was a close associate of Simeon Peter, mainly because he recorded the life of Jesus according to the eyewitness account given by Peter and some of the other apostles.

Day 50—February 19

OT}—Today, we learn what animals are and are not suitable for eating. Some clean animals are cattle, antelope, goat, elk, deer, fish like bass, cod, flounder, grouper, salmon, snapper, trout, and tuna. Clean fish must have scales and fins. Unclean animals are most insects except locusts, grasshoppers, and crickets. Even though people eat catfish, lobster, crabs, and shrimp, back then, God says they should not eat them. Also, rabbits, pigs, and unclean birds. The list goes on…

Leviticus 10-11
Psalm 25:15-22
Proverbs 5:7-9
Mark 1:23-45

NT}—Mark starts with an introduction to John the Baptist and the baptismal of Jesus. Then he jumps right in on the beginning of Jesus's ministry.

Even though the authority of Jesus has command over evil spirits, they can be stubborn and unwilling to listen, but at the end of the day, they must bow down to the name of Jesus and do what they are told. Remember this when you are praying with someone.

Day 51—February 20

OT}—Here, we see how a woman must act after giving birth to a child. Also, back then, the priest were the ones people would go to for health issues, and the priest would then direct the path the person must take according to the law. Today we turn to doctors or medical professionals for help. But unlike then, we are not cast out just because we have an issue.

Leviticus 12-13
Psalm 26:1-6
Proverbs 5:10-12
Mark 2:1-13

NT}—Today, you will read the true meaning of friendship and the faith that four guys had in helping their friend. Determination is a powerful thing with some great results.

Even though Jesus is no longer here on earth in a physical body, his authority is here through Holy Spirit. What does that mean? You and I, being saved, are engrafted in the branch that holds that same authority as when Jesus was here. To do the same works, heal the sick, command the lame to walk, blind eyes to see, and give comfort to the brokenhearted, all in the name of Jesus without it being blaspheming.

Day 52—February 21

OT}—The following two chapters discuss the same things as yesterday on going to the priest with an issue. I am delighted that today our society does not cast us out, for the most part, that is. Over my lifespan, I have had some issues with my skin: acne, psoriasis, and maybe other names. I would have been cast out of the city if I had lived back then. I am grateful that I live in this day and age.

Leviticus 14-15
Psalm 26:7-12
Proverbs 5:13-14
Mark 2:14-28

NT}—Jesus gets right in the middle of some sinners and sparks a controversial conversation.

To put clarity to verse 18, this John is John the Baptist. Even though John was in prison, his followers still followed the Jewish law.

The fast you read about today was one of the four fasts that the Jews observed as a corporate fast.

Day 53—February 22

Prayer: Teach me oh Lord what you want me to learn today. Help me Holy Spirit to unfold today's daily scriptures. Amen!

After reading question: What is God saying to me today?

OT}—Do you remember that on February 12, I mentioned the priest having to tie the rope around them before going into the Holy of Holies? Well, today, you will read why I said that.

Here we also see that just because you are a guest in someone's city or home, does not mean you do not follow the rules they laid down.

Leviticus 16-17
Psalm 27:1-7
Proverbs 5:15-16
Mark 3:1-19

NT}—One of the takeaways I get from the first few verses of this chapter is how insensitive the Pharisees were. They were so stuck in religious ways that they could not care less if a person was made whole.

The people gathered from nearby cities, and because there were so many, Jesus had to preach from a small boat so he would not get crushed.

Day 54—February 23

Prayer: Teach me oh Lord what you want me to learn today. Help me Holy Spirit to unfold today's daily scriptures. Amen!

After reading question: What is God saying to me today?

OT}—God instructs the Israelites not to live as they did in the past; No sex with relatives, orgies, men with men and women with women, respecting parents, taking from another, gossiping, or holding grudges. He goes on with keeping the Sabbath holy and respecting the church, seeking out psychic readings, seances, or even Ouija boards can be on this list. I used to think it was just a game, but the Holy Spirit taught me that it is an open gateway to the dark side.

Leviticus 18-19

Psalm 27:8-14

Proverbs 5:17-18

Mark 3:20-35

NT}—It seemed to be that whenever Jesus was in Capernaum, he stood at Peter's house. Maybe that is why Peter is considered to be Jesus's favorite disciple.

Jesus teaches that we should not speak against Holy Spirit or misrepresent him. Holy Spirit is God inside us, which joins us back to God.

Day 55—February 24

Prayer: Teach me oh Lord what you want me to learn today. Help me Holy Spirit to unfold today's daily scriptures. Amen!

After reading question: What is God saying to me today?

OT}—"You shall consecrate yourselves therefore and be holy; for I am the Lord your God. And you shall keep My statutes and do them. I am the Lord who sanctifies you." (Lev. 20:7-8)

Leviticus 20-21
Psalm 28
Proverbs 5:19-20
Mark 4:1-20

NT}—Jesus teaches in parables.

Over the years, people have asked what the meaning of a parable is. Simply put, a parable is an illustration or comparison set beside truths to explain them. Jesus used them for a spiritual lesson.

There are at least thirty-six parables and over one hundred metaphors used by Jesus throughout the New Testament.

➢ Matthew has 15
➢ Mark has 6; 4 are repeats from Matthew
➢ Luke has 35; 16 repeats and 19 unique

Day 56—February 25

<u>Prayer:</u> Teach me oh Lord what you want me to learn today. Help me Holy Spirit to unfold today's daily scriptures. Amen!

<u>After reading question:</u> What is God saying to me today?

OT}—The Lord speaks to Moses to give Aaron and his sons some direction. Then he tells Moses, multiple times, what to say to the Israelites.

I am so glad that today God speaks directly to me, and I do not need to wait for someone else to tell me what God is saying, or better yet, what his plan is for my life.

Leviticus 22-23
Psalm 29:1-6
Proverbs 5:21-23
Mark 4:21-41

NT}—Jesus continues to explain the seed parable and breaks down the different levels of Christian belief, and how we are not all the same, even if we go to the same church.

Then, on the same day, Jesus uses an illustration of wind and roaring sea to address the lack of faith and understanding of any of the teachings thus far from the disciples.

Day 57—February 26

<u>Prayer:</u> Teach me oh Lord what you want me to learn today. Help me Holy Spirit to unfold today's daily scriptures. Amen!

<u>After reading question:</u> What is God saying to me today?

OT}—Here is where we get something you may have already heard of; "eye for an eye, tooth for a tooth," highlighting the law of retaliation. This principle is no longer in effect like it was back then. Today we have laws and jurisdiction systems that will handle people's wrongdoings, but people still carry it in their hearts, going against God's principles.

Leviticus 24-25
Psalm 29:7-11
Proverbs 6:1-3
Mark 5:1-20

{NT}—Jesus meets a man who has been under Satan's power for years. As soon as they saw Jesus, the evil spirits knew who he was.

In this example of how the spirits can take over someone, we see that they built up a stronghold with many different demons after many years. This is why we need to handle ourselves and not build anger, hate, and other feelings.

Day 58—February 27

Prayer: Teach me oh Lord what you want me to learn today. Help me Holy Spirit to unfold today's daily scriptures. Amen!

After reading question: What is God saying to me today?

OT}—There shall be no idols. You will see the power of unity prayer. And the scattering that is found in verse 26:33.

Some believe this was fulfilled when the Jews were forced to leave their country out of fear of losing their lives if they stood in their homes when King Nebuchadnezzar overthrew Judah. We end this book today in verse 27:34, "These are the commandments which the Lord commanded Moses on Mount Sinai for the Israelites."

Leviticus 26-27

Psalm 30:1-6

Proverbs 6:4-6

Mark 5:21-43

NT}—Jesus brings a little girl back to life, but he must empty the room first.

If you mock God, he will put you out!

As Jesus enters back into Capernaum from the lakeshore, he is greeted by Jairus, a ruler in the synagogue. He was a well-known religious leader who expressed his faith in Jesus to be able to heal his daughter from a deadly disease.

Day 59—February 28

Prayer: Teach me oh Lord what you want me to learn today. Help me Holy Spirit to unfold today's daily scriptures. Amen!

After reading question: What is God saying to me today?

OT}—Numbers, book number four, the Greek word *"Bemidbar,"* meaning *"in the wilderness."* The book accounts for thirty-eight years of wilderness wandering with murmuring and rebellion from the Israelites. Just picture this; if they had just been obedient and trusted God from Egypt, they could have completed the journey to the promised land in forty days.

Today we read that the tabernacle was under the tribe of Levites, and the rest of the tribes of Israel were instructed how they would camp around it.

Numbers 1-2
Psalm 30:7-12
Proverbs 6:7-9
Mark 6:1-29

NT}—Jesus returns to his hometown, Nazareth, but he is not accepted. They could not believe that the carpenter's son could be full of the wisdom and intelligence he was speaking with. They disapproved of him, and it hindered them from acknowledging his authority.

Verse 17 starts to tell a story about King Herod pursuing John the Baptist and ends it in verse 29.

Day 60—March 1

<u>Prayer:</u> Teach me oh Lord what you want me to learn today. Help me Holy Spirit to unfold today's daily scriptures. Amen!

<u>After reading question:</u> What is God saying to me today?

OT}—The Lord starts to get Moses ready to take the promised land by preparing and setting a head count, by taking a census of all the males according to their tribes.

We also get a list of names of the men that helped Moses.

The tribe of the Levites was instructed that they would be responsible for the tabernacle and how they would assist. Aaron and his sons were the only ones who would pack and unpack everything in the tabernacle. Then the male Kohathites, Gershonites, and sons of Merari were assigned each to his work of serving and carrying.

Numbers 3-4
Psalm 31:1-8
Proverbs 6:10-12
Mark 6:30-56

NT}—Jesus offers up to the Father five loaves and two fishes to feed five thousand men, plus women and children. In theory, that could have been anywhere from ten to fifteen thousand or more people. That's a lot of fish!

The book of Mark does not mention Peter walking on water in verses 48-51.

Day 61—March 2

Prayer: Teach me oh Lord what you want me to learn today. Help me Holy Spirit to unfold today's daily scriptures. Amen!

After reading question: What is God saying to me today?

OT}—The Lord talks to Moses about how the Israelites should act if any man's wife goes astray and commits an offense of guilt against him.

You will end today's reading from the Old Testament with one of the most famous blessings leaders will release congregations with, chapter 6, verses 24-27.

Numbers 5-6
Psalm 31:9-16
Proverbs 6:13-15
Mark 7:1-18

NT}—Jesus talks about traditions in how they are manmade and not from God.

You may ask, what is tradition? Merriam-Webster.com dictionary says it is:

a. : an inherited, established, or customary pattern of thought, action, or behavior (such as a religious practice or a social custom)

b. : a belief or story or a body of beliefs or stories relating to the past that are commonly accepted as historical though not verifiable[10]

Day 62—March 3

Prayer: Teach me oh Lord what you want me to learn today. Help me Holy Spirit to unfold today's daily scriptures. Amen!

After reading question: What is God saying to me today?

OT}—After the tabernacle's completion, the first offerings are given up to the Lord, and the Lord directs Moses on how Aaron is to set up the lampstand. Jews call this the *Menorah*. It is the oldest continuously used religious symbol in western civilization. The Menorah symbolizes the creation in seven days, with the center light representing the sabbath.

Numbers 7-8
Psalm 31:17-24
Proverbs 6:16-18
Mark 7:19-37

NT}—Back in Leviticus, chapter 11, you read about what animals were good or not good to eat. You may have thought to yourself, that was then, and this is now so that we can eat that stuff. We know Jesus came, not to abolish the law, but to fulfill it. But today, he makes a statement that has been controversial for years, starting in verse 20 and ending in verse 23, which helps to smooth out that list of unclean foods.

After Jesus clears that up, he continues his influence by heading to Tyre and Sidon, where he deals with a Greek mom begging him to deliver her daughter from unclean spirits.

Day 63—March 4

Prayer: Teach me oh Lord what you want me to learn today. Help me Holy Spirit to unfold today's daily scriptures. Amen!

After reading question: What is God saying to me today?

OT}—God talks about the Passover, instructing what to do when a man is defiled and how a stranger will act. The Lord led the Israelites through the wilderness with a cloud ascending/descending on the tabernacle.

Because they did not have today's technology, Moses used trumpets to communicate with his people. An alarm was blown whenever the Israelites were to assemble and set out on their journey.

Numbers 9-10

Psalm 32:1-6

Proverbs 6:19-21

Mark 8:1-21

NT}—Jesus is moved with compassion to feed four thousand men, women, and children. Some say this might have been the same feeding we read in chapter 6 because of the way it was written in some of the other gospels.

But we read in verses 18 to 21 where Jesus mentions both accounts, and in Matthew 16:9-10, the Jewish people told the disciples about their faith in both versions.

Day 64—March 5

Prayer: Teach me oh Lord what you want me to learn today. Help me Holy Spirit to unfold today's daily scriptures. Amen!

After reading question: What is God saying to me today?

OT}—The Lord shows anger to the Israelites complaining and murmuring.

We read how much love Moses had for his people. Remarkably, Moses was willing to take on the people's burdens as an atonement for their sins. The example of what Jesus did on the cross for us.

Numbers 11-12
Psalm 32:7-11
Proverbs 6:22-24
Mark 8:22-38

NT}—Jesus heals the blind man in Bethsaida and talks about our external life in the kingdom.

Some people asked why Jesus had to touch the blind man a second time. In the aspect of faith, sometimes a person may be standing on the fence with their belief. We can assume that might have been the case because the people brought the man and begged Jesus to touch him. The blind man might have been a nuisance. Either way, the power of Jesus spitting in his eyes worked the first time, but the man's faith was weak.

Day 65—March 6

<u>Prayer:</u> Teach me oh Lord what you want me to learn today. Help me Holy Spirit to unfold today's daily scriptures. Amen!

<u>After reading question:</u> What is God saying to me today?

OT}—God tells Moses to send out scouts to the land of Canaan to spy on the people and the value of the land. Once again, the Israelites grumble over the reports that came back and compared their time back in Egypt.

Numbers 13-14

Psalm 33:1-7

Proverbs 6:25-27

Mark 9:1-25

NT}—Jesus is transfigured before Peter, James, and John. Then Elijah and Moses show up to put an even more twist on their faith.

I always laugh when I read verse 16 in today's reading. In many other accounts, we read that Jesus knew what someone was saying or thinking. So why does he have to ask as if he did not understand what was happening? I believe that because Jesus was not around, the scribes wanted to use it to assert their authority and draw the disciples back into their legalistic mindset. Jesus wanted the disciples to hear how deceiving they were.

Day 66—March 7

Prayer: Teach me oh Lord what you want me to learn today. Help me Holy Spirit to unfold today's daily scriptures. Amen!

After reading question: What is God saying to me today?

OT}—God gives direction about how to bring an offering when they get to the promised land. Also, God's compassion is extended outside the lines to any who calls Israel their home and wants to live according to Israel's customs.

Chapter 15, verse 38, mentions a blue cord, Tekhelet in Hebrew, being added to the tassel. The color blue was always the symbol of heavenly beauty; thus, they were constantly reminded that they were under the direct government of God.

Moses confronts the Levi's for talking about Aaron and all of his sons.

Numbers 15-16
Psalm 33:8-14
Proverbs 6:28-30
Mark 9:26-50

NT}—Jesus and his disciples leave the holy mount towards Capernaum through Galilee. On the way, the disciples discussed and argued which one was the greatest. This opens another opportunity for Jesus to give them another teaching on their lack of faith.

Day 67—March 8

<u>Prayer:</u> Teach me oh Lord what you want me to learn today. Help me Holy Spirit to unfold today's daily scriptures. Amen!

<u>After reading question:</u> What is God saying to me today?

OT}—The Levites are separated from the other tribes because they have no inheritance from the land but only through offerings. This means they have homes, cities, and pasturage to use but not to possess as their inheritance!

Numbers 17-18

Psalm 33:15-22

Proverbs 6:31-33

Mark 10:1-27

NT}—The Pharisees test Jesus about the law to find a weakness in him. The disciples want more information on the matter. Then Jesus turns to the children and loves on them.

Today I want to give you a little note on verse 15. After Jesus relieves the children, he uses them to express entering the Kingdom of God. Depending on what version of Bible you read from, the first part of that verse means the same. You might have "Truly," "Verily," "Assuredly," or just, "I tell you." This statement is seen about 76 times in the New Testament in one form or another. The meaning is all the same; God is saying, "*Listen Up*" to what I am about to say because it is crucial.

Day 68—March 9

Prayer: Teach me oh Lord what you want me to learn today. Help me Holy Spirit to unfold today's daily scriptures. Amen!

After reading question: What is God saying to me today?

OT}—Once again, the people make a complaint to Moses about the lack of water (provision). They still do not trust God whole heartily. This is where God tells Moses that he will not be entering the promised land.

I love Moses's heart, which confirms how big it was. He spends all the time and energy to get the people where they need to be and is told that he does not get to touch it, just gets to see it, and still pours out his love for the people.

Numbers 19-20

Psalm 34:1-7

Proverbs 6:34-35

Mark 10:28-52

NT}—Yesterday, we ended with knowing that all things are possible with God. Then today, we see Peter compares himself to what Jesus was saying yesterday and acts a.little selfish.

The journey continues towards Jerusalem, building their faith and Jesus proclaiming his destiny.

When they pass through Jericho, Jesus heals Bartimaeus, a blind beggar.

Day 69—March 10

Prayer: Teach me oh Lord what you want me to learn today. Help me Holy Spirit to unfold today's daily scriptures. Amen!

After reading question: What is God saying to me today?

OT}—The fight begins, and the people again speak against God and Moses, saying, "Why have you brought us out of Egypt to die in the wilderness?" And, once again, God forgives them, and the journey continues.

Today, we read a story about Balaam, a fortuneteller whom God used to speak to Balak, the king of Moab. When Balaam disobeys God's direction, God uses a donkey to set him straight. I like the illustration in verse 30 of chapter 22. Sometimes we miss our blessings!

Numbers 21-22
Psalm 34:8-14
Proverbs 7:1-3
Mark 11:1-17

NT}—Passing through Bethany, just outside of Jerusalem, Jesus was hungry and went to a fig tree he saw in the distance, but even though the leaves were green, there was no fruit. With a fig tree, the fruit appears simultaneously with the leaves. So, since there was no fruit, Jesus cursed it never to produce fruit again.

Sometimes we can get ahead of God and do things our way with no fruit.

Day 70—March 11

OT}—Today, you continue reading about Balaam and Balak. So far, we see that Balaam is not from the Israel tribe, but he was a prophet and foreteller of events that King Balak would look to for answers. Throughout this story, God continues to speak to Balaam despite his wickedness to give guidance to the king. It shows us that spiritual giftedness does not equal spiritual maturity or holiness of life.

God knew Balak wanted a spiritual curse on Israel, but Balaam could not curse them unless God cursed them first.

Numbers 23-24
Psalm 34:15-22
Proverbs 7:4-5
Mark 11:18-33

NT}—Yesterday, you read about the fig tree and that Jesus cursed it because it did not have any fruit. That is an example to us. Just like the fig tree withered literary overnight, God can and will do the same to us if we do not allow our lives to bear heavenly fruit.

Have faith in God constantly.

Day 71—March 12

Prayer: Teach me oh Lord what you want me to learn today. Help me Holy Spirit to unfold today's daily scriptures. Amen!

After reading question: What is God saying to me today?

OT}—Israel turns away from God towards the god of Baal of Peor and has sex parties. God's anger is kindled against Israel, and he orders all the leaders to be hung. Afterward, Aaron's grandson, Phinehas, kills two of the people who played a part in the plague that killed 24,000 people, and God was pleased with his action and made a covenant of peace for the people.

Numbers 25-26
Psalm 35:1-7
Proverbs 7:6-7
Mark 12:1-23

NT}—Jesus teaches in a parable and is asked a question on the resurrection.

Jesus uses the vineyard parable to point to himself in his last days. Those that were set before him and the people rejected the truth. In verse 6 son would refer to Jesus. The landowner is God. The tower is God's protection over Israel. Tenants are religious leaders. Vinedressers refer to the Israel people. Bondservants would be anyone who tried to put them on the right path, like John the Baptist.

Day 72—March 13

<u>Prayer:</u> Teach me oh Lord what you want me to learn today. Help me Holy Spirit to unfold today's daily scriptures. Amen!

<u>After reading question:</u> What is God saying to me today?

OT}—Here, God allows inheritance to be passed down to daughters for the first time. The daughters of Zelophehad, who had no sons, petitioned the Lord through Moses, asking, "Why should the name of our father be removed from his family because he had no son?" God agreed.

Numbers 27-28
Psalm 35:8-14
Proverbs 7:8-9
Mark 12:24-44

NT}—Jesus answers the resurrection question as well as the one on the most important commandment.

Giving is probably the most talked about action for a believer, "Give, and it shall be given back to you," "Give with a cheerful heart," and many others. Today we see that when you give out of faith, compared to giving out of abundance, God smiles more.

There is immense value in investing everything into Jesus.

Day 73—March 14

Prayer: Teach me oh Lord what you want me to learn today. Help me Holy Spirit to unfold today's daily scriptures. Amen!

After reading question: What is God saying to me today?

OT}—God speaks on what is still happening today all across the land. Also, the great Day of Atonement and the Feast of Tabernacles takes place after *Rosh Hashanah*, New Year. Its origin is commemorated with a loud blast from the shofar, a ram's horn, usually in September. *Yom Kippur*, the Day of Atonement, is eight days after Rosh Hashanah for the cleansing of sins. Sukkot, Feast of Tabernacles, is to commemorate the exodus from Egypt five days later.[11]

Numbers 29-30
Psalm 35:15-21
Proverbs 7:10-11
Mark 13:1-18

NT}—Peter, James, John, and Andrew privately ask Jesus about the signs of the end times. It is hard to comment on today's reading because many have tried and gotten it wrong. I will ask you one question though; Do you think we are in the end times?

➢ False prophets—seen and have them
➢ Wars—plenty of them around the world
➢ Earthquakes in various places—yep
➢ Famines and Calamities—covid helped this one
➢ People being martyred for their faith—most definitely

Day 74—March 15

<u>Prayer:</u> Teach me oh Lord what you want me to learn today. Help me Holy Spirit to unfold today's daily scriptures. Amen!

<u>After reading question:</u> What is God saying to me today?

OT}—With the time spent in the wilderness experience, the Israelites grew into a massive group of tribes. Things were starting to come together for the new land they were to possess, but because of their disobedience and lack of trust, or even better yet, faith, many of the men did not get to go into the new land. God caused them to wander in the wilderness for forty years until they died.

Numbers 31-32
Psalm 35:22-28
Proverbs 7:12-13
Mark 13:19-37

NT}—Jesus continues the conversation on the end times and what it will look like.
- ➢ Brother against brother and father against son—yep
- ➢ Oppression and Tribulation—always
- ➢ More false Messiahs—For-sure

What's left?

Because of our technology, there are not too many places left in the world for preaching the good news. Fire in the sky from the stars falling. Who knows but God, our job is to keep watch and keep sharing!

Day 75—March 16

Prayer: Teach me oh Lord what you want me to learn today. Help me Holy Spirit to unfold today's daily scriptures. Amen!

After reading question: What is God saying to me today?

OT}—Today, you will get to read the journey step-by-step as recorded by Moses. Count their moves to determine how many times the Israelites may have pulled stakes to move before reaching the land of Canaan.

See page fourteen to compare your findings.

Numbers 33-34
Psalm 36:1-6
Proverbs 7:14-15
Mark 14:1-25

NT}—Chief priests and scribes are planning how they will arrest Jesus. Meanwhile, Jesus and the disciples are preparing for Passover.

We hear many Jewish Feasts throughout the Bible, and today is no different. Some people read verse 1 and think it is two separate events, so I wanted to share a little light on them.

Hebrew *Pesach*, meaning Passover, is a seven-day celebration in spring commemorating the liberation from slavery. The Feast of Unleavened Bread starts on the second day of Passover. Also, The Feast of Firstfruits is that week as well.[12]

Day 76—March 17

<u>Prayer:</u> Teach me oh Lord what you want me to learn today. Help me Holy Spirit to unfold today's daily scriptures. Amen!

<u>After reading question:</u> What is God saying to me today?

OT}—We end the Book of Numbers with the Lord instructing Moses to tell the Israelites where the bounty lines will be and what goes to the Levites.

Numbers 35-36

Psalm 36:7-12

Proverbs 7:16-17

Mark 14:26-49

NT}—After the Passover supper, Jesus has communion with the disciples, which is something we still do today in remembrance of that day.

Why take Communion?

> ➤ To commemorate the death of Jesus: Taken of bread symbolizes the broken body of Jesus
> ➤ Drinking of juice or wine: To signify, seal, and apply to believers all the benefits of the new covenant through the shedding of the blood.

After supper, they went to the Garden of Gethsemane, where Judas Iscariot betrays Jesus.

Day 77—March 18

Prayer: Teach me oh Lord what you want me to learn today. Help me Holy Spirit to unfold today's daily scriptures. Amen!

After reading question: What is God saying to me today?

OT}—Today, you start on the fifth and final Book of Moses, Deuteronomy, which means in Greek, *"Second lawgiving,"* where Moses summarizes the essence of Israel's religion. It is a powerful message, hidden in the Bible, that the eleven-day journey took forty years and that God kept Moses with him at Mount Sini for forty days and nights.

Deuteronomy 1-2
Psalm 37:1-7
Proverbs 7:18-19
Mark 14:50-72

NT}—One of the things about the stories told about when Jesus was captured they go right into him being handed over to Pilate. What they fail to mention is that the night they took Jesus, he was in front of the church's counsel and the high priest Caiaphas first. Today's reading makes that clear.

In verses 51 and 52, Mark mentions a man who fled naked. No identity is mentioned and is not mentioned in any of the other Gospels. Some believe that since it was only mentioned here in Mark, it was Mark himself. A question for us to ask when we are face-to-face with God.

Day 78—March 19

Prayer: Teach me oh Lord what you want me to learn today. Help me Holy Spirit to unfold today's daily scriptures. Amen!

After reading question: What is God saying to me today?

OT}—One of the reasons I believe the Israelites' journey took so long was that they were so stuck in their ways as enslaved people; from being in Egypt for so long. They could not see God's Love right in front of them! Even with God telling them straight out what to do and not do, it did not help.

I wonder how many times we do that today ourselves.

Deuteronomy 3-4
Psalm 37:8-14
Proverbs 7:20-21
Mark 15

NT}—Jesus is held for trial, then crucified on calvary after a brutal journey from the palace.

I hate this part of history in seeing what my Lord had to go through so that I have my sins forgiven and receive eternal life. Why is it that we, the people, from the beginning of time, have a hard time believing in true things? We question just about everything and approach things with doubtful thoughts. Then when a tragedy comes along, we can see the truth. That is precisely what happened to the centurion who put Jesus on the cross.

Day 79—March 20

Prayer: Teach me oh Lord what you want me to learn today. Help me Holy Spirit to unfold today's daily scriptures. Amen!

After reading question: What is God saying to me today?

OT}—Moses recalls the Ten Commandments and tries to realign the Israelites with God's instructions.

God spoke directly to the Israelites, but they still had difficulty believing and trusting God's Word. As a father, I love talking to my children, especially when I can share my wisdom and give them direction in their life. What saddens me is when they disregard my words. The people of Israel did the same to God after he did so much for them and spent all that time with Moses laying out the plans for their lives.

Deuteronomy 5-6

Psalm 37:15-21

Proverbs 7:22-23

Mark 16

NT}—After the sabbath, when many believe it is the time that Jesus was coming out of Hades with the keys to the kingdom that Lucifer stole when they were in heaven, Jesus rose. After he appeared to Mary Magdalene, she went to tell the others with excitement, but they did not believe her. Jesus then is saddened and rebuked the eleven remaining apostles with disappointment for their lack of faith.

Day 80—March 21

Prayer: Teach me oh Lord what you want me to learn today. Help me Holy Spirit to unfold today's daily scriptures. Amen!

After reading question: What is God saying to me today?

OT}—Here is something that is too funny to me: God tells them how many nations he will give them to defeat with his help, and they are still afraid. He tells them what not to do when they destroy those nations, and they do not listen.
Talk about being hard-headed!

Deuteronomy 7-8
Psalm 37:22-27
Proverbs 7:24-25
Luke 1:1-25

NT}—Today, we go to gospel number three, Luke.

It is the longest gospel and links to the Book of Acts. Luke was a physician who most likely was not Jewish. He was from Antioch in Syria. The Book of Luke has been recognized as a complete representative account of the life of Jesus.

Luke was associated with Apostle Paul in his ministry and wrote down the account of his activities.

Day 81—March 22

OT}—God tells them that it is not because of their righteousness on why they are getting the land, that it is because of the sins of the other nations, and the promise/ covenant the Lord swore to Abraham, Isaac, and Jacob.

That is what it is like for us today; Jesus is the new covenant for our future.

Deuteronomy 9-10
Psalm 37:28-33
Proverbs 7:26-27
Luke 1:26-52

NT}—Luke starts with his purpose in this writing and jumps right into the accounts that lead to the conception of Jesus.

Some people have questioned whether Mary was a virgin and if she and Joseph were married then. I can only assume that these people do not read the Bible because today, in verse 27, it is evident that Mary and Joseph were not married when Jesus was conceived, and she was a virgin. And talk about trust; just listen to her faith today.

Day 82—March 23

Prayer: Teach me oh Lord what you want me to learn today. Help me Holy Spirit to unfold today's daily scriptures. Amen!

After reading question: What is God saying to me today?

OT}—As you read this part of history, do you see the depth of love Moses had for the Israelites? I believe that love is why God speaks about the difference between Egypt and the new land. And how they had to labor to have a crop, compared to the hills and valleys that will be cared for by God.

Deuteronomy 11-12
Psalm 37:34-40
Proverbs 8:1-3
Luke 1:53-80

NT}—Today, John the Baptist was born, and his father, Zachariah, prophesied.

On March 19, I was talking about the lack of believers. As you have read over the past couple of days, Zachariah, who was filled with God's glory, was no different. God has to silence him to make a point and then allow him to speak today to collaborate with his wife on the name for their son. Sometimes God will throw a curveball in our lives to keep excitement happening.

Day 83—March 24

Prayer: Teach me oh Lord what you want me to learn today. Help me Holy Spirit to unfold today's daily scriptures. Amen!

After reading question: What is God saying to me today?

OT}—God speaks about false prophets and obedience.

In chapter 6, verse 16, God tells us not to test him, but that does not mean he will not test our faith. Today, we see that sometimes a false prophet, or teacher, will be put in our path to see what we do. Are we going to be submissive to them, or will we run from them because we know the truth? This is why it is crucial to know God's Word.

Deuteronomy 13-14
Psalm 38:1-7
Proverbs 8:4-6
Luke 2:1-24

NT}—Jesus is born, and an angel appears to the shepherds who search for the Messiah. The wise men's accounts are different here compared to Matthew 2. Matthew is the nativity set we see today, but the bringing of gifts is in Luke. The main difference between the two Gospels is that jLuke's account is depicted through the eyes of Mary, and Matthew's gives details of Joseph. Luke shows the shepherd. Matthew shows the wise men (Magi). Could they be different? Or are the two accounts (stories) told differently?

Day 84—March 25

OT}—The obedience talk continues. Chapter 15 illustrates the number seven. Seven means "New Beginnings."

Chapter 16 talks about Passover. As I mentioned before, Passover is a seven-day feast. In the spring of the Gregorian calendar. There are a few names, all meaning the same time you may read about. First month:

➤ Babylonian name: Nisanu
➤ Jewish name: Nisan
➤ Canaanite name: Abib[13]

Deuteronomy 15-16

Psalm 38:8-14

Proverbs 8:7-9

Luke 2:25-52

NT}—Today, Mary and Joseph bring Jesus to Jerusalem. Simeon then blesses Jesus and prophecies. After completing everything according to the law of the Lord, they return to Nazareth. Jesus grew in age and spirit, bringing him to twelve years old when he would sit among the teachers listening and asking questions. In Luke's account, there is no mention of them hiding from the king. He jumps right into the dedication and their return to Nazareth.

Day 85—March 26

OT}—The Lord talks to the Levites about their inheritance. Mainly, they will not have any among their brethren, and the Lord is their inheritance, as he promised them.

Chapter 17 are laws about the rulers of Israel.

Deuteronomy 17-18
Psalm 38:15-22
Proverbs 8:10-12
Luke 3:1-20

NT}—Luke records the preaching of John the Baptist just before he was put in prison.

Through all the great work John the Baptist was doing, he never kept the glory for himself. He always pointed to God the Father and Jesus the Messiah. He knew his calling as far back as when Mary visited and leaped in his mother's womb. He knew the purpose of his life and gladly lived it.

Do you know one of the best parts of John's life? His father and mother understood the purpose of his life and supported him until his death.

Day 86—March 27

Prayer: Teach me oh Lord what you want me to learn today. Help me Holy Spirit to unfold today's daily scriptures. Amen!

After reading question: What is God saying to me today?

OT}—The Lord builds their refuge cities as a safe haven for certain offenders to save their lives.

The Lord tells them not to be afraid when they go into battle with armies greater than they were.

Deuteronomy 19-20
Psalm 39:1-7
Proverbs 8:13-15
Luke 3:21-38

NT}—Jesus was baptized with a pleasing message from God out of the heavens.

Have you ever seen people get baptized? I have seen plenty because of my role as a deacon. First, they come in the water like an electrical cord was placed in it, and then they are stiff as a board. No, not all of them, and I am not making fun of them; I just wanted to make a point. Jesus needs to be our example in life, and when John was baptizing him, Jesus was praying the whole time, ushering in the glory of his father.

Today we see the genealogy from God to Jesus;
See Chart on page 9.

Day 87—March 28

Prayer: Teach me oh Lord what you want me to learn today. Help me Holy Spirit to unfold today's daily scriptures. Amen!

After reading question: What is God saying to me today?

OT}—God is continuing to speak in a matter-of-fact tone of voice, which one of the statements is towards a stubborn and rebellious son. I am thankful that through the work of the cross, he no longer directs us towards this kind of correction.

Deuteronomy 21-22
Psalm 39:8-13
Proverbs 8:16-18
Luke 4:1-20

NT}—Here, we hear about Jesus on his forty-day fast. I only know a few people who did a forty-day fast with just water, a challenging task to complete. The most that I have done is twenty-one days.

A 40-day fast is an extreme spiritual breakthrough and some physical health benefits that is a challenge for all Christians. If you ever decide to give it an attempt, please seek out advice and do your research before starting.

As you will see, when we attempt to do good things, spiritual things, the devil is right there to try to stop it.

Day 88—March 29

Prayer: Teach me oh Lord what you want me to learn today. Help me Holy Spirit to unfold today's daily scriptures. Amen!

After reading question: What is God saying to me today?

OT}—I like one of the verses in today's reading where it talks about the father shall not be put to death for the children and vice versa. This is a great topic that I have heard spoken on. If a child sins, are the parents responsible? We can see in the scripture today that the answer is no. Salvation too!

As you read today, you will see that the Lord says after reaping the harvest to leave what is left for others. I remember as a kid; the farmers did that. Then people would leave the fields a mess, so the farmers stopped it.

Deuteronomy 23-24
Psalm 40:1-9
Proverbs 8:19-21
Luke 4:21-44

NT}—Jesus is thrown out of the synagogue and escapes being thrown off the top of the hill. He left his own town to go somewhere where they would appreciate his teachings and listen to what he had to say. Verse 34 says the spirits knew Jesus, and verse 35 goes on to say Jesus had authority over the evil spirits. Since we are filled with the Holy Spirit, we have the same authority today to tell them to be silent!

Day 89—March 30

Prayer: Teach me oh Lord what you want me to learn today. Help me Holy Spirit to unfold today's daily scriptures. Amen!

After reading question: What is God saying to me today?

OT}—In verse 9, we read about a widowed woman who is rejected by her brother-in-law when her husband dies and is unwilling to take her as his wife. It was customary for the nearest kinsman to marry the widow. Because he rejected her, taking off the scandal and spitting in his face in the presence of the elders was a sign of degradation, shame, and disgrace, not just to him, but to the family as well.

The Lord speaks on tithing and the reward for doing it. We still call it the first fruits or the first 10% of our income. We will hear more about tithing and offerings later in the year.

Visit www.anthonyordille.com for more in-depth teaching on tithing in one of my blogs.

Deuteronomy 25-26
Psalm 40:10-17
Proverbs 8:22-24
Luke 5:1-20

NT}—I like today's reading because it reminds me to keep my faith. No matter how many times I may do something with no results; when Jesus speaks to me to try again, I better do it because he has the final word.

Day 90—March 31

Prayer: Teach me oh Lord what you want me to learn today. Help me Holy Spirit to unfold today's daily scriptures. Amen!

After reading question: What is God saying to me today?

OT}—Moses and the elders command the people to keep all the commandments with authority.

These two chapters have been quoted and taught many times throughout the years to show what happens when we do, or do not, keep the commandments.

Chapter 27 is the cursed chapter. Chapter 28 starts off as the blessing chapter during the first fourteen verses, but then for fifty-four verses, goes back to curses if the commandments and statutes are not followed. Which one do you want?

➤ *Cursed:* The cursed life is a result of a life without God
➤ *Blessings:* A blessed life with God results in fullness and abundance

Deuteronomy 27-28
Psalm 41:1-7
Proverbs 8:25-27
Luke 5:21-39

NT}—Today, we see another sad moment where most of the leaders of the Judah faith had the Messiah right under their noses, and they did not believe it was him.

Day 91—April 1

Prayer: Teach me oh Lord what you want me to learn today. Help me Holy Spirit to unfold today's daily scriptures. Amen!

After reading question: What is God saying to me today?

OT}—God speaks straight forward to the Israelites on the covenant that Moses addressed. Then he gives them an ultimatum on the choices they will face.

I believe this word is still for us today, with God giving Jesus to us to say, "Choose life," which comes in three parts: Love the Lord your God, obey his voice, and lastly, cling to him.

Deuteronomy 29-30
Psalm 41:8-13
Proverbs 8:28-30
Luke 6:1-23

NT}—In today's society, with all the different beliefs and cultures, we no longer hold our seventh day of the week as a holy day. As a young kid, most, if not all, of the businesses in our town were closed on Sundays. If you need gas, you better fill your tank up on Saturday, or you will be left on the side of the road when you run out. Today just about everything is open, so I can get a good understanding with today's reading as we hear the Pharisees ask Jesus questions.

Day 92—April 2

<u>Prayer:</u> Teach me oh Lord what you want me to learn today. Help me Holy Spirit to unfold today's daily scriptures. Amen!

<u>After reading question:</u> What is God saying to me today?

OT}—Moses's journey is ended, but not until he gets to address his people one last time. Standing at the finish line, God tells Moses to go up into the mountain to look at the promised land from a distance and remain there until he dies. What a way to finish the race, huh?

Deuteronomy 31-32
Psalm 42:1-6
Proverbs 8:31-33
Luke 6:24-49

NT}—Today, Jesus is talking to us about how we should act as believers in Christ. Be cheerful givers, be kind, and be doers of his word. We should:
- ➤ Invoke blessings and pray for those that curse us
- ➤ Turn the other cheek
- ➤ Give to the needy
- ➤ Do unto others as you would have them do to you
- ➤ Love your enemies
- ➤ Be merciful, sympathetic, tender, responsive, and compassionate
- ➤ Not to judge someone just because they look different
- ➤ Do not condemn, and you will not be condemned

Day 93—April 3

OT}—Today, we end the Book of Deuteronomy with the ending of the story of Moses. Moses is an essential Jewish prophet whom the Lord knew face-to-face. According to scripture, God came and buried him when Moses died, and no man knows where.

His love for the people is immense, steadfast in completing the plan of God, passionate, even impulsive, and so much more. We can all learn from Moses to be better leaders and work on developing his character traits to extend to our churches and families.

Deuteronomy 33-34
Psalm 42:7-11
Proverbs 8:34-36
Luke 7:1-23

NT}—In my time so far as a believer in Jesus Christ, I have seen people who typically say they do not believe in God turn to him in times of tragedy. Today is what we see with the centurion who sent people to Jesus, on his behalf, to ask for healing for a servant. Because the centurion understood authority, he knew Jesus's authority and could not deny the power he had heard about.

Day 94—April 4

Prayer: Teach me oh Lord what you want me to learn today. Help me Holy Spirit to unfold today's daily scriptures. Amen!

After reading question: What is God saying to me today?

OT}—The Book of Joshua continues where Moses left off. Joshua was commissioned as the leader of the Israelites by God, through Moses, and accepted by the people to listen to him just as they had to Moses. It must have been an honor for Joshua to go from second in command to a leader who now talks to God.

When it was time, he led the people into the promised land and orchestrated the taking of at least thirty-one kings, along with their cities and territories. The people loved him as much as they loved Moses.

Joshua 1-2
Psalm 43
Proverbs 9:1-2
Luke 7:24-50

NT}—We must be careful about how we treat people, especially when we know their sins. Just because someone appears different on the outside does not mean the inside is foul. Today you will read where one righteous person judges someone's faith.

Day 95—April 5

Prayer: Teach me oh Lord what you want me to learn today. Help me Holy Spirit to unfold today's daily scriptures. Amen!

After reading question: What is God saying to me today?

OT}—Joshua gets the people ready to cross the Jordan River. God performs the same miracle as with the Red Sea, and they cross over on dry land.

As they crossed, one man from each tribe took up a stone from the riverbed, and after the priests who bore the ark of the covenant of the Lord had come up out of the midst of the Jordan, Joshua stacked them to make a monument. This was a memorial for all generations to know where they came from.

Joshua 3-4
Psalm 44:1-7
Proverbs 9:3-4
Luke 8:1-26

NT}—One of the main things I get walking with the Lord is; that when he is present, nothing around me is crazy. That is what I see in the story of the raging sea when Jesus is in the boat. His peace was not on the disciples until they woke him.

Jesus is always awake in my life today!

Day 96—April 6

<u>Prayer:</u> Teach me oh Lord what you want me to learn today. Help me Holy Spirit to unfold today's daily scriptures. Amen!

<u>After reading question:</u> What is God saying to me today?

OT}—God instructs Joshua to circumcise all males born in the wilderness. God had postponed circumcision in the wilderness because of their disobedience and now has hope for his people to start again. Joshua takes Jericho with the sounding of the trumpets. The fact that Joshua's army could march around the city seven times in one day shows that the city was small. The first six days were once a day, maybe for Jericho to let their guide down, thinking, "Those people are back, do not worry about them. They are no threat; what harm can they do?"

Joshua 5-6

Psalm 44:8-13

Proverbs 9:5-6

Luke 8:27-56

NT}—Jesus continues with healing with three significant accounts:

1. The man who was possessed and running around naked because of many demons inside him
2. The woman with the blood issue whom no physician could heal her
3. The director's daughter, whom Jesus raised from the dead after the family laughed at him

Day 97—April 7

OT}—Joshua attempts to take Ai but fails because of a thief in the family. Achan gets greedy and takes something from Jericho that was consecrated to the Lord, so God allows thirty-six men to fall, and then the army retreats. After Joshua finds and confronts Achan to make restitution with God, they make a second attempt to take Ai.

Joshua 7-8
Psalm 44:14-20
Proverbs 9:7-8
Luke 9:1-36

NT}—Jesus releases power and authority to the apostles to call out demons, cure diseases, and send them out to preach the kingdom of God and bring healing.

Today Jesus has given us, the believer, the same authority, but most of us do not exercise that authority because our faithfulness has diminished. I believe that if we understood our authority, we would see a more powerful church in our society. Instead, some believe Satan's lies and are being deceived when he says things like "Did God surely mean those things for all of us?" or "Surely God's healing power was for generations past."

Day 98—April 8

Prayer: Teach me oh Lord what you want me to learn today. Help me Holy Spirit to unfold today's daily scriptures. Amen!

After reading question: What is God saying to me today?

OT}—The journey continues to take the land, which opens doors to manipulation, conning, and pretending. Because of the overtaken of Jericho and Ai, other cities became fearful for their lives and devised a way to live. Joshua then uses them to his advantage and puts them to work.

And we see in verse 42 of chapter 10 that Joshua took all the land because the Lord fought for Israel.

Joshua 9-10

Psalm 44:21-26

Proverbs 9:9-10

Luke 9:37-62

NT}—I think that maybe some people today are like the apostles in verse 45. Jesus cannot be any clearer that he had given all his authority to do the same work as he did when he was here on earth.

Why then is there a lack of faith?

Jesus answers this question in verse 41. He calls them faithless ones, unbelieving and without trust in God, a perverse, wayward, crooked, and warped generation!

Day 99—April 9

OT}—By this time, other kings are coming together in numbers to attempt to defeat Israel, but the promises of God are more substantial. Over five years, Joshua took the whole land according to all that the Lord had spoken to Moses, and Joshua gave it to Israel according to their allotments by tribes.

Joshua 11-12
Psalm 45:1-9
Proverbs 9:11-12
Luke 10:1-22

NT}—Jesus builds on the ministry to cover more ground because there were many people, both Jew and Gentile, who wanted the gospel and believed in Jesus, so he had to enlarge his team because his time on earth was running out, and he needed to get the word out fast.

We hear a little bit about blessedness today, but do we understand what it is? We use the word blessing, whether looking for one or hoping for one for someone else, for everything. But I believe sometimes we lose focus on the true meaning of what a blessing is when it is being used. God's unmerited favor and protection!

Day 100—April 10

<u>Prayer:</u> Teach me oh Lord what you want me to learn today. Help me Holy Spirit to unfold today's daily scriptures. Amen!

<u>After reading question:</u> What is God saying to me today?

OT}—Because the tribes of Reuben, Gad, and half of the tribe Manasseh chose not to enter the Promised Land, Moses, before he died, gave the land east of the Jordan to them with the condition that they wage battle ahead of the other troops.

With the initial battles behind them, which may have been the most significant or substantial of them all, God tells Joshua to divide the remaining land up to the other nine and a half tribes because he is getting old.

Each tribe took possession of their lands and settled there.

Joshua 13-14

Psalm 45:10-17

Proverbs 9:13-14

Luke 10:23-42

NT}—I have a few questions for you today:
- ➤ What is the basis of salvation?
- ➤ What will get you into heaven?
- ➤ What type of person will God accept to reside in his kingdom?

See if you can answer these questions through today's reading.

Day 101—April 11

Prayer: Teach me oh Lord what you want me to learn today. Help me Holy Spirit to unfold today's daily scriptures. Amen!

After reading question: What is God saying to me today?

OT}—Today's reading starts to lay out the boundary lines and the story behind the possession of the land. Boundaries are easy to see in a physical sense. They are lined with fences, walls, hedges, and even signs. But did you know we have spiritual boundary lines as well? These boundary lines define your soulish realm: mind, will, and emotions, between what is from the spirit (God) and what is from our own will. What is right or what is wrong! Things of this nature are what are defined as boundary lines. Do not cross the line into a natural mindset and your spirit lives on, stuff like that.

Be careful about what side of the spiritual line you are on.

Joshua 15-16
Psalm 46:1-6
Proverbs 9:15-16
Luke 11:1-28

NT}—He said to them, "When you pray, say:
Father, hallowed be Your name. Your kingdom come.
Give us each day our daily bread.
And forgive us our sins,
For we ourselves also forgive everyone who is indebted to us
[who has offended or wronged us].
And lead us not into temptation [but rescue us from evil]."

Day 102—April 12

Prayer: Teach me oh Lord what you want me to learn today. Help me Holy Spirit to unfold today's daily scriptures. Amen!

After reading question: What is God saying to me today?

OT}—The tribe of Joseph is growing in numbers so fast that the land that was given to them is too small. Confronting Joshua with a petition, Joshua tells them to expand to the forest and clear ground for themselves.

Joshua 17-18

Psalm 46:7-11

Proverbs 9:17-18

Luke 11:29-54

NT}—Jesus uses the lighting of a lamp to illustrate how we are to protect what we see, hear, and speak. Verse 35, "Be careful, therefore, that the light that is in you is not Darkness."

What does it mean to allow our light to shine? It means that when you live a truthful, thoughtful, caring life, people will see it and inquire where it comes from. Bam! The door just opened for you to share the love of Jesus.

Day 103—April 13

OT}—Today, they finished dividing up the land. Israelites gave Joshua the city he asked for, Timnath-Serah, in the hills of Ephraim. Then God tells Joshua to appoint the six cities of refuge spoken through Moses (Numbers 35:1-34 and Deuteronomy 4:41-43) and explains why they are needed.

Joshua 19-20
Psalm 47
Proverbs 10:1-3
Luke 12:1-32

NT}—Jesus tells us not to be anxious for nothing. Just as he provides for the birds of the air, how much more will he provide for his beloved ones?

Some people have a hard time with this because they want to keep up with their neighbors, like that old cliche, "Keeping up with the Jones," instead of trusting that God will provide and give what is needed when it is required. There is nothing wrong with abundance, as long as God is the provider. I have heard people say, "God did not give all this to me. I worked for it." Who gave them the ability?

Verse 20 tells it best.

Day 104—April 14

Prayer: Teach me oh Lord what you want me to learn today. Help me Holy Spirit to unfold today's daily scriptures. Amen!

After reading question: What is God saying to me today?

OT}—God spoke to Moses for the Levites in the wilderness to assist Aaron and his sons with the Tabernacle. In return, all the other tribes would give them cities to dwell in and raise their cattle in. The Levites were the only Israelite tribe that received cities but were not allowed to be landowners because God was their inheritance.

Joshua 21-22
Psalm 48:1-7
Proverbs 10:4-6
Luke 12:33-59

NT}—Yesterday, we read about not being anxious about what to eat or drink or being troubled-minded. Today we start with a famous verse we read from Matthew 6:19-20, which is an expanded version.

Then Jesus tells us to be ready. Ready for what, you may ask? Verse 40 answers that question; You must be prepared for the Son of Man is coming at an hour and a moment when you do not anticipate it.

Therefore, my question is, do you think you are ready?

Day 105—April 15

Prayer: Teach me oh Lord what you want me to learn today. Help me Holy Spirit to unfold today's daily scriptures. Amen!

After reading question: What is God saying to me today?

OT}—The story of Joshua comes to an end today. Joshua calls all of Israel together to have one last talk. He tells them to be courageous and steadfast. Also, to keep all the commandments, turning not aside from it to the right hand or the left. Keep looking forward to what God has planned. We need to follow that word for today.

We get another famous verse that is quoted by many, "but as for me and my house, we will serve the Lord." Joshua 24:15b

Sometime after Joshua sent the people away, he died at one hundred and ten.

Joshua 23-24
Psalm 48:8-14
Proverbs 10:7-9
Luke 13:1-17

NT}—Jesus touches on repenting. When you hear the word repent, you may think of what John the Baptist says. "Repent for the kingdom of heaven is at hand." I like the amplified Bible's additional phrase of the meaning (change your mind for the better and heartily amend your ways, with abhorrence of your past sins).

Day 106—April 16

Prayer: Teach me oh Lord what you want me to learn today. Help me Holy Spirit to unfold today's daily scriptures. Amen!

After reading question: What is God saying to me today?

OT}—Hebrew word *Shopetim* means "Judges" or "ruling leaders," which is the title of the book you start into today. It accounts for the period of Israel's history between the death of Joshua and the ministry of Samuel, 1245 BC – 1056 BC.

There is a total of fifteen individuals noted in this book for their leadership.

Judges 1-2

Psalm 49:1-7

Proverbs 10:10-12

Luke 13:18-35

NT}—Jesus continues to explain what the kingdom of God is like and how to get there. Mathew 7:13-14 said it best, "Enter through the narrow gate: for wide is the gate and spacious and broad is the way that leads away to destruction, and many are those who are entering through it. But the gate is narrow (contracted by pressure), and the way is straitened and compressed that leads away to life, and few are those who find it." Verses 23-30 have a deeper perspective.

Now, after reading that, Do you believe there are many paths to Jesus? Some people in this world what us to think there is.

Day 107—April 17

<u>Prayer:</u> Teach me oh Lord what you want me to learn today. Help me Holy Spirit to unfold today's daily scriptures. Amen!

<u>After reading question:</u> What is God saying to me today?

OT}—The tribe of Judah joins forces with Simeon, his brother, to fight against the Canaanites and other territories. After defeating them, they lived among them and turned from serving God. Consequently, God's anger sold them into another round of slavery for eight years. But did they learn their lesson?

Judges 3-5

Psalm 49:8-14

Proverbs 10:13-15

Luke 14:1-17

NT}—Jesus explains that just because it is the sabbath does not mean to turn our backs on others' needs.

We are called to help. Help in any way we can. But first, we must put aside our pride and sit among the sinner, the hurt, and the guilty. Be humble, know who you are in Christ Jesus, and put your hand out; you might catch a fish.

Day 108—April 18

<u>Prayer:</u> Teach me oh Lord what you want me to learn today. Help me Holy Spirit to unfold today's daily scriptures. Amen!

<u>After reading question:</u> What is God saying to me today?

OT}—No matter how often Israel falls away from God throughout the generations, God is always there for them when they cry out. This time God uses Gideon, but I think Gideon is unsure of himself because God has to tell him multiple times that he is with him. Just in chapter 6, Jesus told him four times he was with him and not to fear, and even appeared as an Angel of the Lord to put a stronger emphasis on his demand.

Starting in verse 11, it is evident that the "Angel of the Lord" is a distinct person in Himself (Jesus) from God the Father.

Judges 6-7
Psalm 49:15-20
Proverbs 10:16-18
Luke 14:18-35

NT}—God calls us to come to him with no excuses, no counterfeit mindset, just open arms and the willingness to lay our past down and follow him.

Are you there?

Are you ready?

Day 109—April 19

<u>Prayer:</u> Teach me oh Lord what you want me to learn today. Help me Holy Spirit to unfold today's daily scriptures. Amen!

<u>After reading question:</u> What is God saying to me today?

OT}—Gideon, also known as Jerubbaal, son of Joash the Abiezrite, led the Israelites to victory over Midian, Zebah, and Zalmunna. Afterward, there was peace for forty years, but as soon as Gideon died, they returned to serving other gods.

Gideon had many wives who gave him seventy sons, plus Abimelech from his concubine. Unfortunately, Abimelech kills his brother, all but Jothan, the youngest, and becomes ruler over Shechem. Because of his wickedness, Abimelech is killed, repaying for his actions toward his brothers.

It seems to be that they cannot fend for themselves, huh?

Judges 8-9
Psalm 50:1-7
Proverbs 10:19-21
Luke 15:1-16

NT}—In Jesus, God has given us an inheritance extending to the time we have left on earth. But unlike the parable of the prodigal son, God does not want us to squander it away.

Whether it is our earnings or the gifts of our talents, we are called to reach out to the lost, the hurting, and the needy.

Day 110—April 20

<u>Prayer:</u> Teach me oh Lord what you want me to learn today. Help me Holy Spirit to unfold today's daily scriptures. Amen!

<u>After reading question:</u> What is God saying to me today?

OT}—Again, God arose up leaders for the next forty-five years, and once again, the Israelites turned their eyes to other gods. What does God do? Let us read to see what happens.

Judges 10-11

Psalm 50:8-15

Proverbs 10:22-24

Luke 15:17-32

NT}—When Jesus shows compassion to our brothers and sisters, he calls us not to get jealous, but to rejoice in any blessings they may receive.

We need to stop thinking that someone is better than us or doing more, which is why God blessed them. God is no respecter of person, and what he does for others, he can do for us. It is all about God's timing, not ours.

I love the story that a person believed in something for years, and the day after they stopped believing for it, it came to pass. Too funny!

Day 111—April 21

Prayer: Teach me oh Lord what you want me to learn today. Help me Holy Spirit to unfold today's daily scriptures. Amen!

After reading question: What is God saying to me today?

OT}—Too funny! As we read yesterday, God returns. But after what looks like four leaders over thirty-one years, the Israelites again did evil in the sight of God. So back to the beginning they go.

Judges 12-13
Psalm 50:16-23
Proverbs 10:25-27
Luke 16:1-13

NT}—Jesus said, "He who is faithful in a tiny [thing] is also faithful in much, and he who is dishonest in a tiny [thing] is also dishonest and unjust also in much."

(Luke 16:10)

One of the takeaways from today's metaphor is that God forgave us of all our sins, looking beyond our character defects, and our job is to extend that same mercy to others. Just because someone sinned against us, in whatever way, does not mean we ridicule them because we got hurt.

Forgive because he first forgave us!

Day 112—April 22

Prayer: Teach me oh Lord what you want me to learn today. Help me Holy Spirit to unfold today's daily scriptures. Amen!

After reading question: What is God saying to me today?

OT}—Well, here comes a part of the Bible you most likely heard as a kid, no matter where you were with religion, the story of Samson and Delilah. Samson uses a riddle to answer a question, probably because he does not want to give the answer he held from his parent's knowledge. I believe he thought it to be solvable easily because he had first-hand experience. But it was not easy for them, so they tried to coax him for the answer by using his wife. The logic behind it is, Good vs. evil; out of something evil came something good.

Judges 14-15

Psalm 51:1-7

Proverbs 10:28-30

Luke 16:14-31

NT}—We see here that Hades, the Greek word for hell, is a place of torment and severe mental or physical pain and suffering. This is not where we want to end up, so God expresses that in his Word.

Day 113—April 23

Prayer: Teach me oh Lord what you want me to learn today. Help me Holy Spirit to unfold today's daily scriptures. Amen!

After reading question: What is God saying to me today?

OT}—Did you know that Delilah was Samson's second wife? I did not realize that until I started reading the Bible for myself. I always thought of it as a love story, but a good wife she was not. Her actions caused Samson's death.

Judges 16-17
Psalm 51:8-13
Proverbs 10:31-32
Luke 17:1-19

NT}—First, Jesus says we will have temptations but not to fall into the traps. Then, he tells us to forgive no matter how many times someone may sin against us.

What is the power of forgiveness? There can be many answers to that question, but I have one for the sake of space. Unforgiveness will eat at you from the inside out. It will change your countenance so bad that people will look into your eyes and see hate and darkness. And you know what? The person you cannot forgive is probably sleeping like a baby, so forgive; nothing is worth losing sleep over.

Day 114—April 24

Teach me oh Lord what you want me to learn today. Help me Holy Spirit to unfold today's daily scriptures. Amen!

After reading question: What is God saying to me today?

OT}—Today, we get to the part of the journey where it was a free-for-all; No king, no leadership, and no real direction that led to murder and a horrific act.

Let us see what happens.

Judges 18-19
Psalm 51:14-19
Proverbs 11:1-3
Luke 17:20-37

NT}—I like how Jesus uses past historical events to illustrate his return. We call these the end times; whether or not we physically experience it, it will come.

One of the main things we need to be precise about in our walk with God is to be ready for his return. You may be in the middle of an act of sin when that trumpet blows, Jesus returns, and you miss the mark.

I know it is not easy, but we must keep at it.

Day 115—April 25

OT}— Today, we end the Book of Judges. After a brutal act, the Israelites unite and take revenge. After completing what they set out to do, they all returned to their own tribe and did what was right in their own eyes. Mainly because there was no God.

You cannot have a true king if you have no God because God is king. They kept God as a sign but paid no tribute to him as a king. They were worshipping him, possibly in the outward form, but knowing nothing of goodness's subduing and directing power.

Judges 20-21
Psalm 52:1-5
Proverbs 11:4-6
Luke 18:1-21

NT}—This is where Jesus tells us to be careful about how we present ourselves. Are you arrogant, pompous, or haughty about your walk? Or are you humble?

In verse 14, Jesus said, "For everyone who exalts himself will be humbled, but he who humbles himself will be exalted."

Day 116—April 26

Prayer: Teach me oh Lord what you want me to learn today. Help me Holy Spirit to unfold today's daily scriptures. Amen!

After reading question: What is God saying to me today?

OT}—Book of Ruth, the wife of Boaz, the great-grandfather of David.

During the peaceful time when Judges ruled over Israel, a famine contributed to Elimelech's death and his two sons, Mahlon and Chiliom. Mahlon was Ruth's first husband, and she wanted to stay with her mother-in-law Naomi.

Ruth 1-2

Psalm 52:6-9

Proverbs 11:7-9

Luke 18:22-43

NT}—Some people strive for riches and claim it is because of their work. God says that it is easier for a camel to enter through a needle's eye than for a rich man to enter the kingdom of God, verse 25. Some versions say the eye of a needle. Jesus uses a metaphor, but some places give a great picture of his meaning. One place is a passage through the City of Jerusalem's wall. It is called "Eye of the Needle Gate." Research "needle eye" to understand more.

Day 117—April 27

<u>Prayer:</u> Teach me oh Lord what you want me to learn today. Help me Holy Spirit to unfold today's daily scriptures. Amen!

<u>After reading question:</u> What is God saying to me today?

OT}—Today, we end the Book of Ruth with Naomi telling Ruth to seek after Boaz as a husband. Boaz then is given the right to redeem the land of Elimelech that Naomi sold and takes Ruth as his wife.

Ruth becomes pregnant and gives birth to Obed, a descendant of Jesus. Thirty-one generations before Jesus is born.

See the genealogy of Jesus on page 10.

Ruth 3-4

Psalm 53

Proverbs 11:10-12

Luke 19:1-28

NT}—Zacchaeus, a chief tax collector, has a spiritual awakening. Because he is radically changed, he gives half of his goods away and returns four times the money he has cheated the people out of.

Could you imagine if we all got saved this way?

Day 118—April 28

Prayer: Teach me oh Lord what you want me to learn today. Help me Holy Spirit to unfold today's daily scriptures. Amen!

After reading question: What is God saying to me today?

OT}—As I mentioned in the short history of the Bible at the beginning of the book, the Book of Samuel was split into two parts. 1 Samuel marks the transition of rule over Israel from judgeship to monarchy, starting with the birth of Samuel.

God used Samuel to express his heart. "If one man wrongs another, God will mediate for him; but if a man wrongs the Lord, who shall intercede for him?" (1 Samuel 2:25) "For those who honor Me I will honor, and those who despise Me shall be lightly esteemed." (1 Samuel 2:30b)

1 Samuel 1-2

Psalm 54

Proverbs11:13-15

Luke 19:29-48

NT}—Jesus replied to the Pharisees that if the disciples were silenced, the stones would cry out.

This is not to be taken literally. The expression Jesus is trying to make here is that it is more likely that the impossible would happen than it would be for the King of Kings to enter Jerusalem without honor.

Day 119—April 29

Prayer: Teach me oh Lord what you want me to learn today. Help me Holy Spirit to unfold today's daily scriptures. Amen!

After reading question: What is God saying to me today?

OT}—Samuel's father and mother were Elkanah and Hannah. Hannah was childless for years but kept praying and seeking God to bless her until Samuel came about. Samuel means "*Heard of God*." As Samuel grew, he was taught by Eli, the high priest of Shiloh, the ways of the Lord.

1 Samuel 3-4
Psalm 55:1-8
Proverbs 11:16-18
Luke 20:1-26

NT}—My interpretation of verses 17 & 18 is that Jesus is the cornerstone, and those of us who believe in him will have his covering. But, for those who reject him will be scattered from his presence.

Have you ever heard someone answer a question with a question? It can be irritating. But I believe someone does that because they really do not know what to answer, or they do not know an answer. Jesus does that a lot throughout scripture, not because he does not know the answer, but probably because it is not time for one.

Day 120—April 30

<u>Prayer:</u> Teach me oh Lord what you want me to learn today. Help me Holy Spirit to unfold today's daily scriptures. Amen!

<u>After reading question:</u> What is God saying to me today?

OT}—The Philistines were afraid that the Hebrews would kill or enslave them, so they took the ark of God to Ashdod and set it beside Dagon, their idol.

Dagon was the highest-ranking god of the Philistines. According to ancient mythology, Dagon was half-man, half-fish, and the father of Baal. He is known as the fish god. The first part of his name, dag in Hebrew, means "fish."

Then God reveals himself with power and plagues. Then, after seven months, the Philistines return the ark.

1 Samuel 5-6
Psalm 55:9-16
Proverbs 11:19-21
Luke 20:27-47

NT}—Today is a controversial reading. Is there marriage in heaven? Will my wife be my wife or my husband be my husband? According to today's reading, the answer would be no. I have no answer to those questions; I will have to wait until I go home.

Day 121—May 1

Prayer: Teach me oh Lord what you want me to learn today. Help me Holy Spirit to unfold today's daily scriptures. Amen!

After reading question: What is God saying to me today?

OT}—After nearly 100 years, the ark returns to Jerusalem, and Samuel returns to Ramah to judge Israel instead of being a traveling judge.

Per the people's request, Samuel cries out to the Lord with an offering to help them with the Philistines. During the battle, the Philistines were defeated, and the taken cities were restored to Israel.

Then the elders of Israel came to ask for a king because of Samuel's son's behavior.

1 Samuel 7-8
Psalm 55:17-23
Proverbs 11:22-24
Luke 21:1-19

NT}—Jesus is telling us today that all we see around us will be gone and to be watchful for anyone who will lead us away.

I like verse 19; "By your steadfastness and patient endurance you shall win the true life of your souls."

You cannot get any planer than that!

Day 122—May 2

OT}—Samuel stumbles across the future King of Israel, Saul. He anoints his head with oil in a secret meeting because it is not time for him to be revealed as king to the nation, then sends him off to confirm his calling.

The actual anointing was not until verse six when the Holy Spirit came upon Saul and changed him to be the man God called him to be. As an unspiritual man, God had to put him in the office of a prophet to reveal to the people that he was worthy as their king. In verse twenty-four, Saul was proclaimed king.

1 Samuel 9-10
Psalm 56:1-7
Proverbs 11:25-27
Luke 21:20-38

NT}—As we head towards the mark of our salvation, Jesus tells us to stay steadfast, and with patient endurance, we will win the real life of our souls. Is that not what we ended yesterday with? Then why is it so hard for us to follow the commander-in-chief? Stand on 1 John 4:4.

As we finish reading chapter 21, Jesus continues to answer the question of the end times and what that will look like.

Day 123—May 3

Prayer: Teach me oh Lord what you want me to learn today. Help me Holy Spirit to unfold today's daily scriptures. Amen!

After reading question: What is God saying to me today?

OT}— After the Ammonites were defeated, the people of Israel gathered in Gilgal, and Saul got sworn in as king because the people kept insisting they wanted a king, overlooking that God was their king.

Samuel addresses the people about how much God has been there for them over all the years, and they need to serve him faithfully, or both them and the king will be swept away.

1 Samuel 11-12
Psalm 56:8-13
Proverbs 11:28-31
Luke 22:1-23

NT}—We start with Judas Iscariot accepting money to betray Jesus. Because he was the treasurer and lover of money, Satan knew that when the chief priests offered him silver, he would take it.

Jesus then tells the disciples that before he suffers, which they did not understand, he wanted to eat the Passover dinner with them. He sends them off to prepare a place.

Day 124—May 4

Prayer: Teach me oh Lord what you want me to learn today. Help me Holy Spirit to unfold today's daily scriptures. Amen!

After reading question: What is God saying to me today?

OT}—Over all my years, I have heard a lot about King Saul, but the more I read about him now, the more I learn that the central part of his story is only within a two-year period, even though he reigned over Israel for twenty years.

1 Samuel 13-14

Psalm 57:1-6

Proverbs 12:1-2

Luke 22:24-44

NT}—There are many times I see people trying to get to the front of a line to be the first for whatever the event may be, or pushing themselves for leadership at their job or church. Even though having a goal to be a leader is not sinful, we must do it with spiritual principles.

Today we hear Jesus talk about how we should act.

When Jesus was in the form of a man, he felt the same pain as we feel today. The difference between us is that he knew what was coming. That is why I believe that he must have known that he would sweat blood drops when praying hard in the garden. Wow, the love he has for us!

Day 125—May 5

Prayer: Teach me oh Lord what you want me to learn today. Help me Holy Spirit to unfold today's daily scriptures. Amen!

After reading question: What is God saying to me today?

OT}—Saul is not the man they thought he was, and God regretted making him king, meaning he impeached him. But Saul was not all bad; he did some good things, like defeating many countries and uniting the scattered tribes. It was only his disobedience that got him in trouble.

Since the people still want a king, Samuel goes out searching. This is where David comes into the story.

As you read chapter 16, pay attention to how awesome God is. He is upset that he made Saul king, impeaches him, but then uses him to get David out of the fields to set him up to be anointed king.

1 Samuel 15-16
Psalm 57:7-11
Proverbs 12:3-4
Luke 22:45-71

NT}—I have heard a lot about the disciples falling asleep, which is why they captured Jesus. Using that as an illustration, I believe that sometimes God will cause us to fall asleep in the spirit, so we do not stop his plan.

Day 126—May 6

Prayer: Teach me oh Lord what you want me to learn today. Help me Holy Spirit to unfold today's daily scriptures. Amen!

After reading question: What is God saying to me today?

OT}—As a child, you most likely heard, or even read, about David defeating the giant Goliath. That is one of today's readings that is a great story.

After Samuel finds David and makes him his armor-bearer, David is used by God to do what no other man would do, take down the Philistine giant. The Philistines were tall and muscular men who must have laughed when David stood before them. God set David up years before by letting him kill the lion and a bear, to build up courage and faith so that he can use him now.

1 Samuel 17-18

Psalm 58:1-6

Proverbs 12:5-6

Luke 23:1-27

NT}—Pilate sends Jesus to Herod because he finds no fault in him. After Herod makes a mockery of Jesus, he sends him back to Pilate, where the people insist that Jesus be crucified.

Day 127—May 7

Prayer: Teach me oh Lord what you want me to learn today. Help me Holy Spirit to unfold today's daily scriptures. Amen!

After reading question: What is God saying to me today?

OT}—Saul gets jealous and fearful of David and orders his son to kill him. Jonathan liked David, so instead, he helped him to escape.

See what jealousy will do? It will make you not think straight.

David prayed for Saul, and this is how he gets treated. That is probably what David may have thought to himself.

1 Samuel 19-20
Psalm 58:7-11
Proverbs 12:7-8
Luke 23:28-56

NT}—Jesus is hung between two thieves, both deserving of death. But because one of them gets a revelation on who Christ is, Jesus forgives him of his sins and welcomes him into the kingdom, no sinner's prayer, no baptisms, just because the thief repented in his heart and received Jesus for whom they said he was. That is the depth of faith we can have by reading his Word.

Day 128—May 8

<u>Prayer:</u> Teach me oh Lord what you want me to learn today. Help me Holy Spirit to unfold today's daily scriptures. Amen!

<u>After reading question:</u> What is God saying to me today?

OT}—David is on the run and facing some challenges, but he meets some good folk willing to help him, not all but a few. This makes Saul even more disturbed, and he goes into a frenzy and has Doeg, his chief herdsmen, kill Ahimelech the priest, along with all the other priests in the city of Nog, eighty-five in total.

1 Samuel 21-22

Psalm 59:1-9

Proverbs 12:9-10

Luke 24:1-26

NT}—Christ has risen; he has risen indeed!

Not only did Jesus have many disciples with him, but many women paid him homage during those three and a half years. One name we do not hear much about is Joanna. Joanna was the wife of Chuza, who managed the household of Herod Antipas. She was healed by Jesus, who then supported his ministry. She was one of the women at the cross.[14]

Day 129—May 9

Prayer: Teach me oh Lord what you want me to learn today. Help me Holy Spirit to unfold today's daily scriptures. Amen!

After reading question: What is God saying to me today?

OT}—With David pursuing and not just hiding, it opens a chance for Saul to go after him. After meeting up, they make an oath, and David is still alive. The bottom line is that he owes his life to Jonathan and God.

1 Samuel 23-24

Psalm 59:10-17

Proverbs 12:11-12

Luke 24:27-53

NT}—Jesus talks with Cleopas and one other disciple without them even knowing who he was.

Over three and a half years, Jesus gave many teachings with thousands of words stating things to come, what to look out for, and his destiny. Like, "Destroy this temple, and in three days I will raise it up," but yet on the third day after he walked out of the tomb, they did not believe it was him. He had to prove to them that it was really him.

I wonder how many times we do the same thing today.

Day 130—May 10

Teach me oh Lord what you want me to learn today. Help me Holy Spirit to unfold today's daily scriptures. Amen!

After reading question: What is God saying to me today?

OT}—Samuel's journey ends at the age of ninety-eight, and he is buried in Ramah.

David reaches out to a wealthy man named Nabal for provision, who refuses to help because he is a wicked and foolish man. David sets out to avenge Nabal's unkindness when Abigail, Nabal's wife, intercedes David with provision.

Saul is at it again and just cannot let David go. David stands up to Saul, and then they make peace with each other again and go their separate ways.

1 Samuel 25-26
Psalm 60:1-6
Proverbs 12:13-14
John 1:1-27

NT}—Today is the Book of John, the fourth and final gospel of our reading. It differs from the other three and is mainly referred to for new believers. It contains no parables, has five additional recorded miracles, and numerous personal interviews. I think we will enjoy the next thirty-nine days.

Day 131—May 11

Prayer: Teach me oh Lord what you want me to learn today. Help me Holy Spirit to unfold today's daily scriptures. Amen!

After reading question: What is God saying to me today?

OT}—Because of Saul's persistence, David felt in his heart that he would die at the hand of Saul, so he went to the land of the Philistines, thinking that would stop Saul from seeking him. We know why Saul seeks David, jealousy, but can he accomplish his goal?

After David gets to Gath, the king makes him his bodyguard and tells David that it is imperative for him to go to battle against Israel with the Philistines.

Then Saul seeks the Lord, but God does not answer him, so he turns to witchcraft for answers.

1 Samuel 27-28
Psalm 60:7-12
Proverbs 12:15-16
John 1:28-51

NT}—We see from the very beginning of time that Jesus was present. He did not come by way of Mary; that was only when he came as a man. He has always been part of the Father, and life was formed by his Word right from the start. Sometimes I think we focus on Jesus as the Christ (Messiah), and we lose the fact that he is part of the beginning.

Day 132—May 12

<u>Prayer:</u> Teach me oh Lord what you want me to learn today. Help me Holy Spirit to unfold today's daily scriptures. Amen!

<u>After reading question:</u> What is God saying to me today?

OT}—The philistines do not want to go into battle with David and his men because they do not trust them not to turn against them during battle.

David returns to Ziklag to find it destroyed and his two wives gone. Then sets out to revenge against the Amalekites to get them back.

Saul, and his three sons, die during a battle with the Philistines. Saul gets his head cut off after he kills himself.

1 Samuel 29-31

Psalm 61

Proverbs 12:17-18

John 2

NT}—John jumps right into Jesus' ministry with the first of many miracles, water-to-wine at his cousin's wedding, in which he displayed his greatness and power openly.

Jesus made a profound statement when he was asked for a sign by the Jews, "Destroy this temple, and in three days I will raise it up again."

Day 133—May 13

Prayer: Teach me oh Lord what you want me to learn today. Help me Holy Spirit to unfold today's daily scriptures. Amen!

After reading question: What is God saying to me today?

OT}—We continue the reading straight into Second Samuel. David gets the report that Saul and Jonathan are dead and mourns. Even though Saul was out to kill David, David respected him and most likely loved him. Listen to the lamentation as you read it. Would you think of someone like that if they were trying to kill you? This kind of stuff helps me understand why God loved David.

David is anointed king over the house of Judah, and Saul's son, Ish-bosheth, steps in as king over Israel for a short two-year reign.

2 Samuel 1-2
Psalm 62:1-6
Proverbs 12:19-20
John 3:1-18

NT}—Today's verses bring us to one of the most taught scriptures, John 3:16. But the verse before it has a buildup to that famous verse that draws it in. The words "Eternal life" come from the Greek word "*Zoe,*" meaning "Life of God" or "Abundant Life."

Day 134—May 14

OT}—Even though Saul was dead, the war between Saul's house and David's house continued.

Abner was slain by Joab, son of Zeruiah, for revenge for killing his younger brother, Asahel. Even though Abner was an enemy of David, David made peace with him and mourned his death. Again we hear David have some nice words to say at a burial.

2 Samuel 3-4

Psalm 62:7-12

Proverbs 12:21-22

John 3:19-36

NT}—At the end of all times, there will be a judgment for all mankind. God tells us in today's reading that if we believe in his son, the world's judgment is not to us, just our good works led by God.

Receiving Jesus as the Light of the world is then confirmed by John the Baptist in the rest of the verses. He also confirms in verse 36 what will happen to someone who does not believe in the Son of God.

Day 135—May 15

Prayer: Teach me oh Lord what you want me to learn today. Help me Holy Spirit to unfold today's daily scriptures. Amen!

After reading question: What is God saying to me today?

OT}—Because of David's faithfulness towards the Lord, he finds favor before men, and they anoint him king over Israel after being king over Judah for seven years and six months. David was thirty years old when he became king and reigned for a total of forty years.

In chapter six, David decides to move the ark of God to the house of David. When Uzzah, son of Abinadab, dies because he touched it, David becomes fearful and sends it to the house of Obed-Edom. Then when David hears that God blessed Obed-Edom, he continues with the organist plan.

2 Samuel 5-6

Psalm 63:1-6

Proverbs 12:23-24

John 4:1-29

NT}—Jesus meets a Samaritan woman at the well and asks her for a drink of water. Because back then, the Jewish people would have nothing to do with the Samaritans, she was amazed at his request. Jesus is showing us to cross barriers and knock down walls between believers.

Day 136—May 16

<u>Prayer:</u> Teach me oh Lord what you want me to learn today. Help me Holy Spirit to unfold today's daily scriptures. Amen!

<u>After reading question:</u> What is God saying to me today?

OT}—Now that David was not distracted by his surroundings, God was able to use him for his own gain.

God wants a brick-n-mortar house he can call home. Through the prophet Nathan, God tells David to build it because he has not dwelt in a house since Egypt. Then David sits before God to talk to him about himself.

Highly moved, David campaigns for the funds through war.

2 Samuel 7-8

Psalm 63:7-11

Proverbs 12:25-26

John 4:30-54

NT}—Today, we see the second miracle of Jesus, the healing of a royal nobleman's son.

Were you ever disappointed that someone you talked to about Christ did not accept him then? Today Jesus touches on that a bit, saying that your labor did not go unnoticed.

"One sows and another reaps"

Day 137—May 17

Prayer: Teach me oh Lord what you want me to learn today. Help me Holy Spirit to unfold today's daily scriptures. Amen!

After reading question: What is God saying to me today?

OT}—David returns the love he received from Jonathan to Jonathan's son. David does not stop there; he extends mercy to the son of Nahash, king of the Ammonites, because of the kindness he received from Nahash.

2 Samuel 9-10

Psalm 64:1-5

Proverbs 12:27-28

John 5:1-23

NT}—Jesus speaks to the paralyzed man at the Pool of Bethesda near the Sheep Gate and then heals him, which then starts a small feud.

This man must have been so bad because he was paralyzed from a lingering disorder for thirty-eight years and could not make it to the pool to receive healing. It must have been chaotic around that pool with people pushing and shoving, waiting for the angel to stir it up so the first person in would receive a healing.

Thank God we all can be healed at the same time today by the work of the cross!

Day 138—May 18

<u>Prayer:</u> Teach me oh Lord what you want me to learn today. Help me Holy Spirit to unfold today's daily scriptures. Amen!

<u>After reading question:</u> What is God saying to me today?

OT}—David's lust gets the best of him, and he commits adultery and then turns around to murder her husband. God's anger is expressed by the death of their first child through a generational curse. David knew as soon as he heard that the child was dead that it was because of his actions and turned to God with a repentant heart.

2 Samuel 11-12

Psalm 64:6-10

Proverbs 13:1-3

John 5:24-47

NT}—Every knee shall bow, and every tongue will confess that Jesus is Lord, is the primary topic for today.

As Christians, one of our jobs is to believe in God and in the work of Jesus Christ, trust in his Word, and cling to it. Then our reward is eternal life.

But so many of us live by sight and not by the spirit. Spend some time today thinking about what verse 29 is saying.

Day 139—May 19

Prayer: Teach me oh Lord what you want me to learn today. Help me Holy Spirit to unfold today's daily scriptures. Amen!

After reading question: What is God saying to me today?

OT}—David's family is falling apart; lust, incest, deception, lies, murder, and people pretending to be other people are running throughout the house.

Sometimes desires can get the best of us and cause us to do stupid things. This is why God calls us to renew our minds on a daily basis.

2 Samuel 13-14
Psalm 65:1-7
Proverbs 13:4-6
John 6:1-21

NT}—After Jesus feeds the 5,000 near Bethsaida, the disciples take a boat to Capernaum. A storm rose, and Jesus walked on water towards them as he calmed the waves.

I believe this might be the same account we read in Matthew chapter 14, minus Peter. When I read this, I receive in my spirit that Jesus wants me to stay focused on him and not on what is raging around me. How about you?

Day 140—May 20

Prayer: Teach me oh Lord what you want me to learn today. Help me Holy Spirit to unfold today's daily scriptures. Amen!

After reading question: What is God saying to me today?

OT}—David's son, Absalom, is upset with the king, so he conspires against his father to overthrow him, so David heads for the hills.

2 Samuel 15-16
Psalm 65:8-13
Proverbs 13:7-9
John 6:22-51

NT}—The people are seeking out Jesus in Capernaum. They are determined to find answers to their many questions.

Jesus sees true purpose and tells them not to seek out the natural resources but to seek out the lasting food which endures continually unto life eternal; Jesus himself.

Once, at a church where I was a deacon, we had a unique community outreach service. We were meeting people's needs with money. People called their families and friends to tell them to come to the church because we were handing out money. After giving away thousands of dollars, we had to stop the service because people were there for the wrong reason. I understand this passage firsthand.

Day 141—May 21

Prayer: Teach me oh Lord what you want me to learn today. Help me Holy Spirit to unfold today's daily scriptures. Amen!

After reading question: What is God saying to me today?

OT}—With David on the run, Absalom pursues him with his newly built army. But he is no match to the servants of David and Absalom meets his destiny.

2 Samuel 17-18
Psalm 66:1-7
Proverbs 13:10-12
John 6:52-71

NT}—John shares with us an extended description of Holy Communion, which some of the disciples that were with Jesus must have thought was a little too much to deal with, so they left the association.

How would you handle it if you were sitting around the room lounging when, out of the blue, someone said, take and eat this is my body, and drink for this is my blood? I would run yelling their nothing but a bunch of cannibals in there. But thank God we know the true meaning that Jesus was saying.

Day 142—May 22

Prayer: Teach me oh Lord what you want me to learn today. Help me Holy Spirit to unfold today's daily scriptures. Amen!

After reading question: What is God saying to me today?

OT}—Even though Absalom came against his father, David, the love of a father remained, and David mourned the loss of his son. But in doing so, he became disrespectful to the people. Joab, son of Zeruiah, went to David to straighten him out. King David then listened to his nephew and addressed the people with a sincere heart. The people then cry out that they want David to return as king.

2 Samuel 19-20

Psalm 66:8-14

Proverbs 13:13-15

John 7:1-34

NT}—Jesus goes to the Jewish Feast of Tabernacles alone after his brothers leave, trying to be undetected. About halfway into the feast, Jesus goes to the temple to teach.

The Feast of Tabernacles, also known as "*Sukkot*," or Feast of Booths, is a week-long fall festival commemorating the forty years in the wilderness. Immediately after is the reading of the Torah, known as "*Sh'mini Atzeret*," or "*Simchat Torah*."[15]

Day 143—May 23

<u>Prayer:</u> Teach me oh Lord what you want me to learn today. Help me Holy Spirit to unfold today's daily scriptures. Amen!

<u>After reading question:</u> What is God saying to me today?

OT}—David makes restitution from the effects of Saul to heal the land.

Afterward, he pours out his heart into a song. One of the attributes of David was his music. He loved to play and sing, which made him a great worshiper and contributed to most of the Book of Psalms.

2 Samuel 21-22

Psalm 66:15-20

Proverbs 13:16-18

John 7:35-53

NT}—Now, on the last day of the Feast of Tabernacles, Jesus makes a statement that some were amazed at the depth of his teaching and marveled at what he was saying. Others questioned the scripture and asked for clarification, but with an unbelieving heart. Still, others wanted to arrest him, but no one laid their hands on him because it was not his time!

Day 144—May 24

Prayer: Teach me oh Lord what you want me to learn today. Help me Holy Spirit to unfold today's daily scriptures. Amen!

After reading question: What is God saying to me today?

OT}—Today, we end the Book of Samuel with David's last words as a public platform. In doing so, thirty-seven of his men get honored.

David once again pours out his heart to God for the people asking for mercy. The more we read about David, the more we see his love for the people. He makes a great statement about our offerings to God. It is in the middle of verse 24.

2 Samuel 23-24

Psalm 67

Proverbs 13:19-21

John 8:1-30

NT}—Jesus continued teaching the next day and tried to answer some of the questions they were testing him with.

They must have thought there is no way this man speaks the truth; he just keeps going. H his energy must be from an evil source. They were dry leaders, so there was no way they could see it from God.

We end today's reading with what we call an altar call.

Day 145—May 25

Prayer: Teach me oh Lord what you want me to learn today. Help me Holy Spirit to unfold today's daily scriptures. Amen!

After reading question: What is God saying to me today?

OT}—Today is the First Book of Kings. The Hebrew text regarded the First and Second Kings as one volume, called "Kings." They were divided into T*he Septuagint* and identified as "The Third and Fourth Books of Kingdoms." Both the First and Second Kings cover a period of over four hundred years of history.

Beginning with Solomon, First Kings trace the history of Israel through the divided kingdom to the reign of Ahaziah, son of Ahab, about two hundred years. Before he dies, we start with King David instructing his son Solomon to keep his eyes on God.

On page twelve, there is a list of kings for Israel and Judah.

1 Kings 1-2
Psalm 68:1-7
Proverbs 13:22-25
John 8:31-59

NT}—After Jesus continues his teaching, it seems to take a twist when he illustrates Abraham with himself. By the end of the day, they wanted to stone him, but Jesus outwitted them.

Day 146—May 26

OT}—Out of all the things Solomon could have asked for when God appeared to him in a dream, he requested wisdom. It pleased God, so he made Solomon one of the wisest men on earth, if not the most discerning. And because he only asked for wisdom, God made him a rich and honorable man, even though he was still foolish with some of the things he did during his reign.

After Solomon wakes up, he gets to put wisdom to the test with two women claiming to be the same child's mother.

1 Kings 3-4
Psalm 68:8-14
Proverbs 14:1-3
John 9:1-23

NT}—Jesus leaves the temple and as he is leaving he sees a blind man. After answering a question from the disciples, he spat on the ground to make clay, put it in the man's eyes, and told him to wash it off.

Jesus did so many miracles that I lost count on what number this one is. Actually, there is a list of them on page sixteen.

Day 147—May 27

Prayer: Teach me oh Lord what you want me to learn today. Help me Holy Spirit to unfold today's daily scriptures. Amen!

After reading question: What is God saying to me today?

OT}—Because there was peace in the land, Solomon started to build the house of the Lord that his father sought after. Four hundred eighty years after the Israelites came out of Egypt.

A cubit measure of length is approximately equal to a forearm's length: 18 inches or 44 centimeters.

1 Kings 5-6
Psalm 68:15-21
Proverbs 14:4-6
John 9:24-41

NT}—Now, because it was the Sabbath, the Pharisees start to interrogate the healed blind man on why he can now see since he was born blind, which is unheard of. They then get to address it with Jesus.

I love how the boy's parents reject what the Pharisees were trying to do yesterday and cast blame on something they did wrong. They answer them with; the boy is of age, ask him for yourselves for the answers you seek.

It was as if the Pharisees did not want to know the truth, so they acted, let's throw the parents under the bus. Love it!

Day 148—May 28

OT}—Solomon continues the building spree, completing his house and the Forest of Lebanon house. It took seven years for the temple and thirteen for the rest.

Solomon built God's house first, then his own. The fact that it took much longer for the other places is no reflection on Solomon. David had made every possible preparation for building the temple, significantly reducing the time needed to finish it, and even left Solomon plans and patterns for the temple and loyal friends to help.
Then he calls for the ark of the covenant.

1 Kings 7-8
Psalm 68:22-28
Proverbs 14:7-9
John 10:1-21

NT}—The conversation goes on with Jesus building his defense on why he was sent here.

Here we see Jesus boldly saying that he is the only way to heaven and all other ways are false proclamations. Hence, if we claim we belong to Jesus or are followers, his voice is the only voice we should be listening to.

Day 149—May 29

Prayer: Teach me oh Lord what you want me to learn today. Help me Holy Spirit to unfold today's daily scriptures. Amen!

After reading question: What is God saying to me today?

OT}—The Lord appears to Solomon for the second time, as he did in Gibeon, and tells him he is pleased with the house. But if he wants it to remain standing, he needs to keep the statutes and precepts of God.

1 Kings 9-10

Psalm 68:29-35

Proverbs 14:10-12

John 10:22-40

NT}—About two months later, the Feast of Dedication was starting, and again, Jesus took advantage and went to preach to draw more believers to him.

"*Hanukkah*" is called the Feast of Dedication, also known as the Festival of Lights, and will last eight days. This is where you might hear of the "*Menorah*," a lampstand used during the eight days. It is a Jewish festival commemorating Jerusalem's recovery and rededicating the second temple at the beginning of the Maccabean revolt.[16]

Day 150—May 30

Prayer: Teach me oh Lord what you want me to learn today. Help me Holy Spirit to unfold today's daily scriptures. Amen!

After reading question: What is God saying to me today?

OT}—Solomon grew to supersede all the other kings of the earth in riches and wisdom, but his lust for foreign women drove him away from God, and after a forty-year reign over Israel, he died.

With Solomon gone, his son, Rehoboam, takes over. But the people are not pleased with the outcome of a request they made to the new king. This opens up the door to division.

1 Kings 11-12
Psalm 69:1-7
Proverbs 14:13-15
John 11:1-29

NT}—Jesus raises Lazarus from the dead and points out to Martha that he is the Resurrection and the Life.

Even though Jesus was just in Judea, where they tried to stone him, he needed to go to his friends, so he put everything in place to return.

Day 151—May 31

Prayer: Teach me oh Lord what you want me to learn today. Help me Holy Spirit to unfold today's daily scriptures. Amen!

After reading question: What is God saying to me today?

OT}—We continue with the Book of Kings with Rehoboam as king. He reigned for seventeen years, but his life was cut short to fifty-eight years old because he sinned. After three years into his reign, the kingdom splits into two: Israel gets the northern land, with Jeroboam as king, and Judah gets the southern with Rehoboam remaining as their first king. Jeroboam reigned for twenty-two years before his death.

1 Kings 13-14
Psalm 69:8-14
Proverbs 14:16-18
John 11:30-57

NT}—Today, we see the shortest verse in the Bible, verse 35; "Jesus wept." One of the takeaways from this story is the risen power of Lazarus, but before that is the most moving part, the love Jesus had for his friends. It broke his heart when Jesus saw Mary crying, so he wept.

But why did Jesus delay getting to Lazarus has many puzzled. Some believe Jesus did not care. But the answer is found in verse 15. So they will believe, trust, and rely more on Jesus. Jesus knew that Lazarus would be resurrected and the best time to perform miracle number thirty-three.

Day 152—June 1

Prayer: Teach me oh Lord what you want me to learn today. Help me Holy Spirit to unfold today's daily scriptures. Amen!

After reading question: What is God saying to me today?

OT}—Abijam, Rehoboam's son, takes the position of king over Judah for three years. He was a wicked king. Then a good king, Asa, began his reign of forty-one years. First Kings does not talk about Asa too much, except to tell us he walked like his forefather David. He removed the male prostitutes and all idols, pulled his mother as queen because she worshipped other gods, and he maneuvered a way to stop a war between himself and King Baasha. After Asa, Jehoshaphat takes over for twenty-five years.

As far as the northern land, eight kings were mentioned, and all did evil in the sight of God; Jeroboam, Nadab, Baasha, Elah, Zimri, Tibni, who was a pretender for Omri, and Ahab.

1 Kings 15-16
Psalm 69:15-21
Proverbs 14:19-21
John 12:1-28

NT}—Two months after Jesus called Lazarus from the dead, Jesus went to Bethany to have dinner with his dear friends, where Mary washed his feet with a rare perfume.

Day 153—June 2

OT}—God hides Elijah and commands the ravens to feed him. Then God sends him to Zarephath, located about 8.5 miles south of Sidon and 14 miles north of Tyre. This is where he meets the widow who gives him her last meal, and then God blesses her household for days, and then Elijah raises a dead child. Afterward, God uses him to end the drought after he speaks to Ahab, King of Israel.

1 Kings 17-18
Psalm 69:22-28
Proverbs 14:22-24
John 12:29-50

NT}—John's account of Jesus arriving in Jerusalem is a little different from the others, as you read yesterday. Then when he arrives, he expresses who he is and that he only speaks what he hears the father speak.

One of the critical scriptures today is found in verses 47 and 48. Jesus did not come to condemn and judge the world, but to save it. If someone does not believe in him, their lack of belief will judge them.

Day 154—June 3

Prayer: Teach me oh Lord what you want me to learn today. Help me Holy Spirit to unfold today's daily scriptures. Amen!

After reading question: What is God saying to me today?

OT}—We start today with Elijah being chased after by Jezebel. Elijah runs and wants God to take his life. God speaks to him face-to-face and tells him to take care of some business.

Ahab goes to war with Ben-Hadad, king of Syria. Because Ben-Hadad wanted all that Ahab had; silver, gold, wives, and children. The bottom line is that King Ben-Hadad wanted to destroy King Ahab.

1 Kings 19-20
Psalm 69:29-36
Proverbs 14:25-27
John 13:1-20

NT}—Jesus washes the feet of the apostles. When Jesus is talking about washing one another's feet, he is trying to say that we are to serve one another through whatever talent we have, and when we do, we are no better than the ones we are serving, no matter what position one may have. Serving is a reward, and Jesus says we are blessed if we serve one another.

Day 155—June 4

Prayer: Teach me oh Lord what you want me to learn today. Help me Holy Spirit to unfold today's daily scriptures. Amen!

After reading question: What is God saying to me today?

OT}—You may have heard of a "Jezebel Spirit" in your time as a Christian. Today we read the second incident that involves King Ahab's wife, Jezebel, in a deceitful act. The first one was found in 1 Kings 18:4 and 13, where she campaigns to rid Israel of God and turn them to Baal. She was obsessive, domineering, and controlling to do God's people wrong. Jezebel Spirit: being single-minded to have one's way, no matter who is destroyed in the process.[17]
Also, we read that Jehoshaphat joined forces with Ahab against Ramoth-Gilead with a lousy ending. Ahaziah began his two-year reign over Israel.

1 Kings 21-22
Psalm 70
Proverbs 14:28-30
John 13:21-38

NT}—In verse 23, John wrote. "One of his disciples, whom Jesus loved...." This statement appears five times in the gospel of John and nowhere else except in revelations. Some believe this may be referencing John himself, and John did not want to bring attention to himself. Some say it might have been the nephew of Barnabas, John Mark.
I challenge you to research and study this for yourself.

Day 156—June 5

<u>Prayer:</u> Teach me oh Lord what you want me to learn today. Help me Holy Spirit to unfold today's daily scriptures. Amen!

<u>After reading question:</u> What is God saying to me today?

OT}—We continue with the Second Book of Kings with the stories of Elijah and Elisha. Also, Joram became the ninth king of Israel.

Elisha, a disciple of Elijah who was a prophet and miracle worker, asked for a double portion of Elijah's spirit before Elijah was taken up to heaven in a whirlwind. Elijah is one of the two, outside of Jesus, who have been taken into heaven alive. The other one was Enoch, and some people believe that they are the two witnesses mentioned in Revelations.

2 Kings 1-2
Psalm 71:1-8
Proverbs 14:31-33
John 14:1-21

NT}—In a world with many religions, I have heard the way to heaven is in many paths, but I will always believe verse 6 of today's reading.

"I am the Way and the Truth and the Life;
no one comes to the Father except by (through) Me."

Day 157—June 6

<u>Prayer:</u> Teach me oh Lord what you want me to learn today. Help me Holy Spirit to unfold today's daily scriptures. Amen!

<u>After reading question:</u> What is God saying to me today?

OT}—Joram and Jehoshaphat join forces to go up against the king of Moab after they receive counsel from Elisha.

Elisha then takes the place of the teacher and continues prophesying throughout the land, and he even raises a dead child by laying on top of him.

In Matthew 14, we read that Jesus fed the five thousand, but that is not the first time God multiplied food. Pay attention to the end of today's reading.

2 Kings 3-4
Psalm 71:9-16
Proverbs 14:34-35
John 14:22-31

NT}—Jesus continues to speak on the future events that will take place. He is reassuring the disciples that they will not be left alone because God will send them the Holy Spirit.

Other names for Holy Spirit are; Comforter, Counselor, Helper, Intercessor, Advocate, Strengthener, Standby, and Spirit of Truth.

Day 158—June 7

Prayer: Teach me oh Lord what you want me to learn today. Help me Holy Spirit to unfold today's daily scriptures. Amen!

After reading question: What is God saying to me today?

OT}—Today, we read some of the life of Naaman, the Arabian who was commander of the Syrian army, reigned by King Ben-hadad of Aram Damascus. He did well in the sight of God. He was healed of his leprosy through the prophet Elisha when he dipped himself seven times in the Jordan.

We also continue with Elisha with the recovery of the ax head showing another miracle of provision. God also protects Elisha from the Syrians. The blind Syrians are healed in Samaria afterward Syria sieges Samaria.

2 Kings 5-6
Psalm 71:17-24
Proverbs 15:1-3
John 15

NT}—As Christians, we have been taught to trust God and believe that he is with us by faith. I have seen verse 5 in my life, and I have also sometimes had verses 2 and 6. But no matter what it looks like around me, I will always have faith.

Where is your faith?

Day 159—June 8

Teach me oh Lord what you want me to learn today. Help me Holy Spirit to unfold today's daily scriptures. Amen!

After reading question: What is God saying to me today?

OT}—We read yesterday that Elisha's life was threatened, but King Joram did not go through with it. Instead, he looks to him for answers.

Jehoram takes his father's place, Jehoshaphat, to reign over Judah at age thirty-two. He reigned for eight years—Edom revolts from Judah.

Ahaziah then reigns in Jehoram's place at the age of twenty-two for one year.

2 Kings 7-8
Psalm 72:1-7
Proverbs 15:4-6
John 16:1-16

NT}—Jesus expresses that when he leaves, the Holy Spirit will return. And when he comes, he will; Convict the world, guide into truth, speak only from the father, declare things to come, honor and glorify Jesus, and reveal all things.

Jesus says that not everywhere we go, or the people we encounter, will accept us because of our faith in him.

Day 160—June 9

Prayer: Teach me oh Lord what you want me to learn today. Help me Holy Spirit to unfold today's daily scriptures. Amen!

After reading question: What is God saying to me today?

OT}—Elisha sends another prophet to anoint Jehu as king over Israel and then prophecies. Because of this, Jehu pursues King Joram to dethrone him and kills him with an arrow. Then orders Jezebel to be thrown out of a window. Jehu further proceeds to illuminate every male in the house of Ahab. Even though Jehu removed the house of Baal and all who worshipped Baal, he did not quit the sins that made Israel sin. Jehu reigned for twenty-eight years, after which his son Jehoahaz took his place for seventeen years.

2 Kings 9-10

Psalm 72:8-14

Proverbs 15:7-9

John 16:17-33

NT}—Prayer: When Jesus was here on earth, all things were completed by him, but today, not just the reading for today, we can pray straight to God the Father, in the name of Jesus, and he will hear our prayers, Verses 23-27. This personal relationship has been given to us through the work of the cross. Some people believe they need to pray to idols for God to hear their prayer. God is not untouchable; he is personable and loves when we sit in his lap, as most fathers enjoy.

Day 161—June 10

Prayer: Teach me oh Lord what you want me to learn today. Help me Holy Spirit to unfold today's daily scriptures. Amen!

After reading question: What is God saying to me today?

OT}—Here, we see the first offering box built by Jehoiada, the priest. Twenty-three years before it was made, priests solicited and received money to be used to repair God's house. But in King Joash's reign, no repairs were done. With concern, the king asked them why and ordered no more money to be received. Then he ordered boxes to be built and put scribes and high priests to keep the money count. Today some churches have deacons to fulfill the task.

2 Kings 11-12
Psalm 72:15-20
Proverbs 15:10-12
John 17

NT}—Jesus speaks to his heavenly father on behalf of the completion of his work and the remaining disciples. We also read today in verse 12 that Jesus says Judas Iscariot was the only lost disciple and doomed for destruction. When we get to heaven, we will find out if God had mercy on his soul at the last second.

What do you think?

Day 162—June 11

OT}—Elisha, the prophet, dies after a long illness. Some say he was 100 years old, but we are not sure how old he was, but he held the office of a prophet in Israel for six decades, 892-832 BC. The power of God on his life and ministry was so strong that even after he had no spirit in him, his bones touched another dead person's bones, and that man was restored to life.

Israel seems to be unable to shed leaders who refuse to follow after God.

Today we read about Jehoahaz, Jehoash, and Jeroboam. All three did evil in the Lord's sight and continued to follow their fathers' sins.

2 Kings 13-14
Psalm 73:1-7
Proverbs 15:13-15
John 18:1-17

NT}—Jesus is betrayed by Judas with a kiss in the garden to fulfill what was to come to Jesus. Prophesied in Zechariah 13:7, Isaiah 53:7, Psalm 22:16, and written before crucifixion was invented.

Day 163—June 12

OT}—At the age of sixteen, Azariah (Uzziah) reigns over Judah for fifty-one years. During his reign, Israel had six kings. Jeroboam II for the first thirty-eight years, Zechariah six months, fulfilling the promise to Jehu that four generations with reign over Israel by God. Shallum for one month, being killed by Manahem, who took his place for ten years. Pekahiah was next for two years and was killed by Pekah. At the end of Azariah's reign, Pekah was king over Israel for twenty years when he was killed by Hoshea, who reigned for nine years.

In the second year of Pekah, Jotham became king over Judah for sixteen years. Then Ahaz was after Jotham for sixteen years. Then Hezekiah was next for twenty-nine years.

2 Kings 15-16
Psalm 73:8-14
Proverbs 15:16-18
John 18:18-40

NT}—Jesus is now being questioned by the high priest and answering that he has, nor has he ever had, anything to hide. He has preached openly to the world. Then he is brought to Pilate for sentencing.

Day 164—June 13

Prayer: Teach me oh Lord what you want me to learn today. Help me Holy Spirit to unfold today's daily scriptures. Amen!

After reading question: What is God saying to me today?

OT}—In some of the readings, you may notice a discrepancy in the years when some of the kings reigned. That is because sometimes the kings would co-regency overlapping dates. Whether it was because of the year marked down or because of the age of the king when the throne was given to them, I found this to mainly be between King Jotham of Judah and King Manasseh. 750 BCE and 643 BCE.

2 Kings 17-18

Psalm 73:15-21

Proverbs 15:19-21

John 19:1-22

NT}—Pilate does not believe Jesus did anything wrong, so he orders him to be scourged, hoping that would be enough. Not believing that Jesus was the son of God, the high priests used the law to crucify Jesus because of the claims that Jesus made about himself.

Nowhere in scripture does it mention how many stripes Jesus received. It is assumed 39 because 40 or more lashes would kill someone. The guards were ordered not to kill him.

Day 165—June 14

Prayer: Teach me oh Lord what you want me to learn today. Help me Holy Spirit to unfold today's daily scriptures. Amen!

After reading question: What is God saying to me today?

OT}—Hezekiah prays to God, asking for mercy for healing. God adds fifteen years to his life. Hezekiah's reign over Judah ends with Manasseh, his son, taking over. King Manasseh reigned for fifty-five years. Israel was conquered by the Neaassyrian Empire between the two kings and destroyed in 722 BCE.

2 Kings 19-20
Psalm 73:22-28
Proverbs 15:22-24
John 19:23-42

NT}—Today, we see some of the fulfilling scripture from the Old Testament that was spoken in reference to what was to come to Jesus.

- Psalm 22:18, They cast lots for my clothing
- Psalm 34:20, He keeps all his bones; not one of them is broken
- Exodus 12:46(b), Neither shall you break a bone of it
- Zechariah 12:10, Piercing of his side
- Psalm 22:8, He will be delivered up

Day 166—June 15

<u>Prayer:</u> Teach me oh Lord what you want me to learn today. Help me Holy Spirit to unfold today's daily scriptures. Amen!

<u>After reading question:</u> What is God saying to me today?

OT}—Manasseh was twelve years old when he began his reign. He was not like his father and did evil in the sight of God. He built altars to worship Baal and made a graven image of the goddess Ashram. Offered his son to Molech in a fire and prated witchcraft.

Manasseh dies, and Amon, his son, reigns for two years and follows in his father's footsteps. Josiah, his son, reigns for thirty-one years at eight years old. Josiah, at eighteen, turns towards God and repents.

2 Kings 21-22
Psalm 74:1-8
Proverbs 15:25-27
John 20:1-18

NT}—Here we see where the scripture says, "Other disciple." This wording is why in chapter 13, verse 23, that you read on June 3, many believe that it was John referencing himself. Did you study it out? Who do you think the other disciple is? I believe it is John.

Day 167—June 16

Prayer: Teach me oh Lord what you want me to learn today. Help me Holy Spirit to unfold today's daily scriptures. Amen!

After reading question: What is God saying to me today?

OT}—Josiah dies by the sword of Pharaoh Necho. His son Jehoahaz was anointed king, but it only lasted three months when Pharaoh Necho replaced him with Eliakim, then changed his name to Jehoiakim, who reigned for eleven years. Jehoiachin reigned for three months when he surrendered to the king of Babylon, who then made Mattaniah king and changed his name to Zedekiah for an eleven-year reign.

King Nebuchadnezzar took Jerusalem and burned the temple and city. Some people ran to escape, and others were taken into captivity. This is known as the "Babylonian Exile." Then the Hasmonean Dynasty began in 140 BCE when Judah gained complete independence.

2 Kings 23-25
Psalm 74:9-16
Proverbs 15:28-30
John 20:19-31

NT}—This is where we hear why Thomas got the nickname "Doubting Thomas."

Day 168—June 17

<u>Prayer:</u> Teach me oh Lord what you want me to learn today. Help me Holy Spirit to unfold today's daily scriptures. Amen!

<u>After reading question:</u> What is God saying to me today?

OT}—Starting into the First Book of the Chronicles can be a challenge for some.

The first nine chapters are the genealogy of humanity from Adam to David. The remaining chapters describe the reign of King David.

Chapter one—Adam's genealogical line,
Chapter two—Sons of Israel, also known as Jacob,
Chapter three—Sons of David that were born in Hebron

See chart on page 9.

1 Chronicles 1-3
Psalm 74:17-23
Proverbs 15:31-33
John 21

NT}—Jesus appeared to the disciples three different times after he had risen. On the third time, Jesus asked Peter three times if Peter loved him. I believe that Jesus was trying to get Peter to deeper depths of his spirit to speak out about how much he loved, trusted, and believed in him.

Day 169—June 18

Prayer: Teach me oh Lord what you want me to learn today. Help me Holy Spirit to unfold today's daily scriptures. Amen!

After reading question: What is God saying to me today?

OT}—We continue with the genealogy.

Today is Chapter four—Sons of Judah, the fourth son of Israel from Leah.

Chapter Five—Sons of Ruben, who were the firstborn to Israel through Leah. Because Ruben slept with Bilhah, his father's concubine, his birthright went to the sons of Joseph, the firstborn son of Rachel. I believe that could be why we get the story of Joseph, instead of the story of Ruben, in Genesis.

1 Chronicles 4-5
Psalm 75:1-5
Proverbs 16:1-3
Acts 1

NT}—Today, we start reading Acts, the basic history of the spread of Christianity during the thirty years immediately following the death and resurrection of Jesus Christ. Acts is part two of a two-volume work addressed to Theophilus, with Luke being the first volume. Most believe Luke is the author of Acts. Identified as the pivotal book of the New Testament.

Day 170—June 19

<u>Prayer:</u> Teach me oh Lord what you want me to learn today. Help me Holy Spirit to unfold today's daily scriptures. Amen!

<u>After reading question:</u> What is God saying to me today?

OT}—Today, we read Chapter six—sons of Levi, third son of Israel from Leah.

And Chapter seven is—Sons of Issachar, the fifth son of Israel from Leah.

1 Chronicles 6-7
Psalm 75:6-10
Proverbs 16:4-6
Acts 2:1-23

NT}—Holy Spirit takes his place on earth with a mighty entrance. This part of the Trinity, which cannot be seen, had to come in like the rushing of a violent tempest blast so the 120 people that were in the upper room, with thousands more outside, would know the sign that Jesus told them, "When I leave another will take my Place."

Holy Spirit is the assurance of our connection to Jesus. Holy Spirit is not a tool; we do not use him like a Jeannie. We should know him just as we know a friend. Holy Spirit always points to Jesus and never to himself, and he will take the focus off himself.

Day 171—June 20

<u>Prayer:</u> Teach me oh Lord what you want me to learn today. Help me Holy Spirit to unfold today's daily scriptures. Amen!

<u>After reading question:</u> What is God saying to me today?

OT}—We continue with the genealogy.
Chapter 8, Sons of Benjamin, who is the second son of Israel from Rachel.

Also, Chapter 9 extends to the genealogies of the Levites and temple servants. Also mentions; the Tribe of Ephraim, the Tribe of Manasseh, who formed the house of Joseph and are considered to be one of the ten lost tribes, sons of Joseph, grandsons of Jacob,

1 Chronicles 8-9
Psalm 76:1-6
Proverbs 16:7-9
Acts 2:24-47

NT}—Peter gets to preach his first sermon to the multitude. Three thousand people accepted Christ in their hearts and were baptized. Therefore, the first church of Christ was started, and God blessed them in number.

With water being scarce in most of Israel, it is possible that they were baptized in cisterns that collected water through a series of small channels. Some by Peter and the leaders, some self-administered with their own confessions of faith.

Day 172—June 21

<u>Prayer:</u> Teach me oh Lord what you want me to learn today. Help me Holy Spirit to unfold today's daily scriptures. Amen!

<u>After reading question:</u> What is God saying to me today?

OT}—After the Philistines slay Saul's sons, he kills himself, so the Philistines do not get credit for his death. Ish-bosheth reigned for two troubled years, and then the people wanted David as their king. So we start the reign of David around 1003 BC. David is anointed king over Israel and goes to Jerusalem to take over the city. They took over the city and became known as "The City of David."

1 Chronicles 10-11

Psalm 76:7-12

Proverbs 16:10-12

Acts 3

NT}—You may have heard this statement, "Silver and gold I have not, but what I do have, is freely yours." That comes from today's reading when Peter and John healed a crippled man at one of the gates of the temple called Beautiful.

When the man began to walk, he went into the temple leaping and praising God. This gives Peter a chance to speak to the people about their failure to believe in Jesus when he walked among them.

Day 173—June 22

<u>Prayer:</u> Teach me oh Lord what you want me to learn today. Help me Holy Spirit to unfold today's daily scriptures. Amen!

<u>After reading question:</u> What is God saying to me today?

OT}—The people come together to make David a king, and after a three-day feast, David addresses the people to bring the Ark of God from Baalah to the city. Uzza, son of Abinadab, where the ark was for twenty years, was transporting the ark with his brother Ahio. When Uzza put his hand out to stable the ark, he died. David was afraid of God, so he did not bring it onto the city of David.

1 Chronicles 12-13
Psalm 77:1-7
Proverbs 16:13-15
Acts 4:1-18

NT}—Well, Jesus is gone, but the arrogance of the Sadducees and other leaders continues.

Peter and John are arrested and thrown in prison, but not before more are added to the church.

They are on trial to defend the authority that Jesus gave them to heal. Then Peter, filled with Holy Spirit, gave them an earful. Because Peter and John were uneducated, the leaders recognized that they had been with Jesus.

Day 174—June 23

<u>Prayer:</u> Teach me oh Lord what you want me to learn today. Help me Holy Spirit to unfold today's daily scriptures. Amen!

<u>After reading question:</u> What is God saying to me today?

OT}—The Philistines cannot relax, they go up against David as the new king, but God delivers them into David's hand to help defeat them twice. David reconsiders bringing the ark to the city, then he prepares a place and tells them nobody but the Levites should carry it since God chose them to carry it.

As they enter the city, there is a caravan of singers and musical instruments celebrating the delivery of the ark. This is where David starts to leap for joy as the ark enters the city, and his wife, Michal, despises him in her heart.

1 Chronicles 14-15
Psalm 77:8-14
Proverbs 16:16-18
Acts 4:19-37

NT}—Peter and John are told to stop preaching. They turned around and prayed to God instead, and the power of God fell on them, so they continued to speak the Word of God with freedom, boldness, and courage.

Day 175—June 24

<u>Prayer:</u> Teach me oh Lord what you want me to learn today. Help me Holy Spirit to unfold today's daily scriptures. Amen!

<u>After reading question:</u> What is God saying to me today?

OT}—After the ark is put in the tent that David put up, he makes offerings to God. After the offerings with thanksgiving, praises, and direction, God tells David, through Nathan the prophet, not to build a house for the ark because his offspring would be the one to make it. David then goes into the tent to speak to God, praising him for all he has done and will do for David and his family.

1 Chronicles 16-17

Psalm 77:15-20

Proverbs 16:19-21

Acts 5:1-23

NT}—Ananias tries to deceive the church, and because he wrongfully appropriated some of the proceeds from the sale of property, he dies. Because his wife knew, she died as well.

It never pays to lie; the truth will always surface and be exposed. Especially when we walk with God!

Day 176—June 25

<u>Prayer:</u> Teach me oh Lord what you want me to learn today. Help me Holy Spirit to unfold today's daily scriptures. Amen!

<u>After reading question:</u> What is God saying to me today?

OT}—Davis's kindness is not received by the king of Ammonites, which sparks a war. In the Jewish tradition, men grew their beards, dating back to Leviticus 19:27, where God told them not to cut their hair. Some of that tradition is still in existence today for various reasons in various religions. Thereby, when King Hanum shaved David's men in 19:4, it was a big deal.

I challenge you to study this further.

1 Chronicles 18-19

Psalm 78:1-8

Proverbs 16:22-24

Acts 5:24-42

NT}—All those preaching were confronted about why they will not stop teaching. The council decided to let them continue in hopes that it was only a phase, and if it were not from God, it would fade away.

Day 177—June 26

<u>Prayer:</u> Teach me oh Lord what you want me to learn today. Help me Holy Spirit to unfold today's daily scriptures. Amen!

<u>After reading question:</u> What is God saying to me today?

OT}—God gives David three choices to choose from because he listens to Satan to take a head count of Israel. God puts his anger out toward the people, then David comes forward to take the blame.

David was a great king in many ways, and today we see his heart expressed for his people.

1 Chronicles 20-21
Psalm 78:9-16
Proverbs 16:25-27
Acts 6

NT}—Steven, and six others, were chosen to take care of any of the widows in the community because they were being overlooked by all the excitement that was taking place with the building of the church.

Steven was a deacon in Jerusalem who did many great things for the church. He was the first Christian martyr. Because some leaders did not care too much for him, they plotted against him by getting some men to say that Steven was using slanderous, abusive, and blasphemous language against Moses and God.[18]

Day 178—June 27

Prayer: Teach me oh Lord what you want me to learn today. Help me Holy Spirit to unfold today's daily scriptures. Amen!

After reading question: What is God saying to me today?

OT}—Because David stood up to take the blame and repented in yesterday's reading, God withdrew his wrath. It prompts David to prepare the building of God's house. He talks with his son Solomon, which means "*peaceable*," to tell him all God had told him about the temple. David then prophesies to Solomon and commences a blessing. Solomon, years later, takes the throne and starts to build.

1 Chronicles 22-23
Psalm 78:17-24
Proverbs 16:28-30
Acts 7:1-25

NT}—The high priest asked Steven if the charges were accurate that we read yesterday, and he gave the high priest a lesson on their heritage in reply to a question.

Today, Stephen greatly compresses Old Testament accounts of two land purchases and two burial places at Hebron and Shechem, and the journey of Joseph leading to all of Israel residing in Egypt through the time Moses kills an Egyptian.

Day 179—June 28

Prayer: Teach me oh Lord what you want me to learn today. Help me Holy Spirit to unfold today's daily scriptures. Amen!

After reading question: What is God saying to me today?

OT}—Today, we read about the genealogy of Aaron. With Aaron, and his sons being in charge of the service of the house of the Lord, it was time to divide and disperse their duties.

This was done by casting lots. The casting of a lot is a form of coin tossing or drawing names from a hat like we use today.

Some scholars believe it may have been some sticks, dice, or stones to help make decisions.

1 Chronicles 24-25
Psalm 78:25-32
Proverbs 16:31-33
Acts 7:26-60

NT}—Steven continues to give a history lesson, but when he calls them out, the Jews are infuriated, and the outcome is not too good. They drugged him out of the city and stoned him to death. It is believed that this is where Steven became the first Christian martyr.

Day 180—June 29

Prayer: Teach me oh Lord what you want me to learn today. Help me Holy Spirit to unfold today's daily scriptures. Amen!

After reading question: What is God saying to me today?

OT}—We start today with the names of the gatekeepers.

We also read a list of the Israelite's heads of father houses, commanders, and officers who served the king in all matters of the divisions.

Gatekeepers were responsible for protecting the temple in a practical and spiritual sense. They ensured that only those ready to serve and worship God could go to the temple and its associated buildings.[19]

1 Chronicles 26-27
Psalm 78:33-40
Proverbs 17:1-2
Acts 8:1-24

NT}—With the death of Stephan, Paul was not only consenting to his death but is also pleased and entirely approving. That caused great persecution against the church. Afterward, all but the apostles scattered throughout Judah and Samaria and continued teaching the Word of God.

Day 181—June 30

<u>Prayer:</u> Teach me oh Lord what you want me to learn today. Help me Holy Spirit to unfold today's daily scriptures. Amen!

<u>After reading question:</u> What is God saying to me today?

OT}—David publicly announces that Solomon is to sit upon the throne, build God's house, and then hands over the plans.

David provided everything Solomon needed to build the temple and its courts, from money to materials and even labor. Solomon sits on the throne, and his father dies at seventy-one after a forty-year reign.

1 Chronicles 28-29

Psalm 78:41-48

Proverbs 17:3-4

Acts 8:25-40

NT}—After some time passed, the gospel started to spread, and some apostles were splitting off on their own.

Today I felt to give the meaning of a eunuch since there is a lot of one mentioned today. A eunuch is a man who has been castrated and used as a servant, or enslaved person, for female living areas and/or queen of a royal court. Because they were castrated, the ruler did not need to be concerned with lust or sexual matters since they had no desires.[20]

Day 182—July 1

Prayer: Teach me oh Lord what you want me to learn today. Help me Holy Spirit to unfold today's daily scriptures. Amen!

After reading question: What is God saying to me today?

OT}—Continuing with Chronicles, we jump right in on the reign of Solomon. Within the first nine chapters, Solomon asks for wisdom and knowledge to rule over Israel and preps to build the temple. Solomon reigned for forty-one years.

In chapter 2, verse 10, it mentions 20,000 baths. A bath is about eight gallons, three quarts of our measure. It would take around ten acres of vineyard to yield one bath. This would equal 175,000 gallons of wine and also of oil. And a measure of crushed wheat could bake one loaf of bread.

2 Chronicles 1-2

Psalm 78:49-56

Proverbs 17:5-6

Acts 9:1-22

NT}—Saul, before he became Paul, started a campaign of persecution against the church in Jerusalem for their faith in Jesus Christ, harassed the believers about some of the teachings, and wanted to arrest them and bound them with chains. That is when Jesus stands up from his throne and yells down to Saul, "Why are you persecuting me?" Jesus blinds him for three days, and when his sight returns, he proclaims Jesus as the son of God.

Day 183—July 2

<u>Prayer:</u> Teach me oh Lord what you want me to learn today. Help me Holy Spirit to unfold today's daily scriptures. Amen!

<u>After reading question:</u> What is God saying to me today?

OT}—After Solomon settled in and finalized some of the detail, he began to build the temple on the second day, of the second month, in the fourth year of his reign. It measured 90 feet in length by 30 feet wide and 45 feet high. It took Solomon about seven years to build it, and a total of twenty years for the whole project. He laid it out and furnished it just as his father David planned it.

2 Chronicles 3-4

Psalm 78:57-64

Proverbs 17:7-8

Acts 9:23-43

NT}—After Saul diverted death, he got his vision back and repented. He started to proclaim Jesus as the Messiah and was preaching in Damascus. It appears that he may have been preaching in other areas, including his hometown of Tarsus. Saul had to prove himself to be part of the team, which took some time.

We end the chapter with Peter traveling to Lydda, where he healed Aeneas from being paralyzed for eight years. Then he journeyed to Joppa to raise Tabitha from the dead.

Day 184—July 3

Prayer: Teach me oh Lord what you want me to learn today. Help me Holy Spirit to unfold today's daily scriptures. Amen!

After reading question: What is God saying to me today?

OT}—The work on the temple is completed, and King Solomon calls for the ark of the covenant to be brought up by the Levites from the city of David. Solomon then prays for God to take up residency in his new place to call home.

In Hebrew, the seventh month is when they have a feast to celebrate, it is today's July.

Pop quiz: Do you know what was in the ark? You will know after today's reading if you do not.

2 Chronicles 5-6
Psalm 78:65-72
Proverbs 17:9-10
Acts 10:1-24

NT}—Cornelius, a centurion of the Italian Regiment in Caesarea, is visited by an angel of God around 3:00 pm because of his generous gifts to the poor, and God was pleased. This angel instructed him to send men to Joppa to take Peter back to Cornelius so he could pray a warning for Peter to act on.

Peter has his first vision.

Day 185—July 4

Teach me oh Lord what you want me to learn today. Help me Holy Spirit to unfold today's daily scriptures. Amen!

After reading question: What is God saying to me today?

OT}—Yesterday, we ended with Solomon finishing his prayer to God. Just as he had finished, God took his rightful place and filled the whole house with glory.

Not only did Solomon complete the house of the Lord, but he also finished his own house. He then works on rebuilding and fortifying other cities that were given to him.

I once experienced God's glory at a church where we had a prayer tunnel with some great intercessors. The glory of God fell in the sanctuary, and it was tough to stand without wobbling, so I can relate when I read this passage today.

2 Chronicles 7-8
Psalm 79:1-7
Proverbs 17:11-12
Acts 10:25-48

NT}—Cornelius tells Peter about his visit from the angel of God. In verse 34, Peter replies with a profound statement: "I now perceive and understand that God shows no partiality and is no respecter of persons."

God is still that way today!

Day 186—July 5

<u>Prayer:</u> Teach me oh Lord what you want me to learn today. Help me Holy Spirit to unfold today's daily scriptures. Amen!

<u>After reading question:</u> What is God saying to me today?

OT}—Today, we finish up with the reign of Solomon and go into the history of the southern kingdom of Judah, starting with the reign of Rehoboam, Solomon's son. Rehoboam was a wicked king, and three years into his reign, Jeroboam returned from Egypt asking him to lighten up on how he was treating the Israelites. After seeking counsel, he followed through with the advice of the young men that grew up with him, instead of the wise older men. So, Israel rebelled against the house of David and split on their own with Jeroboam as their king.

2 Chronicles 9-10

Psalm 79:8-13

Proverbs 17:13-14

Acts 11

NT}—Here, we see a denominational dispute, even though there was one purpose. Jesus was being accepted outside the Jewish church, and some Jewish Christians were unhappy. Peter explains why he was preaching to the Gentiles.

Day 187—July 6

After reading question: What is God saying to me today?

OT}— During the reign of Rehoboam, there were wars between Judah and Israel, even though God told them to have peace. Rehoboam sets out to fight the rebellious tribe of Israel because he wants the kingdom back, but God calls it off. Instead, he started building fortified cities which did not help him when the king of Egypt came up against Jerusalem. Rehoboam dies at fifty-eight years old after reigning over Judah for seventeen years.

In today's scripture, the wrath of God is devastating, but when we repent, God will be merciful. As you read today, you will see that the Levites were kicked out of Israel. That is because Jeroboam wanted his own priests to be over his demon worship idols.

2 Chronicles 11-12
Psalm 80:1-7
Proverbs 17:15-16
Acts 12

NT}—Herod, the king, who was not a good king, kills James, the brother of John, and puts Peter in prison during Passover week. After some time passes, and just before Herod is to judge Peter, God breaks him out and sends a plague of worms to kill Herod.

Day 188—July 7

Prayer: Teach me oh Lord what you want me to learn today. Help me Holy Spirit to unfold today's daily scriptures. Amen!

After reading question: What is God saying to me today?

OT}—After the death of Rehoboam, Abijah became king of Judah for three years and continued his father's wars with King Jeroboam. Even though in Kings, chapter 15, Abijah is said to have been an evil king. The recorded report in today's reading shows a measure of faith and wisdom. God uses him to destroy Jeroboam.

After Abijah died, Asa, his son, regained for forty-one years. He honored God, and after ten years he went to war, starting with the Ethiopians.

2 Chronicles 13-14
Psalm 80:8-13
Proverbs 17:17-18
Acts 13:1-26

NT}—After Barnabas and Saul return to Antioch from Jerusalem, they are sent out to the mission field by Holy Spirit as they were worshiping the Lord. Along the way, they meet a wizard, a false prophet named, Bar-Jesus, who wants to hear more about salvation and how to attain it through Christ.

Note: Barnabas was one of the Cypriots who founded the church in Antioch where he preached.

Day 189—July 8

<u>Prayer:</u> Teach me oh Lord what you want me to learn today. Help me Holy Spirit to unfold today's daily scriptures. Amen!

<u>After reading question:</u> What is God saying to me today?

OT}—After Asa became king, a prophecy was spoken to him that brought hope again to Judah and Israel until the thirty-fifth year of the reign of Asa. Then a new king arose in Israel that came against Judah, and King Asa turned to Ben-hadad, king of Syria, for help.

2 Chronicles 15-16
Psalm 80:14-19
Proverbs 17:19-20
Acts 13:27-52

NT}—Paul continues sharing the gospel in Pisidia, and the people keep wanting to hear more preaching, so after the service, many of the Jews followed them. Almost the entire city gathered the next Sabbath to hear what they had to say.

At this time, the eagerness from the people concerning eternal salvation through Christ started to spread throughout the whole region.

We are drawn to bad news, but our spirits crave good news. We need good news to bring us back to goodness, which could be why the gospel spread like wildfire.[21]

Day 190—July 9

<u>Prayer:</u> Teach me oh Lord what you want me to learn today. Help me Holy Spirit to unfold today's daily scriptures. Amen!

<u>After reading question:</u> What is God saying to me today?

OT}—After the death of Asa, his son, Jehoshaphat, becomes king. Jehoshaphat was a good king and walked in the ways of God like his great-great-great-great grandfather David. King Jehoshaphat and King Ahab of Israel fought against Syria, where Ahab did not survive.

2 Chronicles 17-18

Psalm 81:1-8

Proverbs 17:21-22

Acts 14

NT}—Because some of the unbelieving Jews were trying to alter the message, Paul and Barnabas remain in Iconium to continue preaching. During that time they healed a cripple man who never walked. Some people started yelling and calling them Herne's "God of speech." Now they had to try to make the people of Iconium see that they were not gods, just servants of the living God.

Not believing them, the people stoned Paul and dragged him out of the town, thinking he was dead. After shaking the dust off, Paul leaves for Derbe. Then, after some time, they return to Iconium for another round of teaching.

Day 191—July 10

<u>Prayer:</u> Teach me oh Lord what you want me to learn today. Help me Holy Spirit to unfold today's daily scriptures. Amen!

<u>After reading question:</u> What is God saying to me today?

OT}—After Jehoshaphat returned to Jerusalem safely, and some time passed, the Moabites, Ammonites, and Meunites came against Judah. Jehoshaphat gets another victory but then ruins it with God by joining King Ahaziah, who was wicked, to build ships to go to Tarshish for the gold, which ended in disaster when the ships were wrecked at Zion Geber.

2 Chronicles 19-20
Psalm 81:9-16
Proverbs 17:23-24
Acts 15:1-21

NT}—After Paul and other disciples finally started to touch the hearts of many people, both Jew and Gentile, the question of whether or not the Gentiles should follow the Mosaic custom and be circumcised was challenged in Jerusalem.

Peter stands up and makes a strong case that God was the one who opened the door for the Gentiles to accept salvation through the same faith that the Jews had.

Day 192—July 11

After reading question: What is God saying to me today?

OT}—After twenty-one years, Jehoshaphat's reign ends when he dies at age sixty. His son Jehoram reigns in his place and does evil in the sight of God. He became an unwanted king in Judah because of his wicked ways, and God removed him after eight years.

Ahaziah took the reign and was just as wicked. He only reigned for one year but stirred up some trouble before being slain by King Jehu. Then his mother, Athaliah, found out her son was dead, so she destroyed all the royal family of Judah.

2 Chronicles 21-22
Psalm 82
Proverbs 17:25-26
Acts 15:22-41

NT}—We have seen up to this point that Paul and Barnabas do not agree on some of the things each other was doing or wanted to do. Today it reached the point that it was time to break up the team, and they went their separate ways.

Day 193—July 12

Prayer: Teach me oh Lord what you want me to learn today. Help me Holy Spirit to unfold today's daily scriptures. Amen!

After reading question: What is God saying to me today?

OT}—After the daughter of King Ahaziah hid the infant son of Ahaziah, and he turned seven years old, Jehoiada, the priest anoints him as king. Then they remove his grandmother, Athaliah, from the throne by killing her.

Judah returns to doing good in the sight of God.

2 Chronicles 23-24
Psalm 83:1-6
Proverbs 17:27-28
Acts 16:1-19

NT}—Paul leaves with Silas to go to Derbe and Lystra. After Timothy gets circumcised, he joins Paul as a missionary because he is Greek.

Even though Paul and Barnabas served well together, God used their split to expand the church.

Paul now has the vision to go to Macedonia because they needed his help. Macedonia was a country lying to the north of Greece, afterward enlarged and formed into a Roman providence. They were eager to hear about salvation.

Day 194—July 13

Prayer: Teach me oh Lord what you want me to learn today. Help me Holy Spirit to unfold today's daily scriptures. Amen!

After reading question: What is God saying to me today?

OT}—Forty years pass, young King Joash, also known as Jehoash, dies, and Judah gets a new king.

Twenty-five-year-old Amaziah, who reigned for twenty-nine years, did right in God's eyes but was not perfect. He got revenge on the servants who killed the king of his father.

2 Chronicles 25-26

Psalm 83:7-12

Proverbs 18:1-3

Acts 16:20-40

NT}—Paul and Silas get thrown into prison because of their preaching. The Lord breaks them out, which opens the opportunity for the jailer to get saved, and his family. Since Paul and Silas were Roman citizens, they were permitted to leave without being harmed.

I had not found an answer to why Paul and Silas did not tell the Magistrates they were Roman citizens upfront before they were beaten.

Day 195—July 14

<u>Prayer:</u> Teach me oh Lord what you want me to learn today. Help me Holy Spirit to unfold today's daily scriptures. Amen!

<u>After reading question:</u> What is God saying to me today?

OT}—Yesterday, we read about King Uzziah, who reigned over Judah for fifty-two years, which brings us to King Jotham. He was a good king during his sixteen-year reign with some building, but we do not get too much information about him. It jumps right into King Ahaz, who shared the last parts of his sixteen-year reign with his son Hezekiah.

2 Chronicles 27-28
Psalm 83:13-18
Proverbs 18:4-6
Acts 17:1-15

NT}—Paul and Silas continue to Thessalonica. After a few weeks of explaining the reason for Christ and quoting passages, some unbelieving Jews were aroused by jealousy and wanted to confront them about their teachings.

Paul and Silas escape with the help of some of the people, and when they fail to find them, the owner of the house where they are staying takes the fall.

Day 196—July 15

<u>Prayer:</u> Teach me oh Lord what you want me to learn today. Help me Holy Spirit to unfold today's daily scriptures. Amen!

<u>After reading question:</u> What is God saying to me today?

OT}—Hezekiah, as we see, is another king who tried to do good. He proclaimed that he would make a covenant with God so God's anger would turn away from Judah because of the sins of the fathers before him, so they rejoiced in Jerusalem, mainly for the first time since Solomon.

2 Chronicles 29-30
Psalm 84:1-6
Proverbs 18:7-9
Acts 17:16-34

NT}—Paul waits for Silas and Timothy in Athens. As he remains, his spirit is grieved because of the idols in the city. With demand, he took a stance to anyone who would listen that they were worshipping and making reverent to demons. One of the inscriptions on an altar was engraved "To the unknown god."

Because of Paul's love and belief in Jesus and steadfastness in who God is, he must have gone ballistic!

Day 197—July 16

<u>Prayer:</u> Teach me oh Lord what you want me to learn today. Help me Holy Spirit to unfold today's daily scriptures. Amen!

<u>After reading question:</u> What is God saying to me today?

OT}—King Hezekiah shared the last part of his twenty-nine-year reign with his son Manasseh. I believe it may have been because Hezekiah was ill during his previous years, as many as twelve years.

At certain times in my research, I found that kings reign simultaneously as other kings. I learned through the Bible that there were times that it was necessary because of an illness or age, like Jehoash, who was only seven when he was in line for the throne. This is called "co-regency," or temporary king.[22] On page twelve of my list of kings, you may see a co-regent next to a king.

2 Chronicles 31-32

Psalm 84:7-12

Proverbs 18:10-12

Acts 18

NT}—Paul journeys to Corinth and meets up with Silas and Timothy. After hanging out for a while, Paul sailed for Syria, journeyed to Ephesus, Caesarea, and back to Antioch, then through the territory of Galatia and Phrygia.

Day 198—July 17

<u>Prayer:</u> Teach me oh Lord what you want me to learn today. Help me Holy Spirit to unfold today's daily scriptures. Amen!

<u>After reading question:</u> What is God saying to me today?

OT}—Now Judah is back in trouble. After King Hezekiah gets God to look good on Judah, Manasseh comes along and puts them back on the wrong path. The sad thing is that this king was evil and the longest king to reign over Judah.

Thank goodness we do not have to read about those wicked years today because the passage goes right to Josiah as king in the next chapter, who turns things around.

2 Chronicles 33-34

Psalm 85:1-7

Proverbs 18:13-14

Acts 19:1-23

NT}—Paul continues to the upper inland districts and Ephesus. We have seen how passionate Paul is about the gospel and how straightforward he can be. After confronting some disciples about how they were baptized, Paul decided to stay in Ephesus, preaching from a room because they needed the truth.

This is where it comes from if you have heard of people getting healed by anointed handkerchiefs.

Day 199—July 18

Prayer: Teach me oh Lord what you want me to learn today. Help me Holy Spirit to unfold today's daily scriptures. Amen!

After reading question: What is God saying to me today?

OT}—As we see, Josiah did right to the people of Judah. We finish the Book of Chronicles with chapter thirty-six, completing the next twenty-one years of Judah before Jerusalem's destruction and the people's exile to Babylon.

Four wicked kings finish this part of the Davidic line:
- ➤ Jehoahaz—three months
- ➤ Eliakim/Jehoiakim, the name changed by the king of Egypt —eleven years
- ➤ Jehoiakim—three months
- ➤ Zedekiah—eleven years

2 Chronicles 35-36

Psalm 85:8-13

Proverbs18:15-16

Acts 19:24-41

NT}—In the province of Asia, worshiping other gods was rampant, and the work that Paul and others were doing was changing the atmosphere. Thus, a silversmith, Demetrius, started a protest with other businessmen to stop Paul because it was hurting their businesses.

Day 200—July 19

<u>Prayer:</u> Teach me oh Lord what you want me to learn today. Help me Holy Spirit to unfold today's daily scriptures. Amen!

<u>After reading question:</u> What is God saying to me today?

OT}—The Book of Ezra most likely was written by Ezra, Jewish Scribe and priest because of the reference made in the first person.

As we read in the last chapter of Second Chronicles, King Cyrus said God charged him to build him a house in Jerusalem. Ezra starts with a proclamation to the people about that word.

Then we see a list of people who returned to Jerusalem and Judah after the exile.

Ezra 1-2

Psalm 86:1-9

Proverbs 18:17-18

Acts 20:1-17

NT}—Paul continues to travel even though some are against him. But Paul stays solid and steadfast on the work of Christ by encouraging them, loving on them, and even at times, confronting them about their evil ways.

Day 201—July 20

Teach me oh Lord what you want me to learn today. Help me Holy Spirit to unfold today's daily scriptures. Amen!

After reading question: What is God saying to me today?

OT}—The Samaritans, whom the Jews did not associate with because of past events, wanted to help build the temple. But Zerubbabel, Jeshua, and other leaders said no thanks. The Samaritans then take offense and start trouble. So much so that the building stopped.

Ezra 3-4

Psalm 86:10-17

Proverbs 18:19-20

Acts 20:18-38

NT}—Paul reassures the people that the Holy Spirit is leading him. He tells them to be watchful for wolves in sheep's clothing after he is gone.

Paul is so filled with the Holy Spirit that he knows ahead of time that he will end up in prison. Does that stop him? No, he builds on that and keeps confessing his faith and the work of the cross to spread the gospel as fast as he can.

Day 202—July 21

<u>Prayer:</u> Teach me oh Lord what you want me to learn today. Help me Holy Spirit to unfold today's daily scriptures. Amen!

<u>After reading question:</u> What is God saying to me today?

OT}—Because of controversy between the Samaritans and church leaders, a letter is sent to King Darius I to decipher the truth, and God again prevails. King Darius I, ordered a search in the archives to see if King Cyrus made a decree to have the house of God be built. As the record shows he did. The king then makes his own decree and orders that Tattenai and associates, who addressed this in the first place, stay away and that they will also help the Jews with provision. The king also decreed that anyone who tried to stop them be reprimanded.

Ezra 5-6

Psalm 87

Proverbs 18:21-22

Acts 21:1-20

NT}—After leaving the province of Asia, Paul returns to Jerusalem, ready to be prosecuted for the Lord.

Paul knew that they would arrest him if he set foot in Jerusalem. Being so set in his spirit, he was not afraid to be arrested, bounded, imprisoned, and even die in the name of the Lord Jesus. He goes anyway.

Day 203—July 22

<u>Prayer:</u> Teach me oh Lord what you want me to learn today. Help me Holy Spirit to unfold today's daily scriptures. Amen!

<u>After reading question:</u> What is God saying to me today?

OT}—We get a history lesson on where Ezra came from and whom he associated with. Verse one through five is genealogy. Ezra was a skilled scribe and one of the later Jews who returned from captivity to Judea and Jerusalem. Because God's favor was on Ezra, King Artaxerxes granted him all his requests for Jerusalem. But I wonder if the generosity from the king was not self-motive.

We also get an understanding of some of the work he did.

Ezra 7-8

Psalm 88:1-6

Proverbs 18:23-24

Acts 21:21-40

NT}—Paul is arrested, bound with two chains, and taken to prison. But what did he do wrong?

It was a mess; people were yelling, throwing things, and making wrongful accusations about Paul; it must have been like a riot. It got so bad that Roman soldiers and centurions rushed to the temple to stop the chaos. That is when they took Paul in for questioning.

Day 204—July 23

<u>Prayer:</u> Teach me oh Lord what you want me to learn today. Help me Holy Spirit to unfold today's daily scriptures. Amen!

<u>After reading question:</u> What is God saying to me today?

OT}—Now, because the Israelites, priests, and Levites have crossbred outside of their native land, Ezra goes to prayer. He comes back with a covenant that the people make an oath that they will adhere to. They will separate themselves from the people of the land and foreign (heathen) wives. We see the genealogy of the sons of Immer, a Jewish priest.

Ezra 9-10

Psalm 88:7-12

Proverbs 19:1-3

Acts 22

NT}—Before going to jail, Paul addresses the people. Paul then acted in his own defense that being bound in chains was wrong because he was a Roman citizen.

That is when Paul starts to address them, telling them he was a Jew born in Tarsus of Cilicia but reared in Jerusalem at the feet of Gamaliel. That means that by the time he was thirteen, he learned the Torah, the first five books of the Bible, by one of the most prestigious rabbis of the day.

Day 205—July 24

<u>Prayer:</u> Teach me oh Lord what you want me to learn today. Help me Holy Spirit to unfold today's daily scriptures. Amen!

<u>After reading question:</u> What is God saying to me today?

OT}—The Book of Nehemiah, meaning in Hebrew "*Yah Comforts,*" was a governor of Persian Judah. He was a layman who served the Persian king, Artaxerxes. He is credited for assisting in the rebuilding of Jerusalem because of the relationship he had with the king and queen. He was able to be released from his duties for some time, with provisions so that he could assist in the building.

Nehemiah 1-3
Psalm 88:13-18
Proverbs 19:4-6
Acts 23:1-16

NT}—As Paul stands in front of the council Sanhedrin to defend himself, he claims he is a faithful and loyal Jew citizen. Because Paul claims to be a Pharisee, a son of Pharisees, it causes the Pharisees and the Sadducees to get angry. We now see a great division because of different beliefs, and the commandant orders his troops to bring Paul back to the barracks so Paul does not get hurt.

The next day they were going to bring Paul back to the Sanhedrin to continue questioning him, but some men plotted to kill him on the way. Paul's nephew learns of the plot, so he runs to tell Paul.

Day 206—July 25

Teach me oh Lord what you want me to learn today. Help me Holy Spirit to unfold today's daily scriptures. Amen!

After reading question: What is God saying to me today?

OT}—Nehemiah was a prayer warrior who loved and trusted God and believed in the word that God wanted to rebuild Jerusalem. He stood up for the people and tried to protect them from those who came against the wall building.

Nehemiah 4-5

Psalm 89:1-7

Proverbs 19:7-9

Acts 23:17-35

NT}—As we read yesterday, there was a conspiracy to kill Paul, who taught about the resurrection and power of Jesus. After Paul learns of the plot to kill him, he asks the centurion to take his nephew to the commandant to share what he knew.

When the commandant heard of the conspiracy, he ordered two centurions to gather two hundred footmen to be ready by the third hour (about 9 pm), so they could move him at night to go to Caesarea to bring him to Felix, the governor. This order keeps Paul safe and shows the power behind being a Roman citizen and the blessing he had in his life.

Day 207—July 26

<u>Prayer:</u> Teach me oh Lord what you want me to learn today. Help me Holy Spirit to unfold today's daily scriptures. Amen!

<u>After reading question:</u> What is God saying to me today?

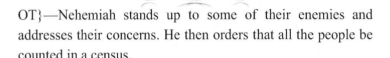

OT}—Nehemiah stands up to some of their enemies and addresses their concerns. He then orders that all the people be counted in a census.

We see the genealogy of those who came from Babylon.

Nehemiah 6-7

Psalm 89:8-14

Proverbs 19:10-12

Acts 24

NT}—Paul's trial begins in Caesarea with Tertullus, a lawyer the Jews employed as the plaintiff, being heard in front of Felix, the governor. Tertullus's words are not too kind, calling Paul a pest, a real plague, an agitator who disturbed all the Jews worldwide, and a ringleader of the Nazarenes.

Paul then has the opportunity to defend himself cheerfully, with good courage, and with some wise statements. He knew that he did nothing wrong and that it was only because of the message regarding the resurrection of the dead that indicted him for such a trial.

Day 208—July 27

<u>Prayer:</u> Teach me oh Lord what you want me to learn today. Help me Holy Spirit to unfold today's daily scriptures. Amen!

<u>After reading question:</u> What is God saying to me today?

OT}—Because time had passed for Israel as they were in captivity, some people either did not remember or did not know the Law of Moses. They assembled the Israelites so Ezra, the priest, could read from the Book of Law. Ezra then prays to God for mercy.

Nehemiah 8-9

Psalm 89:15-21

Proverbs 19:13-15

Acts 25

NT}—After two years, Felix is succeeded by Porcius Festus, and the chief priests try to get Paul moved back to Jerusalem for trial because they made plans to ambush him on the way so they could kill him. But Festus saw through their plan and kept him in Caesarea.

Paul gets to speak again in his own defense with Festus, who then decides to send him to Caesar because Paul made an appeal to see him.

Since King Agrippa and his sister, Bernice, were coming to town to pay respects to Festus, Festus tells him of the case. Then King Agrippa wants to talk to Paul himself.

Day 209—July 28

<u>Prayer:</u> Teach me oh Lord what you want me to learn today. Help me Holy Spirit to unfold today's daily scriptures. Amen!

<u>After reading question:</u> What is God saying to me today?

OT}—We get a list of all the leaders who set their seals to the covenant made with God and those who dwelt at Jerusalem.

Nehemiah 10-11

Psalm 89:22-29

Proverbs 19:16-18

Acts 26:1-18

NT}—After King Agrippa calls Paul to hear about the case, Paul speaks to King Agrippa in his defense.

You may have heard this phrase: "A man who is his own lawyer has a fool for a client."

The first verse of this chapter states, "At that Paul stretched forth his hand and made his defense." I will go out on a limb here and say that when Paul stretched out his hand, he was stretching it out towards God for him to talk through Paul as his lawyer. Why do I say that? Paul was no fool!

Day 210—July 29

OT}—The list continues with the priests and Levites.

Nehemiah finishes his work and most likely returns to his duties with the king and queen of Persia. But not before celebrating to dedicate the wall of Jerusalem.

Today we end the Book of Nehemiah with the rest of his policies and program.

To recap some of Nehemiah's aptitudes, he was humble, self-motivated, full of faith, willing to take the lead, confident in knowing what God wanted, fearless, organizer, and obedient.

Nehemiah 12-13
Psalm 89:30-37
Proverbs 19:19-21
Acts 26:19-32

NT}—Paul continues to explain his actions to King Agrippa. This is so awesome about Paul. Even though he is on trial, he tries to convert the king and anyone listening.

I love verses 24-29; Festus calls him mad and says, "Your great learning is driving you insane."

Day 211—July 30

<u>Prayer:</u> Teach me oh Lord what you want me to learn today. Help me Holy Spirit to unfold today's daily scriptures. Amen!

<u>After reading question:</u> What is God saying to me today?

OT}—Today is the Book of Esther, Hebrew Hadassah meaning "*Myrle*." Esther is used to defending the Jews from being slaughtered.

The beginning of this book might just be the first women's liberation movement recorded. The queen of the Persian Empire refused to appear in front of the king and his guest. She was cast out of her queen position, opening the door for a new queen, "Queen Esther."

Esther was reared by her uncle (some versions say cousin) Mordecai after her father and mother died. Her real name was Hadassah, Hebrew meaning "myrtle." Mordecai changed it to hide her identity when she was chosen to go before the king.

Esther 1-2
Psalm 89:38-45
Proverbs 19:22-24
Acts 27:1-23

NT}—Paul's defense helped save his life from the courts but is put into a dangerous situation when they take to sail to Italy. But their trust in God's Word helps them to hold on.

Day 212—July 31

OT}—The story of Esther is known for verse 14 in chapter4, "For such a time as this and this very occasion." Another topic is that Esther's uncle, Mordecai, was the main reason she got in as queen, but her beauty put her there. Mordecai was just a mouthpiece that opened the door to the kings' chambers so God could deliver the Jews from destruction. That is because King Ahasuerus decided to promote Haman to second in command, and Mordecai refused to bow down to him, which triggered a decree to kill all the Jews in the province of Persia.

Esther 3-4

Psalm 89:46-52

Proverbs 19:25-27

Acts 27:24-44

NT}—Paul urges the people on the ship to eat to build up strength. Afterward, they all became more cheerful and were encouraged to eat for themselves, which was a good thing because shortly after that, they had to throw a lot of food off the ship to help it not sink. After being tossed around like a wet towel, they arrive safely on land.

Day 213—August 1

Teach me oh Lord what you want me to learn today. Help me Holy Spirit to unfold today's daily scriptures. Amen!

After reading question: What is God saying to me today?

OT}—As we read yesterday, it was against the law that anyone to enter the king's inner court without being called should be put to death. When Esther entered, her beauty mesmerized the king so that she could speak freely. Queen Esther invites the king and Haman to dinner. Esther is priming the pump to get to the place to spill the beans about Haman's plot against the Jews.

One night when the king is restless and recalls the good deed from Mordecai and honors him through the man that hates him the most, Haman.

Esther 5-6

Psalm 90:1-9

Proverbs 19:28-29

Acts 28

NT}—Paul finally and safely arrives in the City of Rome. Though the journey was intense, Paul was treated with respect, allowing him to preach to the local Jews. Even though Paul was still a prisoner, they did not treat him as a common criminal. Instead, they allowed him to live in his own rented house with bounded chains accompanied by a guard.

Day 214—August 2

<u>Prayer:</u> Teach me oh Lord what you want me to learn today. Help me Holy Spirit to unfold today's daily scriptures. Amen!

<u>After reading question:</u> What is God saying to me today?

OT}—Esther gets to hold a dinner for the king and Haman, where she reveals her true identity and the harm Haman plans on doing to the Jewish people. The king is flabbergasted and orders Haman to hang. The king then promoted Mordecai, which should have been done when he promoted Haman.

Once again, we see how God moves mountains to save the Israelites from death.

Esther 7-8

Psalm 90:10-17

Proverbs 20:1-2

Romans 1:1-14

NT}—The Letter of Paul to the Romans, written by Paul around 57 AD, was for all the believers in the City of Rome. The content of Romans is centered on the theme of God's revelation of righteousness. Paul was completing his third missionary journey and most likely wrote this letter from Philippi in preparation for his visit to Rome.

Paul gives a lengthy introduction and tells them that he is eager to preach to all who are in Rome.

Day 215—August 3

Prayer: Teach me oh Lord what you want me to learn today. Help me Holy Spirit to unfold today's daily scriptures. Amen!

After reading question: What is God saying to me today?

OT}—Because of Mordecai's position, his persistence in guiding his niece, and the love that Esther had for her heritage, the Jews are saved from being massacred.

I must add this: "Promotion, Promotion, Promotion," when you do your work (job) from the heart, doors will open.

Esther 9-10

Psalm 91:1-8

Proverbs 20:3-4

Romans 1:15-32

NT}—Paul tells them that the gospel is not just for the Jews but for the Greeks (Gentiles) as well. He then brings out a short history lesson about how their Godless life and what the result was.

With God's handiwork, he has made it discernible about his eternal power and divinity. Mankind has no excuse to say they do not know how to live a God-filled life without any defense or justification.

Day 216—August 4

<u>Prayer:</u> Teach me oh Lord what you want me to learn today. Help me Holy Spirit to unfold today's daily scriptures. Amen!

<u>After reading question:</u> What is God saying to me today?

OT}—Today, we start the Book of Job, uncertain who the author is or the timeframe it took place. Job is a story of hope, faith, repentance, and trust. It asks, "Why do things happen to good people?" or in some people's hearts, "Why does God allow bad things to happen in the world?" Even though the answer to those questions is unclear, Job helps us continue the faith that God loves us.

Job 1-2

Psalm 91:9-16

Proverbs 20:5-6

Romans 2

NT}—This is my interpretation of Romans Chapter 2.

Those who do not know the difference will not be held accountable. But those who know the difference, then teach something else and do not share the whole truth, will be the ones accountable. Not just for themselves, but those they did not teach the truth to.

Day 217—August 5

Prayer: Teach me oh Lord what you want me to learn today. Help me Holy Spirit to unfold today's daily scriptures. Amen!

After reading question: What is God saying to me today?

OT}—As we read yesterday, the Book of Job starts with who Job was and turns into a conversation between God and Satan in heaven. We see that Satan knows anyone that God has in his protection. We also see that God does not take from us; he only is a giver. Satan comes to steal, kill, and destroy (John 10:10). Job loses everything except his wife, friends, and life. Then after being with his friends for seven days in silence, they start a long day of conversations, and Job curses the day he was born.

Job 3-4
Psalm 92:1-8
Proverbs 20:7-8
Romans 3

NT}—Paul expresses that all men are accountable under sin, no one is righteous, and no person will be made righteous in the sight of God by keeping the law.

Some atheists disbelieve there is a God. Even their lack of belief will nullify, make ineffective, and void the faithfulness of God and his fidelity to his Word, verse 3.

No one will escape God's judgment, no matter who they are!

Day 218—August 6

<u>Prayer:</u> Teach me oh Lord what you want me to learn today. Help me Holy Spirit to unfold today's daily scriptures. Amen!

<u>After reading question:</u> What is God saying to me today?

OT}—Job's friend Eliphaz continues to talk. He comes across as mild and modest, and then he seems to put a spin on the way he started with an exhortation to confess any hidden iniquities. Job answers him with an attitude.

Job thinks his friends came to comfort him, but as soon as the conversations start, they begin a long miserable debate about why Job is going through his suffering.

What a long day that must have been!

Job 5-6
Psalm 92:9-15
Proverbs 20:9-10
Romans 4

NT}—Being righteous will open more doors than observing the law's commands.

Abraham received the promise that his descendants would be unnumbered, not by observing the law, but only by the righteousness of faith.

Day 219—August 7

<u>Prayer:</u> Teach me oh Lord what you want me to learn today. Help me Holy Spirit to unfold today's daily scriptures. Amen!

<u>After reading question:</u> What is God saying to me today?

OT}—Job finishes with Eliphaz, then Bildad chimes in, basically saying that Job is being tested for a greater reward.

When giving advice:
1. Be helpful
   a. Being helpful requires some sensitivity
2. Be empathetic
   a. Sympathy - I feel sorry for you
   b. Empathy - I feel what you feel
3. Be humble
4. Be teachable
   a. A refusal to budge is a sign of insecurity

Job 7-8

Psalm 93

Proverbs 20:11-12

Romans 5

NT}—Faith, by grace through God, is how we firmly and safely stand. Through Adam, sin entered the world, bringing death to all mankind, but through Jesus, life came forth. The unmerited favor from God allows us to accept Christ by faith to bring salvation.

Day 220—August 8

<u>Prayer:</u> Teach me oh Lord what you want me to learn today. Help me Holy Spirit to unfold today's daily scriptures. Amen!

<u>After reading question:</u> What is God saying to me today?

OT}—Job then replies to them, questioning who he is in God, how little God is in man's life and the unsearchable secrets God has.

With God being superior, who does he answer to? Who can tell him what to do or even say? This is where Job's thinking is; his despair has altered his thinking. He justifies what he is saying: he has the right to free expression.

Job 9-10

Psalm 94:1-8

Proverbs 20:13-14

Romans 6

NT}—Because of God's grace, we can walk away from sin. We live in a sinful world, and sometimes it is difficult walking this out, but God tells us that we are no longer slaves to sin and need to yield our bodies towards righteousness.

"For the wages of sin is death, but the free gift of God [that is, His remarkable, overwhelming gift of grace to believers] is eternal life in Christ Jesus our Lord." (Romans 6:24)

Day 221—August 9

<u>Prayer:</u> Teach me oh Lord what you want me to learn today. Help me Holy Spirit to unfold today's daily scriptures. Amen!

<u>After reading question:</u> What is God saying to me today?

OT}—Then Job's friend Zohar replies to Job's response to Bildad. He accuses Job of wickedness, and his punishment is too good for him. Job then replies with a strong answer, "Who are you?"—"No doubt you are the only wise people in the world, and wisdom will die with you," Verse 2. Then Job comes right out and says, "I am not inferior to you, you are no better than me."

Job 11-12
Psalm 94:9-16
Proverbs 20:15-16
Romans 7

NT}—We have heard the word *Law* many times throughout the Bible. I felt today to share a short meaning with you. The word "*Law*" in the Old Testament refers to the "*Torah,*" which generally is God's instruction. In the New Testament, it is "*Nomos,*" referring to the "*Mosaic Law,*" which is an extension of the Ten Commandments given to Moses, with a total of 613 commands that no one will be able to follow.

Hence, through the Law, we recognize what is right and wrong. The Law is Holy and just, but because the Law, in itself, cannot save us, we need to surrender the flesh to Jesus.

Day 222—August 10

<u>Prayer:</u> Teach me oh Lord what you want me to learn today. Help me Holy Spirit to unfold today's daily scriptures. Amen!

<u>After reading question:</u> What is God saying to me today?

OT}—Job continues to reply to Zohar with the attitude that *you are no better than I am,* except you are deceitful and lie. Your words are not helpful and bring me no peace. Job keeps defending his actions and telling his friends that he is not stupid and knows what he is saying. He just wants to question God on the issues at hand and does what he believes lines up with God.

Job 13-14

Psalm 94:17-23

Proverbs 20:17-18

Romans 8:1-18

NT}—I like the start of today's reading; "Therefore there is now no condemnation [no guilty verdict, no punishment] for those who are in Christ Jesus [who believe in Him as personal Lord and Savior]. For the law of the Spirit of life [which is] in Christ Jesus [the law of our new being] has set you free from the law of sin and of death."

When we go before the judgment throne of God, we will be found innocent of the accusations of our sins. But the word "therefore" is connected to yesterday's reading, which ties it to how we live today.

Day 223—August 11

<u>Prayer:</u> Teach me oh Lord what you want me to learn today. Help me Holy Spirit to unfold today's daily scriptures. Amen!

<u>After reading question:</u> What is God saying to me today?

OT}—Eliphaz replies, asserting that Job does not fear God. If he did, he would not be facing this suffering. He belittles Job's self-justification. Job responds that his friends are miserable comforters with useless words.

Job 15-16
Psalm 95:1-6
Proverbs 20:19-20
Romans 8:19-39

NT}—Here is a scripture, 8:28, that has been used out of context by many. It is a little nonsensical how things like death and disease can work together for our good, like suffering, chronic pain, depression, and the list goes on and on. Consequently, it does not say all things are good, but God is redeeming all things. We need to go back to verse 27 to complete that statement.

We should not use Romans 8:28 to console ourselves or others when faced with tragedies and trials, to say that God will turn things around. But instead, all things will be worked out for our good.

Turning it over to Holy Spirit, who knows what we need when we need it.

Day 224—August 12

Teach me oh Lord what you want me to learn today. Help me Holy Spirit to unfold today's daily scriptures. Amen!

After reading question: What is God saying to me today?

OT}—Job is still answering his friends with a broken spirit. They were not being helpful and empathetic.

Then Bildad's response says that Job must have done something wrong since God punishes him.

Mankind continually puts the outcome of situations on God, blaming him for things they do not understand and even the inevitable parts. Just because they prayed for healing or someone to recover, and it did not come to pass, they blame God. Sometimes things are meant to be, and not even God will change them. That does not mean that someone did something wrong.

Job 17-18

Psalm 95:7-11

Proverbs 20:21-22

Romans 9

NT}—Paul says that if he could take their place for the wrongs they do, he would. That is how much love Paul had for the saved, as well as for the unsaved.

Day 225—August 13

<u>Prayer:</u> Teach me oh Lord what you want me to learn today. Help me Holy Spirit to unfold today's daily scriptures. Amen!

<u>After reading question:</u> What is God saying to me today?

OT}—Job answers with a plea to be left alone by God and wants his friends' pity, then turns it around by putting his trust in God.

Zophar gets mad, then lectures Job about the temporariness of evil for man's pleasure.

Job 19-20
Psalm 96:1-7
Proverbs 20:23-24
Romans 10

NT}—Paul starts with the same expression for Israel with the desire that all Israel would be saved.

We also see a verse used many times to bring someone into the kingdom. We call it the *sinners' prayer*, but there really is no actual sinner's prayer; it just fits.

Romans 10:7-10
"If you believe in your heart, and confess with your mouth, confess Jesus is Lord, and God raised him from the dead, you will be saved."

Day 226—August 14

Prayer: Teach me oh Lord what you want me to learn today. Help me Holy Spirit to unfold today's daily scriptures. Amen!

After reading question: What is God saying to me today?

OT}—Job now tries to defend himself by standing up to his friends with a stronger voice. He ends by telling them to comfort him with compassion, not empty words; almost like, why did you come here to waste time?

Eliphaz speaks for the third time and last time. He reflects on the old Hebrew idea that suffering always implies sinful nature. But he is wrong.

Job 21-22

Psalm 96:8-13

Proverbs 20:25-26

Romans 11:1-18

NT}—As you see so far, Paul loves to bring up the past works of God and Israel. He uses it as a reference to build up the people, much as Jesus did with the parables.

Romans 11 is the restoration of Israel and the remnant of grace. God has not cast away his people whom he foreknew. Even though as a group overall, in Pauls's day, Israel rejected their Messiah. Yet a substantial remnant embraces the gospel, and God has worked through a faithful remand as he did in the time of Elijah.

Day 227—August 15

Prayer: Teach me oh Lord what you want me to learn today. Help me Holy Spirit to unfold today's daily scriptures. Amen!

After reading question: What is God saying to me today?

OT}—Job responds that no matter what he did or did not do, God is unchangeable, and God is with the wicked and the good no matter what.

I believe that Job knew in his heart that no matter how he felt about God's action, or lack of, God was still with him. That was something I do not think his friends understood.

Job 23-24

Psalm 97:1-6

Proverbs 20:27-28

Romans 11:19-36

NT}—Paul uses the olive tree to illustrate how we are drafted in with Christ, and all things are from the main branch being alive through him. When you read this today, consider the goodness and severity of God. Only through God's love can we be reconciled back to him. The same love he had for the Israelites back then is the same love he has for us.

Jesus is our primary source of life, and we are to stay connected to him if we want to stay alive.

Day 228—August 16

<u>Prayer:</u> Teach me oh Lord what you want me to learn today. Help me Holy Spirit to unfold today's daily scriptures. Amen!

<u>After reading question:</u> What is God saying to me today?

OT}—Bildad answers for the third time on the idea that none can be righteous before God.

Job answers him with sarcasm and argues with him, defending who God is.

Job 25-26

Psalm 97:7-12

Proverbs 20:29-30

Romans 12

NT}—Because we are part of Jesus, we are not to conform to this world but be transformed by renewing our minds. Some people stop there, but Romans 12:2 goes on to say, "So that you may prove for yourselves what is the good and acceptable and perfect will of God...."

You cannot come to the throne room of God if you do not humble yourself. Pride is the root of many issues in our lives. Surrendering ourselves to humility is not a form of defeat. In God's kingdom, it is a form of victory.

Do you recall Proverbs 16:18, "Pride comes before the fall?

Day 229—August 17

Prayer: Teach me oh Lord what you want me to learn today. Help me Holy Spirit to unfold today's daily scriptures. Amen!

After reading question: What is God saying to me today?

OT}—Job is still answering Bildad and defending his belief in God with, "As long as my life is still whole within me, and the breath of God is yet in my nostrils, my lips shall not speak untruth, not shall my tongue utter deceit."
Now that is faith!

Job 27-28
Psalm 98:1-5
Proverbs 21:1-3
Romans 13

NT}—Some people have a hard time doing what is right according to our governments. We know in Mark 12:17 that Jesus told them to give to Caesar what is Caesar's, meaning paying taxes. But there is more to that. We must submit to authorities at all levels, following the speed limits, our bosses, police officers, etcetera. Paul said in verse 2 that he who resists authorities resists what God has appointed and arranged in divine order.

Then Paul brings out some commandments to grow in. "Do not indulge in the flesh. Put a stop to thinking about the evil cravings of your physical nature to gratify its desires [lust]."

Day 230—August 18

<u>Prayer:</u> Teach me oh Lord what you want me to learn today. Help me Holy Spirit to unfold today's daily scriptures. Amen!

<u>After reading question:</u> What is God saying to me today?

OT}—Job remembers better days: blessed relationships with God and people. Job reflects on former times with a sense of security and confidence, even with authority and leadership in the community.

But now, his friends do not respect him; they mock him, and plague him on mercy.

Job 29-30

Psalm 98:6-9

Proverbs 21:4-6

Romans 14

NT}—Jesus calls us not to judge each other in doubtful things. We are to receive the weaker brother or sister but not to carry on a debate with them regarding any unsure thing. Judging them is inappropriate because we are not their master. It is wrong as a matter of conscience. Another reason is that we all face judgment before Jesus. At the same time, do not use your liberty to stumble another brother or sister.

And like we read in Luke 6:37, don't judge, and you shall not be judged.

Day 231—August 19

After reading question: What is God saying to me today?

OT}—Job is still speaking, but his controversial words end some of the conversations.

Job's three friends are finished at this point, but there was one more friend, Elihu, who joined them later and has not spoken until now. Elihu was upset at Job because Job justified himself and even made himself out to be better than God.

Elihu was also mad at the other three because they made Job out to be wrong without proof.

Job 31-32

Psalm 99

Proverbs 21:7-9

Romans 15:1-16

NT}—Paul teaches how we are to lift each other up just as Christ has welcomed and received us, never ceasing and always ready to help. Jesus was a servant, and if we say we are followers of Christ, we ought to follow his example and become servants.

Serving someone is a privilege and an honor, especially when they are in need.

Day 232—August 20

<u>Prayer:</u> Teach me oh Lord what you want me to learn today. Help me Holy Spirit to unfold today's daily scriptures. Amen!

<u>After reading question:</u> What is God saying to me today?

OT}—Elihu turns his attention, saying that Job was wrong in thinking he was without sin and that God would not answer.

Then Elihu shifts to declaring God's justice.

Job 33-34

Psalm 100

Proverbs 21:10-12

Romans 15:17-33

NT}—Paul ends his letter with the hope that he will see them the next time he passes through Rome and thanks them for their provisions.

Paul's gratitude, purpose, and mission emerge in this epistle. Convinced that all men, no matter who they are, are lost without Christ, Paul is thankful that this righteousness of God has been imparted to him. He is not ashamed of the gospel but is determined to make Christ known to all men and women.

Day 233—August 21

<u>Prayer:</u> Teach me oh Lord what you want me to learn today. Help me Holy Spirit to unfold today's daily scriptures. Amen!

<u>After reading question:</u> What is God saying to me today?

OT}—Elihu turns back to Job, condemning his thinking about God. Elihu brings out many of the attributes of God, emphasizing his greatness.

Job 35-36

Psalm 101

Proverbs 21:13-15

Romans 16

NT}—I have heard from churches that they do not believe women should have leadership positions. I guess they never read today's scripture and many others, for that matter. Paul introduces Phoebe as a deaconess.

I used to be part of a deacon ministry at a large church in Texas, and right before I left the area, they anointed their first deaconess. That, to me, is Awesome!

As we finish today's reading, we end the Book of Romans with a powerful declaration. "To the only wise God be glory forever through Jesus Christ the Anointed One!"

Day 234—August 22

<u>Prayer:</u> Teach me oh Lord what you want me to learn today. Help me Holy Spirit to unfold today's daily scriptures. Amen!

<u>After reading question:</u> What is God saying to me today?

OT}—Elihu starts to direct Job to hear the voice of God. Elihu might just be the better friend of the four because even though he was straightforward with Job, he brought the focus to God.

Then God chimes in to have a chat with Job, first, with a series of questions.

Job 37-38

Psalm 102:1-7

Proverbs 21:16-18

1 Corinthians 1

NT}—The First Letter of Paul to the Corinthians was split into two writings by Paul to the church in Corinth before he wrote Romans. During Paul's extended ministry in Ephesus, around 55 AD, he sent this letter responding to a letter he received concerning the conditions in the church of Corinth and requesting counsel.

Paul came to Corinth during his second missionary journey and was there for a year and a half. It was during this time that he established the church.

Day 235—August 23

<u>Prayer:</u> Teach me oh Lord what you want me to learn today. Help me Holy Spirit to unfold today's daily scriptures. Amen!

<u>After reading question:</u> What is God saying to me today?

OT}—God is still speaking to Job about who he is and all the work he did.

Job then respectfully answers God, knowing that everything he said in the last thirty-seven chapters was like a spoiled brat.

God then tells Job to grow up and be a man with his answers.

Job 39-40
Psalm 102:8-14
Proverbs 21:19-21
1 Corinthians 2

NT}—Paul speaks plainly to the people of Corinth, who were young in their faith, so that they can understand his teaching with a blessing and words of encouragement. He is hoping to lift their spirits.

His main concern was that they would not put their faith in the wisdom of men and human philosophy but the power of God.

Day 236—August 24

<u>Prayer:</u> Teach me oh Lord what you want me to learn today. Help me Holy Spirit to unfold today's daily scriptures. Amen!

<u>After reading question:</u> What is God saying to me today?

OT}—After God builds an even stronger case, Job answers him like a man. Job understands who God is, but in chapter 42, something changes his thinking. Job is surrendering his thoughts to what God was saying in previous chapters. God then restored to Job twice as much as he had before. Job never found out why he suffered but knew it was much better to know God than to see the answer.

Job's life experiences:

1) Revelation, 2) Recognition, 3) Repentance, 4) Redemption
Take away:

When we go from hearing to seeing is when the transition takes place. God is a God of restoration, but what he did for Job does not mean he will restore everything to us.

Job 41-42
Psalm 102:15-21
Proverbs 21:22-24
1 Corinthians 3

NT}—When we are first born of the spirit, we feed like little children, but then as we grow, we need solid food and provide for ourselves, just what you are doing now. But we always need to be mindful that God is the only one who gives the increase to help us to grow.

Day 237—August 25

<u>Prayer:</u> Teach me oh Lord what you want me to learn today. Help me Holy Spirit to unfold today's daily scriptures. Amen!

<u>After reading question:</u> What is God saying to me today?

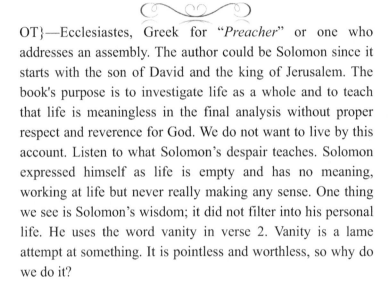

OT}—Ecclesiastes, Greek for *"Preacher"* or one who addresses an assembly. The author could be Solomon since it starts with the son of David and the king of Jerusalem. The book's purpose is to investigate life as a whole and to teach that life is meaningless in the final analysis without proper respect and reverence for God. We do not want to live by this account. Listen to what Solomon's despair teaches. Solomon expressed himself as life is empty and has no meaning, working at life but never really making any sense. One thing we see is Solomon's wisdom; it did not filter into his personal life. He uses the word vanity in verse 2. Vanity is a lame attempt at something. It is pointless and worthless, so why do we do it?

Ecclesiastes 1-2
Psalm 102:22-28
Proverbs 21:25-27
1 Corinthians 4

NT}—Paul said yesterday that they were still like little children not able to feed themselves. Today Paul tries to bring them higher in their faith so that when he goes to them, he can show up with a loving spirit and not a rod of correction.

Day 238—August 26

<u>Prayer:</u> Teach me oh Lord what you want me to learn today. Help me Holy Spirit to unfold today's daily scriptures. Amen!

<u>After reading question:</u> What is God saying to me today?

OT}—Here, we have a chapter where we heard a famous song from Pete Seeger in the late 1950s. Turn! Turn! Turn! As well as being quoted by many others in different venues. The definition of chapter three is that there is a right time for everything, as found in verses 1-8. But verse 9 says life is tiresome. There is no hope for new things. As Christians, we must look beyond the sun, to the son!

Note: Life is not meant to be balanced, God is on one side, and everything is on the other side. We should be on the side that God is on.[23]

Ecclesiastes 3-4
Psalm 103:1-7
Proverbs 21:28-31
1 Corinthians 5

NT}—Paul calls them proud and arrogant because they are allowing sexual immorality within their church and tells them they should not be associating themselves with anyone who is known to be guilty of sin.

In our world today, it can be a struggle not to fall into immoral because it is all around us. That is why it is crucial to stay in the word of God daily.

Day 239—August 27

Prayer: Teach me oh Lord what you want me to learn today. Help me Holy Spirit to unfold today's daily scriptures. Amen!

After reading question: What is God saying to me today?

OT}—Here, we see the author trying to pass down some wisdom through actions. This is from a natural man whose interests are unstable, and the wisdom of "Proverbs" is not the wisdom of "Ecclesiastes."

How impressive throughout Ecclesiastes is the evidence that, while Solomon is doing his utmost to prove that life is futile and not worth living, Hoy Spirit is using him to show that these conclusions are the tragic effect of living" Under the sun"—ignoring God, dwelling away from God the Father, oblivious of the Holy Spirit and yet face to face with the mysteries of life and nature.[24]

Ecclesiastes 5-6
Psalm 103:8-14
Proverbs 22:1-3
1 Corinthians 6

NT}—Paul draws their attention to become mature in who they are in Christ. He is teaching them that their bodies are no longer theirs but belong to Christ. This means they should honor God by honoring their bodies!

Day 240—August 28

<u>Prayer:</u> Teach me oh Lord what you want me to learn today. Help me Holy Spirit to unfold today's daily scriptures. Amen!

<u>After reading question:</u> What is God saying to me today?

OT}—Solomon puts more emphasis on death than life, that the end is better than the effort to go through life. God has made everything crooked, so who can make it straight? He is looking to human solutions for world problems that only can be corrected from a biblical understanding.

People do not like when bad things happen to them; who does? But our sorrow can be turned into gladness when we have the right mindset.

> "Weeping may endure for a night, but joy will come in the morning." (Psalm 30:5)

Ecclesiastes 7-8
Psalm 103:15-22
Proverbs 22:4-6
1 Corinthians 7:1-20

NT}—Paul then turns to the matters they originally wrote him; infidelity, sex outside of marriage, and fulfilling the lust of the flesh.

He talks a little bit about how a marriage should be.

Day 241—August 29

Prayer: Teach me oh Lord what you want me to learn today. Help me Holy Spirit to unfold today's daily scriptures. Amen!

After reading question: What is God saying to me today?

OT}—The United States Declaration of Independence mentions "That all men are created equal." Solomon might just be the first person to make that statement. He says in verse 2, "All things come alike to all. There is one event to the righteous and to the wicked, to the good and to the clean and to the unclean; to him who sacrifices and to him who does not sacrifice. As is a good man, so is the sinner; and he who swears is as he who fears and shuns an oath." If this is the case, why do we believe, trust in, adhere to, and seek out the righteousness of God?

Ecclesiastes 9-10
Psalm 104:1-7
Proverbs 22:7-9
1 Corinthians 7:21-40

NT}—The scripture for today has been, and still is, controversial in the marriage arena. I have heard it go in both directions, good and bad. I think Paul is saying it is better to be alone because the cares of a relationship will not affect the relationship between God and us. But if you join with someone in marriage, do not let it come between God and yourself through sin.

Day 242—August 30

After reading question: What is God saying to me today?

OT}—Solomon had a wisdom about him that was eerie. It is sad to see that a man who had so much, filled with great insight, ruler of many, and a lot going for him, thinks the way he does about his life and life in general.

We end Ecclesiastes with, "For God shall bring every work into judgment, with every secret thing, whether it is good or evil." As much as Solomon's thinking was off throughout the whole book, it looks like he came to an understanding that it would be worth obeying God.

Ecclesiastes 11-12
Psalm 104:8-14
Proverbs 22:10-12
1 Corinthians 8

NT}—In today's reading, Paul is talking about food, but if we take that deeper into the Word, we will see that we are not to cause someone to stumble by our actions or anything, e.g., Let us say you like to have a glass of wine with dinner. You meet someone at church who is a recovering alcoholic and invite them over one Sunday for dinner. Do you still have that glass of wine at dinner? I am going to use Paul's words here; Certainly not!

Day 243—August 31

<u>Prayer:</u> Teach me oh Lord what you want me to learn today. Help me Holy Spirit to unfold today's daily scriptures. Amen!

<u>After reading question:</u> What is God saying to me today?

OT}—Today is the Song of Solomon, "The Best of Songs," by Solomon, a series of lyric poems about a young woman and her lover.

Various interpretations have been written, but the most common is an allegory of God's love for the Israelites. In the New Testament, this would be paralleled by Jesus's relationship with the church.

Song of Solomon 1-2

Psalm 104:15-21

Proverbs 22:13-15

1 Corinthians 9

NT}—Paul tells us today that we need to come off our high horses and become like the ones we need to win for Christ. Does this mean we need to lose who we are? No, we need to know whom we are trying to reach and be at their level of understanding so we can talk to them with compassion.

You intuitively measure what is important enough to invest in yourself. Like my pastor once said, "Harvest time is too late to plant seeds."[25]

Day 244—September 1

Prayer: Teach me oh Lord what you want me to learn today. Help me Holy Spirit to unfold today's daily scriptures. Amen!

After reading question: What is God saying to me today?

OT}—Song of Solomon, otherwise known as Song of Songs, has no plot or mention of God.

It could be seen as a Book of Hebrew traditions surrounding marriage, love, and complex relationships.

Here is a note from my Bible that I felt to add:
"Among the multitudes who read the Bible, comparatively few clearly understand the Song of Solomon. Some have thought it to be a collection of songs. Still, it is generally understood to be a sort of drama, the positive interpretation of which is impossible because the identity of the speakers and the length of the speeches are not disclosed."[26]

Song of Solomon 3-4
Psalm 104:22-28
Proverbs 22:16-18
1 Corinthians 10:1-17

NT}—When it comes to temptations, you are weakest in the area where you are most selfish.

Day 245—September 2

Prayer: Teach me oh Lord what you want me to learn today. Help me Holy Spirit to unfold today's daily scriptures. Amen!

After reading question: What is God saying to me today?

OT}—When I read chapter 5, I see God going to the garden, looking for his bride and the church, and hearing the knocking of all who want to know him. Israel and maybe others who turned from him and how he comes looking for us, his beloved and his friend. What do you see?

Chapter 6 talks about a Shulamite, who is a person from Shulem, a village about ten miles from Nazareth. She is the main character in this chapter and is viewed as a lovely young lady exhaustedly waiting for her lover. The theme behind the story it is Israel.

Song of Solomon 5-6
Psalm 104:29-35
Proverbs 22:19-21
1 Corinthians 10:18-33

NT}—Today, we read about idols. An idol is nothing more than a substitute for God.

We must watch how we place people, places, and things in our lives. It is easy to put them first instead of God.

Day 246—September 3

<u>Prayer:</u> Teach me oh Lord what you want me to learn today. Help me Holy Spirit to unfold today's daily scriptures. Amen!

<u>After reading question:</u> What is God saying to me today?

OT}—The man mentioned in today's chapters is head-over-heels with the woman. He is continuously delighted in her beauty and the way she looks.

Song of Solomon 7-8
Psalm 105:1-8
Proverbs 22:22-24
1 Corinthians 11:1-16

NT}—Paul wants to be the example of how we should be as followers of Christ. We see models of headship throughout the verses. Verse 3, Christ is the head of a man, and a husband is the head of his wife only as a reflection of God.

Verse 4, As a man, we do not teach, refute, reprove, admonish, or comfort without Christ.

Verse 5, As a woman, we do not teach, refute, reprove, admonish, or comfort dishonoring her husband.
Either way, we all are subjected to the authority of Jesus.

Too many times, people will take these verses and quote them for their advantage to feed the flesh. No one is greater than the other. Not man over a woman, or woman over a man!

Day 247—September 4

<u>Prayer:</u> Teach me oh Lord what you want me to learn today. Help me Holy Spirit to unfold today's daily scriptures. Amen!

<u>After reading question:</u> What is God saying to me today?

OT}—The Book of Isaiah, a Hebrew prophet, began his ministry in the year of King Uzziah's death and lasted about sixty years. King Manasseh murdered him in a brutal death by sawing him in half. Living about 700 years before Jesus, he prophesied the coming of Jesus. Isaiah is the author of the first thirty-nine chapters, and several unknown authors wrote the remaining chapters.

Isaiah 1-2

Psalm 105:9-16

Proverbs 22:25-27

1 Corinthians 11:17-34

NT}—Paul talks about the importance of taking communion.

This is a time to examine ourselves for any sin in our lives thoroughly. We ask for forgiveness from God and ask that his love and mercy replace any wrongdoing. This allows our hearts to get right with God, and then he fills it with himself.

Day 248—September 5

<u>Prayer:</u> Teach me oh Lord what you want me to learn today. Help me Holy Spirit to unfold today's daily scriptures. Amen!

<u>After reading question:</u> What is God saying to me today?

OT}—Isaiah repeatedly warned his people that Jerusalem and Judah would be ruined because of their speech and their wickedness are against the Lord.

Israel repeatedly got itself in trouble with God. I always look at them when I read the Bible like little kids, we keep telling our kids what will happen if they are disobedient, but they do not listen. Likewise, I find myself asking, when will Israel ever learn?

Isaiah 3-4

Psalm 105:17-24

Proverbs 22:28-29

1 Corinthians 12

NT}—Paul talks about speaking in a heavenly language. We call it *"Tongues."* This remains controversial throughout history and is not approved of in many churches.

Tongues: A spiritual gift to stimulate faith, direction, and edification right from Holy Spirit.

Day 249—September 6

<u>Prayer:</u> Teach me oh Lord what you want me to learn today. Help me Holy Spirit to unfold today's daily scriptures. Amen!

<u>After reading question:</u> What is God saying to me today?

OT}—Isaiah gets a vision and sees the Lord sitting upon a throne. Partway through the vision, he has a revelation about how unclean he is.

The first few verses of chapter 6 have been used in worship for many years and have been used to usher people to this same vision Isaiah had.

Isaiah 5-6

Psalm 105:25-31

Proverbs 23:1-3

1 Corinthians 13

NT}—We see that Paul spoke in tongues, but he expresses that without love, it is worthless.

Also, today is a chapter called "*The Love Chapter.*" Love is a highly needed tool for us to have in our lives. It endures, is patient and kind, never boastful or vain, never unkind, and never fails or comes to an end. When we walk in love, we walk in Christ.

Love:-True affection for God and man, growing out of God's love for and in us.

Day 250—September 7

Prayer: Teach me oh Lord what you want me to learn today. Help me Holy Spirit to unfold today's daily scriptures. Amen!

After reading question: What is God saying to me today?

OT}—God uses Isaiah to speak to King Ahaz with a warning that he will be attacked, but not to worry because it shall not stand, nor shall it come to pass. King Ahaz is unsure if he believes him, so God wants to send a sign, but Ahaz will not ask for one.

Isaiah 7-8

Psalm 105:32-38

Proverbs 23:4-6

1 Corinthians 14:1-20

NT}—Paul tells us to pursue and seek love and make it our aim, our great quest. To desire spiritual gifts, especially that we may prophesy. 1 Corinthians 14 teaches about tongues, prophecy, and public worship.

Tomorrow I will expand on tongues, but today I want to answer the question: "But what does it mean to prophesy?" To be able to prophesy is one of the gifts of the spirit that allows us to share a prophecy with someone to proclaim a message from God. This is mainly through a prophet. Today, God can use this gift to speak through someone filled with the Holy Spirit with an authoritative word.

Day 251—September 8

<u>Prayer:</u> Teach me oh Lord what you want me to learn today. Help me Holy Spirit to unfold today's daily scriptures. Amen!

<u>After reading question:</u> What is God saying to me today?

OT}—Here, we see where Isaiah prophesied Jesus, the Messiah, that would save them. We get to add to the long list of names that Jesus has: Wonderful, Counselor, Mighty God, Everlasting Father of Eternity, and Prince of Peace.

Isaiah 9-10

Psalm 105:39-45

Proverbs 23:7-9

1 Corinthians 14:21-40

NT}—Paul lays out the order of speaking in tongues. Remember, "God is not a God of confusion and disorder, but peace and order."
The Bible makes it clear that tongue speaking should follow definite rules:

> ➤ Praying in tongues in your prayer time is for self-edification. This is not meant for anyone else. If used in worship time, it should be quiet, not disturbing anyone.

> ➤ Speaking in tongues in public or at any open assembly should have an interpreter present; if not, a person should remain silent.

> ➤ If there is an interpreter, it is meant to build up the believers, not used as a rod of correction.

Day 252—September 9

<u>Prayer:</u> Teach me oh Lord what you want me to learn today. Help me Holy Spirit to unfold today's daily scriptures. Amen!

<u>After reading question:</u> What is God saying to me today?

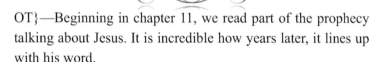

OT}—Beginning in chapter 11, we read part of the prophecy talking about Jesus. It is incredible how years later, it lines up with his word.

See Genealogy Chart on page 9.

Isaiah 11-12

Psalm 106:1-7

Proverbs 23:10-12

1 Corinthians 15:1-29

NT}—Today, we read about Paul getting humble.

I have seen people ask what verse 21 meant. Sometimes the answers to scripture are plain, but other times our intellect clouds our judgment.

I want to expand on that verse:
Adam and Eve sinned and brought sin and death into the world. Jesus, the second Adam, came so all who believe will have everlasting life.

Day 253—September 10

<u>Prayer:</u> Teach me oh Lord what you want me to learn today. Help me Holy Spirit to unfold today's daily scriptures. Amen!

<u>After reading question:</u> What is God saying to me today?

OT}—The City of Babylon was destroyed around 539 BC by King Cyrus the Great, and its ruins are present-day Iraq. The Iraqi government, under Saddam Hussein, excavated the ruins and attempted to reconstruct some of the ancient city. Today the United States Armed Forces built a military base on the ruins of Babylon.[27]

Isaiah 13-14

Psalm 106:8-14

Proverbs 23:13-15

1 Corinthians 15:30-58

NT}—"O death, where is your victory? O death, where is your sting?"

We live in a body that will decay, but if our spirit is right with God, we have a guarantee of everlasting life. Knowing the truth about our resurrection should affect how we live without any question.

Verse 39 says all flesh is not the same. This explains why we do not see animals rise in the resurrection. Mankind is the only flesh with an immortal soul, which is the analogy of living and heavenly bodies.

Day 254—September 11

<u>Prayer:</u> Teach me oh Lord what you want me to learn today. Help me Holy Spirit to unfold today's daily scriptures. Amen!

<u>After reading question:</u> What is God saying to me today?

OT}—The nation of Moab was a country about thirty miles square, north of the Zered River, south of the Amon River, and east of the Dead Sea. It was known for its rich pastureland for sheep and other livestock. The soil was ideal for growing wheat, barley, and other grains.

We see that Ar was the capital, and Isaiah prophesied its ruin.

Isaiah 15-16
Psalm 106:15-21
Proverbs 23:16-18
1 Corinthians 16

NT}—Paul says his goodbyes but assures them they will not be left alone.

Paul's love for Corinth grew deep during that year and a half he was there. He is open with them in giving them direction to safeguard their faith and letting them know they are not alone; and that others, like Timothy and Apollos, will follow until his return sometime soon.

Day 255—September 12

Prayer: Teach me oh Lord what you want me to learn today. Help me Holy Spirit to unfold today's daily scriptures. Amen!

After reading question: What is God saying to me today?

OT}—Today is Isaiah's prophecy for Damascus, the capital of Syria. Damascus is about 130 miles northeast of Jerusalem, one of the oldest cities in the world and the fourth holiest city in the middle east. However, it is destined to become a ruinous heap according to Isaiah 17. It has not happened thus far, but considering recent events, it could be any time for that prophecy to come to pass.[28]

Isaiah 17-18
Psalm 106:22-28
Proverbs 23:19-21
2 Corinthians 1

NT}—Paul writes to the Corinthians in a second letter because of some tension and strife that continued after the first letter. Most likely from Macedonia around the same time as the first letter, 55 AD.

After his introduction, he apologizes for not being able to come in person because of a change of plans.

Day 256—September 13

<u>Prayer:</u> Teach me oh Lord what you want me to learn today. Help me Holy Spirit to unfold today's daily scriptures. Amen!

<u>After reading question:</u> What is God saying to me today?

OT}—Today is Isaiah's prophecy for Egypt. We know Egypt to be the home of Pharaoh, where the Israelites were enslaved for 430 years, but because of how Israel was treated without cause, God passed judgment on the land.

Isaiah 19-20

Psalm 106:29-35

Proverbs 23:22-24

2 Corinthians 2

NT}—Paul addresses the deep heart pain he felt when he heard about a person who committed incest. After expressing his love for them, he tells them to forgive, comfort, and encourage the person to keep him from going deeper into sorrow and despair.

We might say it this way today, to keep him from making a wrong decision and committing suicide.

This chapter starts with Paul explaining why he had a change of plans, then focuses on the strategy of Satan and the victory of Jesus. Ends with Paul briefly characterizing his ministry.

Day 257—September 14

<u>Prayer:</u> Teach me oh Lord what you want me to learn today. Help me Holy Spirit to unfold today's daily scriptures. Amen!

<u>After reading question:</u> What is God saying to me today?

OT}—Today is Isaiah's prophecy for the Desert of the Sea and the Valley of Vision.

Desert of the Sea was Babylon after great dams were raised to control the waters of the Euphrates River, which overflowed it like a sea and would do so again.

Valley of Vision is a reference to the city of Jerusalem. Jerusalem is surrounded by mountains and the valleys running between them.

Isaiah 21-22
Psalm 106:36-42
Proverbs 23:25-27
2 Corinthians 3

NT}—To be forgiven of our sins, we no longer need to put a veil between us and God, i.e., the Holy of Holies. If we walk in repentance with God, the veil is stripped off. But one better, it is *taken away*.

Day 258—September 15

<u>Prayer:</u> Teach me oh Lord what you want me to learn today. Help me Holy Spirit to unfold today's daily scriptures. Amen!

<u>After reading question:</u> What is God saying to me today?

OT}—Today is Isaiah's prophecy for Tyre. Tyre, modern-day Lebanon, is a two-part port city, the first part on the mainland and the second part on an island. God mainly came down on Tyre because they were joyful in the pain that Jerusalem was going through. Nebuchadnezzar destroyed Tyre in 572 BC and lay desolate for seventy years until Alexander the Great in 332 BC, took the ruins of the old city, and made a causeway to the island, thus fulfilling the prophecy exactly.[29]

Isaiah 23-24

Psalm 106:43-48

Proverbs 23:28-30

2 Corinthians 4

NT}—God is saying that nothing from him is hidden from those that are not lost. That is why we need to walk by faith. The definition from Dictionary.com says:

1. Confidence or trust in a person or thing
2. A belief that is not based on proof[30]

The Bible says in Hebrews 11:1, "Now faith is the substance of things hoped for, the evidence of things not seen." Similarly, that leads right into verse 18.

Day 259—September 16

<u>Prayer:</u> Teach me oh Lord what you want me to learn today. Help me Holy Spirit to unfold today's daily scriptures. Amen!

<u>After reading question:</u> What is God saying to me today?

OT}—Isaiah is praising God for his wonderful deeds, righteous judgment, goodness to the weak, and all the things he will do.

Isaiah 25-26
Psalm 107:1-7
Proverbs 23:31-33
2 Corinthians 5

NT}—What is our goal? There are thousands of answers to that question. One of them is found in chapter 5, verse 9, "Therefore, whether we are at home on earth away from him, or away from home and with him, we are constantly ambitious and strive earnestly to be pleasing to him."

- ➢ Home is earth
- ➢ With him is after we die of a natural death

Have you ever heard of the phrase, "Home is where the heart is?" When our heart is focused on Jesus, even though we are here on earth, we are seated with him in heavenly places. When we are seated with him in Heavenly places, our focus is still on Jesus but through love.

Day 260—September 17

<u>Prayer:</u> Teach me oh Lord what you want me to learn today. Help me Holy Spirit to unfold today's daily scriptures. Amen!

<u>After reading question:</u> What is God saying to me today?

OT}—Isaiah continues prophesying the future for Israel. He speaks about the sinful nature of the drunkards of Ephraim, and then he turns to say that the beauty of Ephraim will come from the Lord of Host.

Chapter 28 begins, directed chiefly to the southern kingdom of Judah. Isaiah will first speak of the sin of Israel, then switch the focus to Judah.

Isaiah 27-28
Psalm 107:8-14
Proverbs 23:34-35
2 Corinthians 6

NT}—We are called to be co-labors with Jesus, which means that we work together in God's service with no obstructions for fault finding and blame.

Verse 14 is a topic that is widely used in the church. "Do not be unequally yoked." However, Paul means much more here than only marrying an unbeliever. It applies to any environment where we let the world influence our thinking. When we join with unbelievers in any ungodly way, we are being unequally yoked.

Day 261—September 18

Prayer: Teach me oh Lord what you want me to learn today. Help me Holy Spirit to unfold today's daily scriptures. Amen!

After reading question: What is God saying to me today?

OT}—What happens when you ignore what God is saying in the spirit?

Spiritual blindness!

That is what Isaiah is saying to Jerusalem, to pay attention to their surroundings; Keep an ear open and hear the prophecies, do not lose vision of what is read, and do not relax.

Isaiah 29-30
Psalm 107:15-21
Proverbs 24:1-3
2 Corinthians7

NT}—Paul builds on the promises of God: Cleansing and perfecting. We are to cleanse ourselves from all filthiness and work on perfecting holiness in fear of God. Even though Paul is writing to the Corinth church, these statements still hold true today.

He asks the church of Corinth to welcome him and his team with open arms, and then he thanks them.

Day 262—September 19

<u>Prayer:</u> Teach me oh Lord what you want me to learn today. Help me Holy Spirit to unfold today's daily scriptures. Amen!

<u>After reading question:</u> What is God saying to me today?

OT}—Isaiah prophesies that God is the one who will give victory to triumph, not Egypt.

And after the fallout of Jerusalem, a righteous king will rise. This would be King Hezekiah.

Isaiah 31-32

Psalm 107:22-28

Proverbs 24:4-6

2 Corinthians 8

NT}—Today, in chapter 8, we get a short lesson on giving. This is not the money that one gives to the church, meaning "*tithe*," this is beyond that, extending to the needy. We are called to help those that have less than us, voluntarily and with a cheerful heart. This can be in the form of money, food, supplies, or our time. And most of all, do not boast.

Visit www.anthonyordille.com to read a blog with more in-depth teaching on tithing.

Day 263—September 20

Prayer: Teach me oh Lord what you want me to learn today. Help me Holy Spirit to unfold today's daily scriptures. Amen!

After reading question: What is God saying to me today?

OT}—God's people cry out to him in prayer, asking for mercy to save their city.

Then there is a calling of all nations to hear the indignant of God against all of them. Isaiah mentioned that not one of the details of prophecy will fail.

Isaiah 33-34
Psalm 107:29-35
Proverbs 24:7-9
2 Corinthians 9

NT}—Paul now goes into the offering. This offering he is talking about is not the gift given in the last chapter. This is to ministries that are doing God's work. Not for your local church to run; that comes through the tithe. This would be more on the lines of building funds or expansions, missionaries, a guest speaker, or someone other than the pastor who feeds you God's Word.

I give an offering, not my tithe if I visit a church. That is why you will hear the saying, "Tithes and offerings."

Day 264—September 21

<u>Prayer:</u> Teach me oh Lord what you want me to learn today. Help me Holy Spirit to unfold today's daily scriptures. Amen!

<u>After reading question:</u> What is God saying to me today?

OT}—The land is restored, then the feeble will be strengthened. Rabshakeh is sent to King Hezekiah about the confidence of trust they have with Egypt.

Isaiah 35-36
Psalm 107:36-43
Proverbs 24:10-12
2 Corinthians 10

NT}—Paul is hoping that the Corinthians will change their attitude towards him and his credentials as an apostle so that he may come to them in gentleness, not severity.

Though we walk in the flesh, we do not war in the flesh. One example of this was in Mark 9:29. The carnal weapons Paul refers to are not material, but spiritual weapons for pulling down strongholds. What kind of strongholds? Wrong thoughts and perceptions that contradict the actual knowledge of God and the nature of God.

Through prayer and fasting, we build our arsenal to demolish strongholds when a battle arises, not by our own doings, but through the spirit.

Day 265—September 22

Prayer: Teach me oh Lord what you want me to learn today. Help me Holy Spirit to unfold today's daily scriptures. Amen!

After reading question: What is God saying to me today?

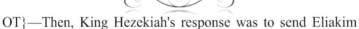

OT}—Then, King Hezekiah's response was to send Eliakim and Shebna to Isaiah seeking God.

Hezekiah's life is spared because Isaiah went to him telling him to get his house in order. Then Hezekiah turned his face to the wall and prayed.

Hezekiah honestly had a repenting heart, so God added fifteen years to his life.

Isaiah 37-38

Psalm 108:1-7

Proverbs 24:13-15

2 Corinthians 11

NT}—Paul is saying today to be watchful for counterfeits, deceitful workers masquerading as apostles of Christ.

We will always have false prophets, teachers, and preachers until the fullness of the antichrist. Our job is to know instantly whether whatever is said is right or wrong. Reading and studying the Word of God is your best defense.

Day 266—September 23

<u>Prayer:</u> Teach me oh Lord what you want me to learn today. Help me Holy Spirit to unfold today's daily scriptures. Amen!

<u>After reading question:</u> What is God saying to me today?

OT}—It is said that chapter 39 is the last chapter written by Isaiah. He gives King Hezekiah a word from God regarding things to come.

God prepares the way for his people.

Isaiah 39-40

Psalm 108:8-13

Proverbs 24:16-18

2 Corinthians 12

NT}—Paul speaks in the third party about being called into heaven to make a reference to boasting.

There must have been some complaints about Paul and others only coming to Corinth to preach for the money only. Because Paul talks about that on his third visit, he is coming to them out of his love for them to feed them spiritually and does not want their money.

He is trying to reassure them that he is not tricking them for financial gain.

Day 267—September 24

Prayer: Teach me oh Lord what you want me to learn today. Help me Holy Spirit to unfold today's daily scriptures. Amen!

After reading question: What is God saying to me today?

OT}—Today is God's glory and reasoning for the coastlands with a call of unity.

Chapter 41 refers to Cyrus the Great, who came from the East but defeated several kingdoms north of Babylon early in his reign. God uses him to restore the Jews to their own land.[31]

In chapter 42, God speaks of his servant. This is the first of the famous prophecies concerning the great future "Servant of the Lord," some believe this is the Messiah.[32]

Isaiah 41-42
Psalm 109:1-8
Proverbs 24:19-21
2 Corinthians 13

NT}—We end Second Corinthians with Paul ending his letter with a firm voice in the authority the Lord has given him for building up their faith and not tearing them down. He wanted to use his authority for edification, not destruction, hoping that the Corinthian Christians would clean up their act before he came to see them.

Day 268—September 25

<u>Prayer:</u> Teach me oh Lord what you want me to learn today. Help me Holy Spirit to unfold today's daily scriptures. Amen!

<u>After reading question:</u> What is God saying to me today?

OT}—Chapter 43 refers mainly to the exile from Babylon. God said that even though he has judged Israel, he will not leave them in captivity. God pays the ransom by giving Egypt over to the Babylonians.

God promised to judge Babylon for how they treated all of Israel's people.

In chapter 44, God is the Israelite's redeemer, claiming that Jerusalem will be inhabited again, and God promises to raise up their ruins.

Isaiah 43-44

Psalm 109:9-16

Proverbs 24:22-24

Galatians 1

NT}—Paul wrote to the Galatians just after his second journey or during his third journey, probably 53-57 AD.

Paul is taken aback by how quickly they turned from God and must have felt compelled to write them.

Day 269—September 26

<u>Prayer:</u> Teach me oh Lord what you want me to learn today. Help me Holy Spirit to unfold today's daily scriptures. Amen!

<u>After reading question:</u> What is God saying to me today?

OT}—God is telling his people to turn towards him, and he will deliver and save them. He will remove their idols and for them to remember that God knows all things from the beginning and to the end.

Chapter 45, verse 7, mentions God and some of his creations. The word evil is a calamity, and it is the moral evil that proceeds from the will of men, but physical evil proceeds from the will of God.[33]

Isaiah 45-46

Psalm 109:17-24

Proverbs 24:25-27

Galatians 2

NT}—Paul highlights his ministry and journeys, trying to express how important the gracious gift from God is. And not to treat it as something of minor importance and defer its very purpose. In doing so, Paul summarizes that his apostolic credentials did not depend on any sort of approval or influence from men.

Paul confronts Peter publicly regarding the acceptance of the Gentiles and reminds Peter that they are justified before God by the work of Jesus, not by their keeping the law.

Day 270—September 27

<u>Prayer:</u> Teach me oh Lord what you want me to learn today. Help me Holy Spirit to unfold today's daily scriptures. Amen!

<u>After reading question:</u> What is God saying to me today?

OT}—Babylon is shown in humiliation, no longer in strength as it once claimed. Babylon thought they were the best of the best, and their wisdom and knowledge were beyond anyone else. God says I do not believe so, daughter.

In chapter 48, God sees the hypocrisy of Judah, no excuse, sinfulness, but God's mercy will be on them because he had made a covenant and will not go back on his word.

Isaiah 47-48

Psalm 109:25-31

Proverbs 24:28-30

Galatians 3

NT}—Then Paul gets a little more excitement in the tone of the letter and confronts their blurred vision of Jesus and his work for them. Paul becomes straightforward with their departure from the faith principle and asks them a loaded question. Did you receive the Spirit by the works of the law or by the hearing of faith? Obviously, it is by faith and not by the works of the law.

I like verse 7, "…That it is the people who live by faith who are the true sons of Abraham."

Day 271—September 28

<u>Prayer:</u> Teach me oh Lord what you want me to learn today. Help me Holy Spirit to unfold today's daily scriptures. Amen!

<u>After reading question:</u> What is God saying to me today?

OT}—In the mention of God's people being saved, we lean to Jesus, the Messiah, who is the one that God will send to save. Chapter 49 seems to be declaring his mission to fulfill his ultimate redemption.

In chapter 50, God questions their heart.

Isaiah 49-50

Psalm 110

Proverbs 24:31-34

Galatians 4

NT}—We are called sons and daughters of God. We are no longer slaves to this world, making us an heir to the Kingdom through Christ.

We must stop thinking like the Israelites when they were in the wilderness, complaining, thinking it would be easier to return to Egypt because everything they needed was provided for them, walking in lack, and being told what to do.

Everything God is, we are. Everything God has, we have. "My daddy's got it all, and so do I!"

Day 272—September 29

<u>Prayer:</u> Teach me oh Lord what you want me to learn today. Help me Holy Spirit to unfold today's daily scriptures. Amen!

<u>After reading question:</u> What is God saying to me today?

OT}—God speaks with a loud voice and says;
"*Listen to Me;* what you have seen in the past was a promise of future blessings. I will never leave, nor forsake you."
"*Listen to Me;* the Lord's salvation and righteousness will be for forever.
"*Listen to Me,*" fear God, not man.
"*Awake,*" to the power and greatness of the Lord.
"*Wake*" up to the reality of God's wrath.

Do you think he was trying to get their attention?

Isaiah 51-52
Psalm 111:1-5
Proverbs 25:1-2
Galatians 5

NT}—Paul says that God has wholly liberated them (us) from slavery. That means that, through Christ, nothing can hold us back from finishing the race and hitting the mark.

The race is the journey we have as Christians, and hitting the mark of righteousness on that last breath we take is what the reward will be.

Day 273—September 30

<u>Prayer:</u> Teach me oh Lord what you want me to learn today. Help me Holy Spirit to unfold today's daily scriptures. Amen!

<u>After reading question:</u> What is God saying to me today?

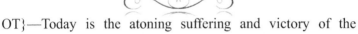

OT}—Today is the atoning suffering and victory of the Messiah, shown in chapter 53. We use verse 5 as a reference for healing in our prayers.

Although chapter 54 is intended to express Zion's joy over redemption, it is also a very personal, long neglected, and often overlooked message for women.[34]

The restoration of Israel and Paul speaks to Israel as a partner in a marriage. We are his bride, and Jesus is the groom.

Isaiah 53-54

Psalm 111:6-10

Proverbs 25:3-4

Galatians 6

NT}—No one is more important than the person standing next to you, wherever you are. No matter your church, ministry, or family role, we are all equal in God's eyes. Being equal means, we are not above someone; we have the same rights, opportunities, and responsibilities.

Day 274—October 1

Prayer: Teach me oh Lord what you want me to learn today. Help me Holy Spirit to unfold today's daily scriptures. Amen!

After reading question: What is God saying to me today?

OT}—Wait and listen! God is speaking and calling all who hear to come for a blessing and be restored. Not only is salvation a free gift from God, but all that is wrapped up in that gift is ours.

- ➤ The gift itself is salvation
- ➤ The box it comes in is Jesus
- ➤ The wrapping paper is Holy Spirit
- ➤ The tape is God

How do we get to salvation? Conformity to the will of God brings salvation.

Isaiah 55-56
Psalm 112:1-5
Proverbs 25:5-6
Ephesians 1

NT}—The Letter of Paul to the Ephesians, written by Paul around 60 AD during his two-year imprisonment in his own house in Rome. Also, it is known as one of the four "Prison Letters." This epistle may have been a circular letter intended for several churches. Paul expresses that we have been chosen before the foundation of the world. We are set apart by God and for God, and Christ is the head of the church, making everything complete.

Day 275—October 2

<u>Prayer:</u> Teach me oh Lord what you want me to learn today. Help me Holy Spirit to unfold today's daily scriptures. Amen!

<u>After reading question:</u> What is God saying to me today?

OT}—Judah's idolatry is like spiritual adultery, but God tells them to cry out and worship the Lord with a loud voice and a repentant heart.

Isaiah 57-58

Psalm 112:6-10

Proverbs 25:7-8

Ephesians 2

NT}—God gives us the free gift of salvation.

We need to ask ourselves what is being saved.
It is:
- A gift
- Eternal life
- Forgiveness
- Justification
- Righteousness
- Redemption
- Total Commitment
- Joint heir
- Fellowship
- Peace
- God's inherited favor (grace)

Day 276—October 3

Prayer: Teach me oh Lord what you want me to learn today. Help me Holy Spirit to unfold today's daily scriptures. Amen!

After reading question: What is God saying to me today?

OT}—God is as close as you make him. Our sins do not keep him away from us; our thinking does.

God tells us to rise to a new life. We are the light on a hill shining into the darkness for all to see.

Isaiah 59-60
Psalm 113
Proverbs 25:9-10
Ephesians 3

NT}—We learn that the Jews persecuted and imprisoned Paul because he was an apostle to the Gentiles and preached the gospel to them. Today God reveals some of his mysteries through his holy apostles and prophets by the Holy Spirit.

We, as Christians, are taught to turn to God in times of trouble to help us get through whatever situation we face. But God is more than that. His work within us can carry out his purpose and do superabundantly, far over and above all that we dare ask or think, infinitely beyond our highest prayers, desires, thoughts, hopes, or dreams. A complete supply from above.

Day 277—October 4

<u>Prayer:</u> Teach me oh Lord what you want me to learn today. Help me Holy Spirit to unfold today's daily scriptures. Amen!

<u>After reading question:</u> What is God saying to me today?

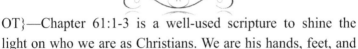

OT}—Chapter 61:1-3 is a well-used scripture to shine the light on who we are as Christians. We are his hands, feet, and voice on earth so that he may be glorified. We take on the empowerment of the Messiah's ministry to continue what he has started.

Isiah prophesied in a time when Jerusalem was still a functioning city but was spiritually corrupt. Today he looks forward to the time when the Babylonians conquer them and prophetically speaks comfort and assurance to the citizens.

Isaiah 61-62

Psalm 114

Proverbs 25:11-12

Ephesians 4

NT}—Paul then pleads with the church to walk worthy of the calling, with behavior that is a credit to the summons to God's service. We need to live our lives as correctly as we can if we are to call ourselves Christians. People are watching, and those that know us will see the change. That is why Paul says to strip ourselves of the former.

Day 278—October 5

<u>Prayer:</u> Teach me oh Lord what you want me to learn today. Help me Holy Spirit to unfold today's daily scriptures. Amen!

<u>After reading question:</u> What is God saying to me today?

OT}—Today is a prayer from captivity asking who this is, why are your clothes red, and remembering the mercy and the might of God.

This prophecy describes the day of the Lord's vengeance. First, judging Edom and then comes to the land of Israel.

Why are your clothes red, is a promise fulfilled when Jesus returns to earth, and this passage is clearly associated with Revelation 19:13 and 15.

Isaiah 63-64
Psalm 115:1-6
Proverbs 25:13-14
Ephesians 5

NT}—Paul wants to express love to the brethren by telling them to be imitators of God by copying him and following his example, just like a child imitates their father.

In a marriage, Paul teaches us how to use encouraging positive words to divorce-proof our marriages.

And guys: headship is not a ruler!

Day 279—October 6

<u>Prayer:</u> Teach me oh Lord what you want me to learn today. Help me Holy Spirit to unfold today's daily scriptures. Amen!

<u>After reading question:</u> What is God saying to me today?

OT}—Today, we end the Book of Isaiah, rejoicing in God's ultimate victory. Hopefully, you got something out of it to edify your spirit.

Sometimes, you might see "New heavens and a new earth" written through prophecies. A footnote in the Zondervan Amplified Bible has that the Hebrew language has no single word to express the concept of cosmos or universe, heavens and earth are substituted, but universe is meant in verse 17.[35]

Isaiah 65-66

Psalm 115:7-12

Proverbs 25:15-16

Ephesians 6

NT}—We are ending Ephesians with four levels of authority; "obey," "put on God's whole armor," "stand firmly," and "pray at all times."
This is the Armor of God:
- ➢ Helmet of Salvation
- ➢ Breastplate of Righteousness (Integrity)
- ➢ Belt of Truth
- ➢ Shod your feet in Preparation
- ➢ Pick up the Shield of Faith and Sword of the Spirit

Day 280—October 7

<u>Prayer:</u> Teach me oh Lord what you want me to learn today. Help me Holy Spirit to unfold today's daily scriptures. Amen!

<u>After reading question:</u> What is God saying to me today?

OT}—The Book of Jeremiah, named after the priest and prophet Jeremiah, son of Hilkiah, offers a piece of extensive information and insight into the religious and political conditions in Judah during the last forty years before the destruction of Jerusalem in 586 BC.

God speaks to Jeremiah, telling him he has been chosen as his instrument to be a prophet to the nations.

Jeremiah 1-2

Psalm 115:13-18

Proverbs 25:17-18

Philippians 1

NT}—The Letter of Paul to the Philippians, the fourth letter written by Paul around 61 AD, during his two-year imprisonment in his own house in Rome, credits Timothy as co-author/co-sender. Also, it is known as one of the four "Prison Letters."

Paul has much to say about the gospel and repeatedly points out its significance through his ministry and their relationship.

Day 281—October 8

<u>Prayer:</u> Teach me oh Lord what you want me to learn today. Help me Holy Spirit to unfold today's daily scriptures. Amen!

<u>After reading question:</u> What is God saying to me today?

OT}—After God appears to Jeremiah to anoint him as a prophet, God directs him to speak to the people to warn the wicked and offer comfort to those who trusted God. Jeremiah 3 is to the backsliders. God uses the divorce illustration to show the severity of their actions, but throughout the chapter, he invites Israel to stop their backsliding ways and return to him. The thought of this return is presented in a good sense.

When we get to chapter 4, which has the same theme as chapter 3, the prophecy shows God inviting Judah and Jerusalem to return to him from a hardened condition and the vanity of hoping to appeal to the invading army of judgment.

Jeremiah 3-4

Psalm 116:1-6

Proverbs 25:19-20

Philippians 2

NT}—Paul exhorts them to humility and unity and commends Timothy for his faithfulness and love towards the welfare of the people. Epaphroditus, who was a co-labor with Paul, was homesick for Philippi and the people, so Paul sent him back to them with his message and for rest.

Day 282—October 9

<u>Prayer:</u> Teach me oh Lord what you want me to learn today. Help me Holy Spirit to unfold today's daily scriptures. Amen!

<u>After reading question:</u> What is God saying to me today?

OT}—The Lord's word through Jeremiah warns of the destruction of Jerusalem, the Daughter of Zion, because the city must be punished for the oppression within her.

Jeremiah 5-6

Psalm 116:7-12

Proverbs 25:21-22

Philippians 3

NT}—Today, Paul speaks from the heart that if there is anyone worthy of God, it would be him because of his birthright as a Hebrew.

Today's hot topic is, But out of the flesh comes loss, and out of the spirit comes the prize that God is calling us upward.

When I got saved and became a follower of Christ, my residence remained unchanged, but my home shifted. I am a resident of this earth, but heaven is my home.

Here is a question that I ask myself; How well do you represent where you come from? How about you?

Day 283—October 10

OT}—God gives the people an opportunity to amend their ways to keep the city. One of God's biggest problems is how they treat the Temple of the Lord. Through Jeremiah, God explained to the people what genuine repentance looks like.

When we get to the end of chapter 8, we see the despair of conquered Judah and Jeremiah's pain-filled mourning over the sufferings of his people.

Jeremiah 7-8
Psalm 116:13-19
Proverbs 25:23-24
Philippians 4

NT}—Paul wraps up the letter with confidence that God will take care of them and provide all their needs according to his riches in glory by Christ Jesus and declares a promise to the Philippians regarding their own financial needs.

God is a God of supernatural provision—a full supply from Heaven above.

Day 284—October 11

<u>Prayer:</u> Teach me oh Lord what you want me to learn today. Help me Holy Spirit to unfold today's daily scriptures. Amen!

<u>After reading question:</u> What is God saying to me today?

OT}—Today, we continue with the lament over Judah, and God pours out his sadness over how rejected he feels. Then he defends his actions and has hopes for the people.

At the end of chapter 9, God points out that his people were like the uncircumcised nations in their lack of knowing God and their wicked conduct. By the end of chapter 10, Jeremiah has a pea to Go for recompense to the invading army.

Jeremiah 9-10

Psalm 117

Proverbs 25:25-26

Colossians 1

NT}—The Letter of Paul to the Colossians has been called the twin epistle of Ephesians. Also, it is known as one of the four "Prison Letters." Written around 60 AD by Paul, and Timothy as co-author, during their two-year imprisonment in his own house in Rome.

Paul may have never been to the city of Colossae, but it could have been evangelized when he was in Ephesus by Epaphras, Timothy, or others.

Day 285—October 12

<u>Prayer:</u> Teach me oh Lord what you want me to learn today. Help me Holy Spirit to unfold today's daily scriptures. Amen!

<u>After reading question:</u> What is God saying to me today?

OT}—God speaks to Judah about their failure to keep the ancient covenant Israel made with God at Mount Sinai in the days of Moses. Jeremiah's assignment was to preach a message of the broken covenant and its consequences in Jerusalem and other cities of Judah.

Then Jeremiah cries out about how they want to persecute him, and he asks God, why does the way of the wicked prosper? God's answer was both powerful and profound. God encouraged Jeremiah to regard his present challenge as a preparation for more significant challenges to come.

Jeremiah 11-12

Psalm 118:1-7

Proverbs 25:27-28

Colossians 2

NT}—Paul tells them to be watchful for deceivers who will defraud them with their words. But for them to know who they are in Christ and stand firm in their faith.

This is extremely important for us today as well. As the end times approach, there is going to be more pressure on the enemy to try to turn believers' hearts from God and serve him.

Day 286—October 13

Prayer: Teach me oh Lord what you want me to learn today. Help me Holy Spirit to unfold today's daily scriptures. Amen!

After reading question: What is God saying to me today?

OT}—God tells Jeremiah that he is done with the people, he is at wit's end and to stop praying for them, and even when they cry out, he will not answer them, but he will consume them by the sword, by famine, and by pestilence.

Then Jeremiah goes back to weeping over the judgment to come, and a plea that God would remember them in their misery unfolds.

Jeremiah 13-14

Psalm 118:8-14

Proverbs 26:1-2

Colossians 3

NT}—Paul speaks words of love telling them they are a new creation, to put off what was old, and to set their minds to what is above, not things that are on the earth.

Until you change your identity, you will not see others as God sees them.[36]

> ➢ You must see yourself as God sees you
> ➢ You must see others as God sees them.

Day 287—October 14

Prayer: Teach me oh Lord what you want me to learn today. Help me Holy Spirit to unfold today's daily scriptures. Amen!

After reading question: What is God saying to me today?

OT}—Several times, God had told Jeremiah not to pray for the people because their fate of judgment and exile was already inevitable. Today Jeremiah is called to be set apart from the people and not to take a wife in Jerusalem.

God promised that Judah would be cast out of his sight by four forms of destruction: Death, sword, famine, and captivity. Some will die by a plague or pestilence, some will die by the sword, some will perish through famine, and the remaining will go into captivity.

I think God is mad!

Jeremiah 15-16

Psalm 118:15-21

Proverbs 26:3-4

Colossians 4

NT}—Paul ends the Letter to the Colossians with directions on how to live as a Christian, letting them know Tychicus, who is part of Paul's ministry, will keep them informed on how the ministry is doing and who will be coming to them helping them with love, and then he blesses them.

Day 288—October 15

<u>Prayer:</u> Teach me oh Lord what you want me to learn today. Help me Holy Spirit to unfold today's daily scriptures. Amen!

<u>After reading question:</u> What is God saying to me today?

OT}—As we continue through the folly of misplaced trust and the depth of Judah's sin, God uses a potter's clay to illustrate himself and the people.

Just as a potter will smash the clay if the vessel he is making does not turn out right to start all over, God will be that potter with his people.

Jeremiah 17-18

Psalm 118:22-29

Proverbs 26:5-6

1 Thessalonians 1

NT}—The First Letter of Paul to the Thessalonians is said to be written by Paul around 51 AD and co-authored by Timothy during the year and a half of ministry in the City of Corinth during the second missionary journey. The letter is one of the earliest letters that Paul wrote.

The letter's theme seems to surround the topic of the second coming of Christ.

Day 289—October 16

<u>Prayer:</u> Teach me oh Lord what you want me to learn today. Help me Holy Spirit to unfold today's daily scriptures. Amen!

<u>After reading question:</u> What is God saying to me today?

OT}—In the previous chapter, God taught Jeremiah at the potter's house. God then told Jeremiah to take a clay bottle to use for a spiritual illustration to confront the leaders about the evil in Jerusalem according to the word from God.

Apparently, Pashhur, son of Immer, the priest and chief officer of the temple, did not like Jeremiah's dramatic sermon about the broken flask because they beat Jeremiah because of the prophecies he was sharing and then put him in jail.

Then the next day, Jeremiah prophesies Babylon's exile.

Jeremiah 19-20

Psalm 119:1-7

Proverbs 26:7-8

1 Thessalonians 2

NT}—Paul is responding to a report from Timothy concerning the conditions there.

Paul speaks to them about the ministry that was for them, despite what happened in Philippi.

Day 290—October 17

<u>Prayer:</u> Teach me oh Lord what you want me to learn today. Help me Holy Spirit to unfold today's daily scriptures. Amen!

<u>After reading question:</u> What is God saying to me today?

OT}—Sometimes, when we face a crisis, we cry out to God for help, but because we are not right with him, he turns away from us.

That is what God did to Jerusalem when Nebuchadnezzar, king of Babylon, was threatening war against Judah.

As you see, the end was coming near to the end of Judah. By this time, Israel, the northern land, had been conquered by the Neon-Assyrian Empire and destroyed. Now Judah is on the verge of replacement because of their Godless ways.

Jeremiah 21-22
Psalm 119:8-14
Proverbs 26:9-10
1 Thessalonians 3

NT}—Paul shows concern for the Thessalonians, but is rekindled in his spirit by the report from Timothy's visit.

Timothy told Paul that the people stood firm in their faith, were loving and kind to each other, and were affectionate to Paul and his team for caring about them.

Day 291—October 18

<u>Prayer:</u> Teach me oh Lord what you want me to learn today. Help me Holy Spirit to unfold today's daily scriptures. Amen!

<u>After reading question:</u> What is God saying to me today?

OT}—Today, we get a vision of people who are leaders in our churches. Jeremiah spoke to leaders in a general sense, but the main emphasis would be on the shepherds as spiritual leaders. God calls them to be good shepherds over the chosen.

What do shepherds do? They lead, they protect the flock, they comfort, and more. Jesus emphasized this in the restoration of Peter on Peter 21, telling him twice to feed his sheep.

What happens if they do not follow this rule? Today's reading will give you that answer.

Jeremiah 23-24

Psalm 119:15-21

Proverbs 26:11-12

1 Thessalonians 4

NT}—Paul tells them that he is grateful for their union with his team and to continue doing what they learned from the ministry, not to veer off from the Lord, and not to surrender to the working of the flesh. Then Paul gives them a glimpse at the second coming of Jesus.

Day 292—October 19

<u>Prayer:</u> Teach me oh Lord what you want me to learn today. Help me Holy Spirit to unfold today's daily scriptures. Amen!

<u>After reading question:</u> What is God saying to me today?

OT}—Jeremiah speaks on the fall of Jerusalem, why, and what will come of the land.

Through Micah's prophecy, God had told them that Mount Zion, the highest hill in Jerusalem, will be plowed like a field.

Note: After Nebuchadnezzar broke down the walls around Jerusalem sometime later, that area literally was plowed under like a field.

Jeremiah 25-26

Psalm 119:22-28

Proverbs 26:13-14

1 Thessalonians 5

NT}—Paul tells them to comfort and encourage one another.

Paul is ending the letter, telling them to be on alert, watchful, cautious, and on guard at all times because the coming of Christ is unknown.

You do not praise God when you see it; you praise him when you pray it, Verse 16-18.

Day 293—October 20

Prayer: Teach me oh Lord what you want me to learn today. Help me Holy Spirit to unfold today's daily scriptures. Amen!

After reading question: What is God saying to me today?

OT}—Jeremiah is given the word from God that he must send to the kings of Edom, Moab, Trye, Sidon, and the king of the Ammonites with a warning of what will happen to their nation if they do not serve Nebuchadnezzar.

God has gotten to the point that he wants King Nebuchadnezzar to rule over all the land until the God-appointed time of punishment for the land comes.

Jeremiah 27-28

Psalm 119:29-35

Proverbs 26:15-16

2 Thessalonians 1

NT}—The Second Letter of Paul to the Thessalonians was written a few months after the first letter while Paul was still in Corinth. Because of how he ended the first letter, the people misunderstood Paul and concluded that the coming of Christ was so imminent that they failed to live with a proper perspective, which is why Paul attempted to correct this view.

Day 294—October 21

<u>Prayer:</u> Teach me oh Lord what you want me to learn today. Help me Holy Spirit to unfold today's daily scriptures. Amen!

<u>After reading question:</u> What is God saying to me today?

OT}—Jeremiah writes a letter to the rest of the leaders in exile, priests, prophets, and captives in Babylon.

The letter was a word from God to build themselves up and pray for peace and welfare of the city. He tells them that if they seek him, he will deliver them.

Jeremiah 29-30

Psalm 119:36-42

Proverbs 26:17-18

2 Thessalonians 2

NT}—Paul tries to turn the focus from the end times to current affairs. He tells them they must focus on the lost ones who do not accept the truth (gospel).

Even though scripture tells us to be watchful for the coming of the Lord, our primary focus is on the here and now. Some people may be so concerned in the end times that they lose focus on taking care of the people that are literally in front of them; the brokenhearted, the hurt, and the lost. We cannot take our eyes off today because we are worried about tomorrow. Also known as; what our reward is going to be. If we take care of today, God promises that he will reward us tomorrow.

Day 295—October 22

Prayer: Teach me oh Lord what you want me to learn today. Help me Holy Spirit to unfold today's daily scriptures. Amen!

After reading question: What is God saying to me today?

OT}—God talks about the rebuilding of his nation.

God loves his people and most likely is saddened that he must discipline them. Through his sadness, he again allows them to get things right.

Jeremiah 31-32
Psalm 119:43-49
Proverbs 26:19-20
2 Thessalonians 3

NT}—We end Second Thessalonians with Paul telling them to pray and commences a blessing on them.

Prayer is a powerful expression of our hearts. Through prayer, situations are changed, hearts turn from bad to good, and sometimes, as we have read throughout the Bible, God's wrath, and man's, has been softened.

Paul knows this, and that is why he asks for prayer.

Day 296—October 23

<u>Prayer:</u> Teach me oh Lord what you want me to learn today. Help me Holy Spirit to unfold today's daily scriptures. Amen!

<u>After reading question:</u> What is God saying to me today?

OT}—While Jeremiah is held in confinement because he faces constant opposition from political and religious leaders about his prophecies, God speaks to him for a second time, giving some positive highlights on the future of Jerusalem.

Jeremiah 33-34

Psalm 119:50-56

Proverbs 26:21-22

1 Timothy 1

NT}—First Letter of Paul to Timothy is the second Pastoral Letter written by Paul around 63-65 AD from Macedonia, perhaps just after his first imprisonment in Rome, to Timothy with instructions for the qualifications and duties of various church officers. Many churches will use the Books of Timothy as a guideline for leadership in their church.

Timothy had a Greek father and a Jewish mother who taught him the scriptures from childhood. This opened the doors for Paul to use Timothy within the ministry.

Day 297—October 24

Prayer: Teach me oh Lord what you want me to learn today. Help me Holy Spirit to unfold today's daily scriptures. Amen!

After reading question: What is God saying to me today?

OT}—God tells Jeremiah to bring a word to the Rechabites, who belong to the Kenite tribe, and accompany the Israelites into the holy land.

In the fourth year of King Jehoiakim's reign, God tells Jeremiah to write a book on all the words he has spoken to Jeremiah against Israel, Judah and all the nations.

Jeremiah 35-36

Psalm 119:57-63

Proverbs 26:23-24

1 Timothy 2

NT}—After the introduction, Paul says that no one is beyond praying, not even kings and anyone in authority. Jesus Christ is the mediator between God and men. When we pray, pray to Jesus, who then goes to the Father on our behalf. One essential characteristic we are to have when we pray is to pray without anger, quarreling, resentment, or doubt in our minds, but to lift up holy hands.

There have been times that I went to church, and my heart was not right because of a situation in my personal life, and as a leader, I kept myself from going to the front to pray for others. This reason is just what Paul is saying in this scripture.

Day 298—October 25

Teach me oh Lord what you want me to learn today. Help me Holy Spirit to unfold today's daily scriptures. Amen!

After reading question: What is God saying to me today?

OT}—Jeremiah is put in prison by King Zedekiah.

Now, because of the words spoken in Jeremiah 21:9, some priests put Jeremiah in a dungeon.

Jeremiah 37-38

Psalm 119:64-70

Proverbs 26:25-26

1 Timothy 3

NT}—Here, we get the qualifications for the office of a bishop and the position of a deacon.

Because everything belongs to God, we are called to be good Stewarts. But if anyone seeks the office of bishop, or even deacon, that stewardship comes with higher demand.

As a deacon, I was taught by my leaders that I was not above the congregation; I was a higher servant who served them.

Day 299—October 26

<u>Prayer:</u> Teach me oh Lord what you want me to learn today. Help me Holy Spirit to unfold today's daily scriptures. Amen!

<u>After reading question:</u> What is God saying to me today?

OT}—Jerusalem is taken captive by Nebuchadnezzar's army, and Jeremiah is set free by King Nebuchadnezzar because of God's favor in his life.

Jeremiah 39-40

Psalm 119:71-77

Proverbs 26:27-28

1 Timothy 4

NT}—Paul gives personal instructions to Timothy. Telling him to devote himself to public and private reading (meditation), exhortation (speaking), and teaching the doctrine (beliefs).

One of the most complex parts of my life, walking as a Christian, is learning the gifts God gave me through Holy Spirit and using them. Some are easy to follow, but others are a struggle, and I fight with my spirit, just like Jacob when he wrestled with God, to fulfill them. But I will keep at it as long as I have breath.

Day 300—October 27

<u>Prayer:</u> Teach me oh Lord what you want me to learn today. Help me Holy Spirit to unfold today's daily scriptures. Amen!

<u>After reading question:</u> What is God saying to me today?

OT}—Today is a "journey to Egypt." Should we go or should we stay? That is the question to Jeremiah.

Also, Captains of the army, Johanan, Jezaniah, and others, approach Jeremiah asking him to intercede for them, asking God for direction.

After ten days, Jeremiah returns with God's answer, saying that as long as they are reasonable, God will be with them, and they do not need to fear the king of Babylon. But if they are not good, evil will come to them.

Jeremiah 41-42

Psalm 119:78-84

Proverbs 27:1-2

1 Timothy 5

NT}—Paul continues to instruct Timothy. He mentions that even though the church is called to take care of the widows and older folk, their families should be the first ones to do so, then the church.

Day 301—October 28

Prayer: Teach me oh Lord what you want me to learn today. Help me Holy Spirit to unfold today's daily scriptures. Amen!

After reading question: What is God saying to me today?

OT}—When Jeremiah finishes with a word from God, they call Jeremiah a liar. With that, they did not listen to remain in Judah. Instead, they journeyed to Egypt, and God's wrath fell on them.

Jeremiah 43-44

Psalm 119:85-91

Proverbs 27:3-4

1 Timothy 6

NT}—Paul talks about the love of money and that it is the root (source) of all evils. Through greed and craving to be rich, some have been led astray and turned from their faith. The curse of greed:

➢ Hearts fixed on money
➢ Eager to have money
➢ Lust after money
➢ Graving for money
➢ Longing for money (to be rich)

Money is good, but it can be a curse as well. We should not crave to have it to fill a void in our hearts, but instead, seek God for his purpose to have money. Sometimes a person is so focused on being rich that they lose sight of what God's plan is for their life.

Day 302—October 29

<u>Prayer:</u> Teach me oh Lord what you want me to learn today. Help me Holy Spirit to unfold today's daily scriptures. Amen!

<u>After reading question:</u> What is God saying to me today?

OT}—Today's reading is the word that Jeremiah spoke to Baruch concerning and against the Gentile nations, Egypt, and the army of Pharaoh Necho, king of Egypt, telling them to stand up and fight.

Jeremiah 45-46

Psalm 119:92-98

Proverbs 27:5-6

2 Timothy 1

NT}—The Second Letter of Paul to Timothy is the third Pastoral Letter written by Paul around 66-67 AD while he was imprisoned in Rome for the second time. I believe it is shortly before his death.

At this point in Paul's life, he seems to know that his ministry is ending.

Paul longs to see Timothy again, recalls Timothy's faith, and tells him not to lose it.

Day 303—October 30

Prayer: Teach me oh Lord what you want me to learn today. Help me Holy Spirit to unfold today's daily scriptures. Amen!

After reading question: What is God saying to me today?

OT}—Today's reading is the word that Jeremiah spoke to the Philistines and Moab.

Jeremiah 47-48

Psalm 119:99-105

Proverbs 27:7-8

2 Timothy 2

NT}—We see here that Paul thought of Timothy like a son and most likely loved him like one as well.

Paul calls Timothy to be like a soldier who has committed their life to the one who enlisted him.

Sometimes people will have controversial opinions over stupid questions or topics. That is fine because no question is ridiculous, but arguing and fighting over them is silly. Paul says that as servants of the Lord, we must not be quarrelsome but be kind to one another, mild-tempered, and above all else, keep the peace.

A Christian should not like to argue!

Day 304—October 31

Prayer: Teach me oh Lord what you want me to learn today. Help me Holy Spirit to unfold today's daily scriptures. Amen!

After reading question: What is God saying to me today?

OT}—Today's reading is the word that Jeremiah spoke concerning and against the Ammonites, Babylon, and the land of the Chaldeans.

Jeremiah 49-50

Psalm 119:106-112

Proverbs 27:9-10

2 Timothy 3

NT}—Paul tells Timothy that there will be perilous times of great stress and trouble, but to continue to hold to the things that he learned.

Some of the things we read today, especially in verses 2 through 7, are going on right now. We as Christians should read this and learn from it so that we are not transitioned into someone of this character.

If you want the full blow of these verses, read them in the Amplified Bible.

Day 305—November 1

Teach me oh Lord what you want me to learn today. Help me Holy Spirit to unfold today's daily scriptures. Amen!

After reading question: What is God saying to me today?

OT}—We end the Book of Jeremiah with some historical appendix. God's forecast through Jeremiah of what was going to happen, and all the details of the prophecy were carried out, is recorded by Daniel. Only an empty-headed fool could say in their heart, "There is no God."[37]

Jeremiah 51-52
Psalm 119:113-119
Proverbs 27:11-12
2 Timothy 4

NT}—Paul charges Timothy, as a preacher of the Word, to show people what way their lives are wrong and to convince them, by rebuking and correcting warnings, to not waiver in their faith.

I would love to see more of this preaching in our churches, rather than a feel-good message that only tickles the ear. Some preachers only care about the seats being filled because the more they are filled, the more money comes in, so they preach nothing but love. We must be reminded of our wrongdoings and what will happen if we do not correct our path.

Day 306—November 2

<u>Prayer:</u> Teach me oh Lord what you want me to learn today. Help me Holy Spirit to unfold today's daily scriptures. Amen!

<u>After reading question:</u> What is God saying to me today?

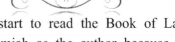

OT}—Today, we start to read the Book of Lamentations. Many believe Jeremiah as the author because he lived in Jerusalem and warned his people about the coming destruction for forty years. The author reflects on the terrible calamity that has fallen on Jerusalem and recognizes that this is the judgment of a righteous God. Knowing that God is merciful, he appeals to God in prayer.

Lamentations is a poetic book on the fall of Jerusalem with the passionate expression of grief and sorrow.

Lamentations 1-2
Psalm 119:120-126
Proverbs 27:13-14
Titus 1

NT}—The Letter of Paul to Titus is the first Pastoral Letter written by Paul around 63-65 AD to Titus at Crete. It looks like it was written in Macedonia after Paul was released from his first imprisonment in Rome. Almost the exact instructions are given here as he gave Timothy about the church leaders. This letter indicates that the church was unorganized and composed of members who needed many admonitions.

Day 307—November 3

Teach me oh Lord what you want me to learn today. Help me Holy Spirit to unfold today's daily scriptures. Amen!

After reading question: What is God saying to me today?

OT}—After the devastation and desolation of Jerusalem, through God's wrath, they turn towards hope in God and ask for mercy.

The Book of Lamentations, like so many of even the saddest of the psalms, does in fact, end with the language of hope and restoration.[38]

Lamentations 3-5

Psalm 119:127-133

Proverbs 27:15-16

Titus 2

NT}—Paul gives Titus what his pastoral responsibilities should be to the church and the congregation.

Unlike I was saying on November 1 about some pastors only tickling the ears, Paul tells Titus to teach wholesome doctrine, to build the character for right living that identifies true Christians. To urge more mature Christians to be temperate, serious, sensible, self-controlled, and sound in the faith, love, steadfastness, and patience of Christ.

Do you think we can be that way? With an open mind to God's Word, we can.

Day 308—November 4

After reading question: What is God saying to me today?

OT}—The Book of Ezekiel is named after the prophet Ezekiel, whose name means *"God is Strong."* The setting of the messages is after the fall of Jerusalem. Ezekiel proclaimed a new message of hope and restoration. This is one of those books that needs to be studied for complete understanding.

Note: As mentioned in Ezekiel, the four faces of the living creatures are symbolic of four portraits of Jesus, as given in the four Gospels.

Ezekiel 1-2

Psalm 119:134-140

Proverbs 27:17-18

Titus 3

NT}—We end this letter with a word for Titus to remind the people to stay righteous.

Before coming to Christ, we were deluded and misled in our thinking. Just as the Israelites were enslaved people in Egypt and Babylon, we were slaves to cravings, pleasures, jealousy, envy, and hating one another in some way. In Paul's teaching, as well as others, he teaches us to be the opposite. Our goal in life; is to not be like the world and our old selves. Are you up for the challenge?

Day 309—November 5

<u>Prayer:</u> Teach me oh Lord what you want me to learn today. Help me Holy Spirit to unfold today's daily scriptures. Amen!

<u>After reading question:</u> What is God saying to me today?

OT}—God tells Ezekiel that he must speak the words he gives him to the people, or their blood will be on his hands. God calls Ezekiel "Son of man" eight times in today's reading and 90 times in the entire book. As generally interpreted by Jesus, "Son of man" denotes mankind generally in contrast to deity or godhead, with particular reference to their weakness and frailty.[39]

God said he would regather the Israelites from the ends of the earth and establish them in their land. Some feel that this was fulfilled on May 14, 1948.

Ezekiel 3-4

Psalm 119:141-147

Proverbs 27:19-20

Philemon 1

NT}—The Letter of Paul to Philemon, written by Paul and co-authored by Timothy, around 60 AD during their two-year imprisonment in his own house in Rome. Also, it is known as one of the four "Prison Letters." It is addressed to Philemon, Apphia, his wife, and Archippus, who appeared to be leaders at a home church. The letter's purpose was to appeal to their hearts for permission to receive Onesimus, an enslaved person, as a brother in Christ.

Day 310—November 6

<u>Prayer:</u> Teach me oh Lord what you want me to learn today. Help me Holy Spirit to unfold today's daily scriptures. Amen!

<u>After reading question:</u> What is God saying to me today?

OT}—God instructs Ezekiel to cut his hair and use it as a sacrifice, and then tells him to prophecy to the mountains of Israel. Mountains here could be referencing problems, issues, concerns, and lacks. Therefore, in Matthew 17:20, we are to say to the mountain, move and be cast into the sea (Jesus).

In reference to verse 10 of chapter 5, we can only assume that these words are referring to a severe famine and drought, where cannibalism will take place, and a terrible work of judgment to those that are left.

Ezekiel 5-6
Psalm 119:148-154
Proverbs 27:21-22
Hebrews 1

NT}—In the Letter to the Hebrews, the author is not mentioned in the book but is traditionally attributed to Paul when he was in Italy because of how well he was known to the recipients. The letter was written sometime in the late 60s AD before the fall of Jerusalem in 70 AD.

Day 311—November 7

<u>Prayer:</u> Teach me oh Lord what you want me to learn today. Help me Holy Spirit to unfold today's daily scriptures. Amen!

<u>After reading question:</u> What is God saying to me today?

OT}—Ezekiel gets the word for the end of Israel. As we read today, we see in chapter 7 that no matter what, there is no return for the land of Israel because of their works and lack of obedience toward God. God removes everything from them with no hope of a "Cancelled note" in place.

I get a solid visual for many people who are asleep in the knowledge of God from verse 6, "The end—after sleeping so long awakes against you. See, it has come!"

Ezekiel 7-8
Psalm 119:155-161
Proverbs 27:23-24
Hebrews 2

NT}—Lifting Jesus as the sole expression of the glory of God, the author expresses that even though the law spoken to Moses was authentic and proved sure, we ought to pay much closer attention to the truths spoken by Jesus.

Jesus became like us so he could become our High Priest, representing us before God and always making atonement for our sins.

Day 312—November 8

Prayer: Teach me oh Lord what you want me to learn today. Help me Holy Spirit to unfold today's daily scriptures. Amen!

After reading question: What is God saying to me today?

OT}—Ezekiel talks about a vision where the Spirit of God cried in his ears and showed things to come. God is angry and reveals it to Ezekiel when Ezekiel asks if God will destroy all who were left.

As noted on November 4, chapter 10 will symbolize four portraits of Jesus.

Ezekiel 9-10

Psalm 119:162-168

Proverbs 27:25-27

Hebrews 3

NT}—We see whomever the author wrote Hebrews was well versed in the Old Testament, who may have been a Jew as well because of the knowledge of Moses and the teachings.

In the previous chapter, we saw Jesus as our heavenly High Priest. Since this is true, it teaches something about who we are. Understanding who we are, compared to who Jesus is and what he did, is essential to a healthy Christian life. It keeps us from the same depths of discouragement the Hebrew Christians faced.

Day 313—November 9

<u>Prayer:</u> Teach me oh Lord what you want me to learn today. Help me Holy Spirit to unfold today's daily scriptures. Amen!

<u>After reading question:</u> What is God saying to me today?

OT}—Then the Spirit brings Ezekiel to the East Gate of the Lord's house to show him some of the men who give wicked counsel to the people.

As you see in verse 4, God tells Ezekiel to prophesy. In a sense, we see that God uses people to get the word out. We cannot remain silent; we must hear what the spirit is saying and speak it out.

Ezekiel 11-12

Psalm 119:169-176

Proverbs 28:1-2

Hebrews 4

NT}—God calls us to enter his rest, much as he did on the seventh day, but not physical rest, a spiritual rest of belief. When we enter God's rest, we experience and get to know God for ourselves. Part of God's rest is learning his Word because it is full of power, making it active, alive, operative, energizing, and effective. Verse 12 says, "It is sharper than any two-edged sword, penetrating to the dividing line of the soul, spirit, and joints and marrow. Down to the deepest parts of nature, exposing and judging our heart's thoughts and purpose." Resting is part of our Christian walk.

Day 314—November 10

<u>Prayer:</u> Teach me oh Lord what you want me to learn today. Help me Holy Spirit to unfold today's daily scriptures. Amen!

<u>After reading question:</u> What is God saying to me today?

OT}—How does someone know if they are wrong on what they prophesy if someone who hears from God does not tell them? Ezekiel is commandant to prophesy to the false prophets who follow their spirit. He shares a word with leaders about their idols.

Ezekiel 13-14
Psalm 120
Proverbs 28:3-4
Hebrews 5

NT}—In the priesthood principles under the law of Moses, we see that pastors, teachers, and priests are chosen to act on behalf of the people relating to the things of God. They are chosen, not self-appointed. They must answer to Jesus, our High Priest, and not become ignorant or go astray.

They are not exempt from learning God's principles. The writer tells them they need to go back to the basics of the Word because they do not know how to feed themselves.

Day 315—November 11

<u>Prayer:</u> Teach me oh Lord what you want me to learn today. Help me Holy Spirit to unfold today's daily scriptures. Amen!

<u>After reading question:</u> What is God saying to me today?

OT}—Ezekiel gets a word to speak to Jerusalem, hoping they will realize their idolatrous abominations are disgusting, detestable, and shamefully vile.

God, Jesus, and Holy Spirit will use vineyard, branches, and trimming of wood as a metaphor for believers to be fruitful, and when there is no fruit, God will destroy the branch. Jesus is the vine, and all his resources will flow to the branch. If the branch refuses to take from the vine, it will wither and die, just like a physical tree branch.

Ezekiel 15-16

Psalm 121

Proverbs 28:5-6

Hebrews 6

NT}—Our goal as Christians is to strive for spiritual maturity, advancing steadily toward completeness and perfection.

Just as an anchor holds a large ship in place, God promises that if we hold fast to his teachings, Jesus will be our anchor to keep us in place with the Father. That anchor cannot slip, and it cannot break down, no matter what.

Day 316—November 12

<u>Prayer:</u> Teach me oh Lord what you want me to learn today. Help me Holy Spirit to unfold today's daily scriptures. Amen!

<u>After reading question:</u> What is God saying to me today?

OT}—God tells Ezekiel to speak in a parable to the house of Israel, like we have seen Jesus do in the New Testament, referring to the kings of that time (around the Babylon exile).

Ezekiel 17-18

Psalm 122

Proverbs 28:7-8

Hebrews 7

NT}—Today, we get a short lesson on the order of a high priest, dating back to Abraham, on the receiving of tithes that most likely affected the reason for a high priest after the order of Melchizedek.

Jesus became the final, unchangeable high priest without taking an oath because God designated Jesus himself. We no longer need a high priest to offer sacrifices to God for our sins; Jesus is that sacrifice.

The seed was already placed in Abraham's loin.

Day 317—November 13

<u>Prayer:</u> Teach me oh Lord what you want me to learn today. Help me Holy Spirit to unfold today's daily scriptures. Amen!

<u>After reading question:</u> What is God saying to me today?

OT}—I love how God will use imagery to express a point. Sometimes when I read, if I can see a picture of what is being said, I better understand the story. Today that is what is happening in chapter 19:

- ➢ Lions—Jerusalem and Judah
- ➢ Her cubs—were the kings
- ➢ Devoured man—were the wars
- ➢ Vine and branches—good works until the kings went bad
- ➢ Fire out of the rod—God's wrath

Ezekiel now speaks to the forest of the South, the Negeb, also known as Negev.

Ezekiel 19-20

Psalm 123

Proverbs 28:9-10

Hebrews 8

NT}—This is our topic for today's reading in the matter of Jesus as the High Priest.

Verse 13, "When God speaks of A new covenant, He makes the first one obsolete. And whatever is becoming obsolete (out of use, annulled) and growing old is ready to disappear."

Day 318—November 14

<u>Prayer:</u> Teach me oh Lord what you want me to learn today. Help me Holy Spirit to unfold today's daily scriptures. Amen!

<u>After reading question:</u> What is God saying to me today?

OT}—Ezekiel then faces towards Jerusalem and prophesies.

Because of their wickedness, God will cut them down.

The sword that is referenced is Babylon. Babylon will take down Jerusalem.

In verse 30 of chapter 22, with no one to stand in the gap for their sins to ask God with a repenting heart for forgiveness, it would lay on the wickedness of the kings.

Ezekiel 21-22
Psalm 124
Proverbs 28:11-12
Hebrews 9

NT}—To better understand chapter 9, if you do not know it now, I suggest researching the Tabernacle to get a visual of the whole layout. Because Jesus became the last sacrifice, we no longer need to follow the Tabernacle rituals. But it is great to know them.

Day 319—November 15

<u>Prayer:</u> Teach me oh Lord what you want me to learn today. Help me Holy Spirit to unfold today's daily scriptures. Amen!

<u>After reading question:</u> What is God saying to me today?

OT}—Here, we see in chapter 23 two symbolic sisters, one representing Israel and the other Judah. This is a powerful description of how Judah followed the sinful nature of Israel.

Ezekiel 23-24
Psalm 125
Proverbs 28:13-14
Hebrews 10

NT}—In verses 11 and 12 of the amplified Bible, there is a great example, before Jesus became the sacrificial lamb, about priests being the only ones that could approach God seeking the atonement of sins.

Today, through Christ being offered a single sacrifice for our sins, we have been given the authority to enter the Holy of Holies for ourselves.

Day 320—November 16

<u>Prayer:</u> Teach me oh Lord what you want me to learn today. Help me Holy Spirit to unfold today's daily scriptures. Amen!

<u>After reading question:</u> What is God saying to me today?

OT}—Ezekiel prophesies against the Ammonites and Tyre.

Ammonite is any member of an Ancient Semitic people whose principal city was Rabbath Ammon in Palestine and who was in discord with the Israelites. In the 13th century BC, they established a kingdom north of Moab.[40]

We learned about Tyre on September 15 if you would like to review it.

Ezekiel 25-26

Psalm 126

Proverbs 28:15-16

Hebrews 11

NT}—*Faith in Action!* Hebrews chapter 11 is known as the faith chapter. Verse one says, "Now faith is the substance of things hoped for, the evidence of things not seen."

Need to build up your faith? Please read the chapter daily until it can withstand the most brutal storms and not crumble.

Day 321—November 17

<u>Prayer:</u> Teach me oh Lord what you want me to learn today. Help me Holy Spirit to unfold today's daily scriptures. Amen!

<u>After reading question:</u> What is God saying to me today?

OT}—Ezekiel continues speaking to Tyre and then Sidon, which is still in Lebanon, because they were acting in the same manner as Tyre.

Because Tyre is mainly an island, it became covered by the sea, and early travelers told of seeing houses, towers, and streets disappear, and probably to date, still under the waters as a lost city.[41]

Ezekiel 27-28
Psalm 127
Proverbs 28:17-18
Hebrews 12

NT}—From the demonstrations of enduring faith in chapter 11, Christians need to run the race of faith by laying aside all distractions, mainly unbelief, and keep their eyes on Jesus, their Savior, for inspiration. Strive to live in peace and lift each other up with the same purpose in mind.

Let Jesus be the ultimate example of inspiration and encouragement to stand back up when the cross becomes too heavy to carry.

Day 322—November 18

<u>Prayer:</u> Teach me oh Lord what you want me to learn today. Help me Holy Spirit to unfold today's daily scriptures. Amen!

<u>After reading question:</u> What is God saying to me today?

OT}—Egypt struggled against its oppressors for a while, but its power was already broken. It has never been for any length of time independent.[42]

Ezekiel prophesies to Pharaoh and all of Egypt.

Ezekiel 29-30

Psalm 128

Proverbs 28:19-20

Hebrews 13

NT}—Today, we end the book of Hebrews with a word about love. Let love be your rudder through your course of life. We are not in this alone, nor are our brothers and sisters in Christ.

Have you ever heard the phrase, "Our doors are always open?" Well, that is a standard we are to live by. We are to extend hospitality to all we meet. Sometimes it may be a room. Other times it may be a meal, maybe even a ride, or just lending an ear. Whatever the need is, we are to be there with open arms and an expression of love.

Day 323—November 19

<u>Prayer:</u> Teach me oh Lord what you want me to learn today. Help me Holy Spirit to unfold today's daily scriptures. Amen!

<u>After reading question:</u> What is God saying to me today?

OT}—Ezekiel continues with Pharaoh, king of Egypt.

Eden has been mentioned several times thus far, so I wanted to share a footnote from my Bible that the traditional site of Eden was within the bounds of the Assyrian Empire. However, this in no sense implies that Assyria was in God's garden, as discussed in Genesis 2:8.[43]

Ezekiel 31-32

Psalm 129

Proverbs 28:21-22

James 1

NT}—The Letter of James, written by James, half-brother of Jesus, was written to the twelve tribes that became scattered among the Gentiles.

James's main concern was about Christians observing the Law. James was at Pentecost and afterward took over the leadership of the Jerusalem church after Peter left Palestine.

Day 324—November 20

<u>Prayer:</u> Teach me oh Lord what you want me to learn today. Help me Holy Spirit to unfold today's daily scriptures. Amen!

<u>After reading question:</u> What is God saying to me today?

OT}—Again, in scripture, we see the sword representing Nebuchadnezzar.

Ezekiel is the watchman to warn them of the judgments of God that will be coming. Ezekiel speaks to the Israelite captives in Babylon, the shepherds of Israel, and all the leaders, who were to protect the people but failed.

Chapter 34, verses 21-31, references the end times.

Ezekiel 33-34
Psalm 130
Proverbs 28:23-24
James 2

NT}—James touches base on how we should act as a church to all who visit, with no partiality, prejudgment, or snobbery.

We are all the same, no matter how we look, or where we come from.

Verses 15 and 17 say what our lives should reflect for the benefit of others.

Day 325—November 21

OT}—Ezekiel prophesies to the mountain range of Seir in Edom and the mountains of Israel.

Edom was prophesied to be made desolate with no hope for restoration, but Israel had the promise to be renewed. The Edomites were the descendants of Esau, and the Israelites were the descendants of Jacob. The ancient family feud is carried through the ages, and Jacob walks away.

Ezekiel 35-36

Psalm 131

Proverbs 28:25-26

James 3

NT}—Today's main topic is not all called to be teachers.

Teachers of every level in the church have a higher calling. Therefore their standard for being a Christian is higher. They need to control their tongue at every level of their life. James uses the metaphor of the tongue being like a rudder of a ship, small, but has the capability to turn the ship in the direction the helmsman determines.

What direction are your teachers steering you?

Day 326—November 22

<u>Prayer:</u> Teach me oh Lord what you want me to learn today. Help me Holy Spirit to unfold today's daily scriptures. Amen!

<u>After reading question:</u> What is God saying to me today?

OT}—Ezekiel talks about when God brought him out in the spirit of the Lord and set him down in the middle of the valley, where he prophesied to the bones.

God uses Ezekiel to speak to dry bones, representing the whole house of Israel, to live again with God's breath and spirit. Then taking two sticks, he writes Judah on one and Joseph on the other, and God joins them as one, representing the return of one nation.

After this, see if you can see Jesus in the rest of chapter 37. Remember, Jesus comes from the line of David.

Ezekiel 37-38
Psalm 132:1-6
Proverbs 28:27-28
James 4

NT}—James speaks about quarrels and arguments within the church. He is telling us to humble ourselves and do right by each other. Yes, they are still there. Why? Because not enough people live by God's principles. If people would just learn to love, we would be just fine.

Day 327—November 23

<u>Prayer:</u> Teach me oh Lord what you want me to learn today. Help me Holy Spirit to unfold today's daily scriptures. Amen!

<u>After reading question:</u> What is God saying to me today?

OT}—Ezekiel prophesies against Gog, ruler of Rosh, Meshech, and Tubal. Gog and Magog are mentioned in Revelation 20:8. We can look at Ezekiel prophesying the end times when Satan gets released from the thousand-year confinement and starts a war.

A cubit is about 18 inches or 44 cm. Handbreadth is about 2.5 to 4 inches or 6.35 to 10.16 cm. A reed measures six cubits.

Ezekiel 39-40

Psalm 132:7-12

Proverbs 29:1-2

James 5

NT}—And one of my favorite scriptures is in verses 13 through 15, "Is any among you sick? Call in the elders of the church so they can anoint them in oil in the name of Jesus and pray with faith that the Lord will restore them, and if they have committed sins, they *will be forgiven!*"

Again, the power of prayer is at hand, but there is something about anointing oil coupled with faith that pushes healing along. The anointing oil is an emblem employed by Jesus and the Old Testament prophets and priests to administer the power of God. The holy and consecrated oil is an instrument by which Holy Spirit is released into another person.[44]

Day 328—November 24

<u>Prayer:</u> Teach me oh Lord what you want me to learn today. Help me Holy Spirit to unfold today's daily scriptures. Amen!

<u>After reading question:</u> What is God saying to me today?

OT}—The vision continues. As I mentioned before, study the Tabernacle to understand this word today.

Because Ezekiel was a priest, he was allowed to go into the Holy Place with the angel. But because he was not a high priest, he was not permitted in the Most Holy Place, so the angel went in alone.

Ezekiel 41-42

Psalm 132:13-18

Proverbs 29:3-4

1 Peter 1

NT}—The First Letter of Peter, written by Apostle Peter to the churches in the northern part of Asia Minor. Very possible that Peter was in Rome when he wrote this letter around 63 AD, shortly before his death.

Apparently, the believers in that area were facing suffering and persecution, and Peter wanted to shed some hope.

Day 329—November 25

Prayer: Teach me oh Lord what you want me to learn today. Help me Holy Spirit to unfold today's daily scriptures. Amen!

After reading question: What is God saying to me today?

OT}—Ezekiel is still sharing his vision about Jerusalem.

Whenever they set up the Tabernacle, the entrance always faced east, so when the walls of Jerusalem and the temple were built, the main entrance was from the East.
Note: The gate for the Garden of Eden was on the East side.

In chapter 44, verse 1, the word "shut" comes to pass. In Christ's time, the Golden Gate was the main path. But by 1542-1543 AD, when Sultan Suleiman the Magnificent rebuilt the wall of Jerusalem, tradition says that the road which once led to this gate had fallen into disuse, and what is now St. Stephen's Gate was the accepted entrance. Therefore, they walled up the Golden Gate and have remained so ever since.[45]

Ezekiel 43-44
Psalm 133
Proverbs 29:5-6
1 Peter 2

NT}—Peter tells them that no matter what wickedness there is, they should not allow it to stump their spiritual growth. They are a chosen race, a royal priesthood that God purchased because they are special.

Day 330—November 26

<u>Prayer:</u> Teach me oh Lord what you want me to learn today. Help me Holy Spirit to unfold today's daily scriptures. Amen!

<u>After reading question:</u> What is God saying to me today?

OT}—Ezekiel is still on the restoration of Israel.

Chapter 45: We start with the land for the priests:

v 1-5—The portion for the priest

v 6—The portion for the whole house

v 7-8—The portion of the prince

v 9-12—A call for justice and fairness

v 13-17—The offering of the prince

v 18-20—Atonement for sins done in ignorance

v 21-25—The Passover offering[46]

Chapter 46: Worship at the temple:

v 1-8—The prince and the offering

v 9-11—Feast days and festivals

v 12—The prince and the east gate

v 13-15—The daily burnt offering, inheritance, and offerings

v 16-18—Inheritance is given to sons and the servants

v 19-20—The place offerings were prepaid

v 21-24—The kitchens of the temple[47]

Ezekiel 45-46

Psalm 134

Proverbs 29:7-8

1 Peter 3

NT}—Then Peter talks to them about marriage.

Day 331—November 27

Prayer: Teach me oh Lord what you want me to learn today. Help me Holy Spirit to unfold today's daily scriptures. Amen!

After reading question: What is God saying to me today?

OT}—We finish the Book of Ezekiel today.

Chapter 47: The River from the temple:

v 1-2—The River source: The temple

v 3-5—The River's increasing depth

v 6-12—The poor of the river

v 13-14—The promise of land and two portions for Joseph

v 15-20—The borders of the land on every side

v 21-23—The command to divide the land[48]

Chapter 48: The division of the land:

v 1-8—Seven northern tribes

v 9-12—The district of the Lord

v 13-14—The area for the Levites

v 15-20—The land apportioned for the city, 1.5 miles square

v 21-22—The portion for the prince

v 23-29—The five southern tribes

v 30-34—The gates of the city

v 35—The name of the city[49]

Ezekiel 47-48

Psalm 135:1-7

Proverbs 29:9-10

1 Peter 4

NT}—Another teaching on how we should treat each other.

Day 332—November 28

OT}—The Book of Daniel, by Daniel, reflects on his experiences and revelation of his dreams and visions dating from about 605-530 BC. Daniel was a devout Jew who prayed and read the scriptures.

Daniel interpreted the king's dream. The interpretations of the dreams and visions point to many events which will only be fulfilled when the everlasting kingdom is established. That is why the Book of Daniel is accepted as a predictive prophecy.

We are starting with events during Nebuchadnezzar's reign, and he is marked as the "Head of gold."

Daniel 1-2
Psalm 135:8-14
Proverbs 29:11-12
1 Peter 5

NT}—Now we end First Peter with Peter warning the church leaders to tend to the flocks (the congregation) needs.

Day 333—November 29

Prayer: Teach me oh Lord what you want me to learn today. Help me Holy Spirit to unfold today's daily scriptures. Amen!

After reading question: What is God saying to me today?

OT}—The king makes an image of himself out of gold as a worshiping idol.

Shadrach, Meshach, and Abednego are thrown into the fiery furnace because they refuse to bow down to the golden image of Nebuchadnezzar. God delivers them and they get promoted.

When we stand firm in our faith, God will be right there in the midst, no matter what the outcome looks like. He is our deliver from all circumstances.

Daniel 3-4
Psalm 135:15-21
Proverbs 29:13-14
2 Peter 1

NT}—The Second Letter of Peter, most likely written in Rome between 65 and 68 AD, right before Peter's death, was addressed to the same readers as the first letter.

The theme of this letter seems to be *knowledge*; the words "Know" and "knowledge" occur more than sixteen times.

Day 334—November 30

<u>Prayer:</u> Teach me oh Lord what you want me to learn today. Help me Holy Spirit to unfold today's daily scriptures. Amen!

<u>After reading question:</u> What is God saying to me today?

OT}—Chapter 5 is the eve of the fall of Babylon, and Daniel is called to interpret another dream, this time for King Belshazzar. In chapter 6, Daniel is put on trial and gets a promotion by the new king of Babylon, King Darius.

Between chapter 4 and chapter 5, King Nebuchadnezzar died. He was replaced with his son, Evil-Merodach, 562-560; then the king's son-in-law, Neriglissar, 560-556; then that king's son, Labashi-Marduk, two months; then the person who murdered him, Nabonidus, 556-539; then his son Belshazzar was appointed coregent by his dad. As mentioned in verse 1, he was only a descendant by marriage, leaving that statement questionable. The cogency is why Belshazzar was called king and exercised kingly authority, even though Nabonidus held the throne.[50]

Daniel 5-6

Psalm 136:1-7

Proverbs 29:15-16

2 Peter 2

NT}—Peter warns of false prophets, and many will turn from the truth because of them. Peter mentioned how God would not accept them because of their wickedness.

Day 335—December 1

Prayer: Teach me oh Lord what you want me to learn today. Help me Holy Spirit to unfold today's daily scriptures. Amen!

After reading question: What is God saying to me today?

OT}—Daniel shared one of his dreams when Belshazzar reigned over Babylon about the four winds and the four beasts, and the one after that dream when he envisioned being in Shushan Persia. I highly suggest that you research these two dreams to get a full explanation of the meaning.

Daniel 7-8
Psalm 136:8-14
Proverbs 29:17-18
2 Peter 3

NT}—Continuing with being deceived, How is it that a person could be fooled so easily? It does not matter if we are in the church or the world; that applies to everyone. Some people, prophet or otherwise, know how to use deceitful words. They promise liberty when they themselves are slaves of depravity and defilement.

Today we end Second Peter with Peter giving them the highlight of his letters and ensuring they guard themselves against the false prophets. Peter mentions being found at peace when Jesus returns. This peace is serene confidence, free from fears, agitating passions, and moral conflicts.[51]

Day 336—December 2

Prayer: Teach me oh Lord what you want me to learn today. Help me Holy Spirit to unfold today's daily scriptures. Amen!

After reading question: What is God saying to me today?

OT}—Today, we read Daniel's prayer and about the seventy weeks found in verse 24. Seventy weeks, 490 years, the prophecy concerns the Jewish people and Jerusalem to finish the transgression, end sin, atone for wickedness, bring in everlasting righteousness, seal up vision and prophecy, and anoint the holiest. This points to the final fulfillment of the second coming of Jesus.[52] The same references to the end times that we read in Revelation 19:11-16 and Zechariah 14:9. Then the great tribulation starts.

Daniel 9-10
Psalm 136:15-20
Proverbs 29:19-20
1 John 1

NT}—The First Letter of John, written by Apostle John, with no set audience. We can only assume by its content that it was addressed to a group of churches, mainly Gentile. The first letter indicates that they were confronted with the error of Gnosticism. In the gospel message, this led to two false theories concerning the person of Christ—Docetism, regarding the human Jesus as a ghost; that is, viewed that Christ only seemed to have a body, and cerinthianism; making Jesus a dual personality at times human and at times divine.

Day 337—December 3

<u>Prayer:</u> Teach me oh Lord what you want me to learn today. Help me Holy Spirit to unfold today's daily scriptures. Amen!

<u>After reading question:</u> What is God saying to me today?

OT}—We end the Book of Daniel today as we finish with the great tribulation vision and return of the Lord.

Are you ready?

Daniel 11-12

Psalm 136:21-26

Proverbs 29:21-22

1 John 2

NT}—Today is a good read to keep our thinking in check. John is trying to get them to see the difference between knowing Christ and saying they do not know him.

He also repeatedly mentions why he is writing and emphasizes fellowship.

I am firm on my belief about Hebrews 10:25, "Not forsaking the assembling of ourselves together...," because it is through fellowship where we grow. Just fellowshipping with God is not enough; we need a human touch sometimes. Proverbs 27:17, "As Iron sharpens iron, so a man sharpens the countenance of his friend."

Day 338—December 4

<u>Prayer:</u> Teach me oh Lord what you want me to learn today. Help me Holy Spirit to unfold today's daily scriptures. Amen!

<u>After reading question:</u> What is God saying to me today?

OT}—God's love for back sliding Israel is the theme of the message of the Book of Hosea. Hosea was a prophet from the Northern Kingdom, Ephraim, and the author. Hebrew meaning for Hosea is "*Salvation.*"

We start with his family life. He was the son of Beeri; his ministry was during the reign of King Jeroboam II and overlapped with Amos.

Hosea 1-2

Psalm 137:1-5

Proverbs 29:23-24

1 John 3

NT}—The destiny of our relationship with God is to enjoy the glory of God. It is an excellent benefit to a Christian to take a good, intense look at the love of God that he placed on us.

If we knowingly sin or practice evildoing, John says we are of the devil; we take his character form. Because the reason Jesus came was manifested, to destroy, loosen, and dissolve the devil's works, we are to decide to abide in sin or God.

Day 339—December 5

<u>Prayer:</u> Teach me oh Lord what you want me to learn today. Help me Holy Spirit to unfold today's daily scriptures. Amen!

<u>After reading question:</u> What is God saying to me today?

OT}—Gomer, Hosea's wife, is an adulteress, and God tells Hosea to love her even as the Lord loves his people.

This infidelity portrays the apostasy of Israel in her covenant relationship with God.

Hosea 3-4

Psalm 137:6-9

Proverbs 29:25-27

1 John 4

NT}—One of the main things taught to me as a new believer in Christ, when I accepted Jesus as my Lord and Savior, was to test all spirits.

John says that today when you hear teaching, it must line up with the Word of God. If something does not sound right, research the scriptures to see if the teaching was right or wrong. If wrong, do not eat the word they spoke and move on.

Remember what you read a few days ago in Second Peter, chapter 2, about the false prophets turning people from their doctrines? What was their destiny?

Day 340—December 6

Prayer: Teach me oh Lord what you want me to learn today. Help me Holy Spirit to unfold today's daily scriptures. Amen!

After reading question: What is God saying to me today?

OT}—A word comes to the house of Israel to repent and return to God.

In verse 11 of chapter 5, Hosea talks about the tribe of Ephraim in its despair. The amplified Bible has *vanities,* and *fifth,* referring to man's evil command. "Vanities" is the rendering of *The Septuagint,* the earliest Greek translation of the Old Testament, and "fifth" is the rendering of *The Dead Sea Scrolls.*

Hosea 5-6
Psalm 138
Proverbs 30:1-3
1 John 5

NT}—John said that if we believe in Jesus, we are born-again children of God. If we love him, we ought to love the other children of God.

He ends this first letter with a command to stay away from false gods (idols), anything that will take first place in our life.

Day 341—December 7

<u>Prayer:</u> Teach me oh Lord what you want me to learn today. Help me Holy Spirit to unfold today's daily scriptures. Amen!

<u>After reading question:</u> What is God saying to me today?

OT}—The problem among the people and leaders of Israel was that they forgot that God saw and remembered their sins. We often intentionally forget that God sees and remembers when we sin. Therefore, it may be a secret before people, but not before God. Today God reveals some truths about what will be revealed when he heals Israel. Let this be an example for us today.

Hosea 7-8

Psalm 139:1-8

Proverbs 30:4-6

2 John

NT}—The Second Letter of John, written by John around the same time as the first letter, is a short letter addressed to the "elect" (chosen) lady (Cyria) and her children. Even though it sounds like it may be a family, scholars lean more toward the meaning of a church leader and the congregation.

John is giving advice and a warning for seducers, deceivers, and false leaders. If someone comes to us, denying the actual doctrine and promoting a false doctrine of Jesus, John says we should give no hospitality or aid to the ones who encourage their incorrect version of Jesus.

Day 342—December 8

<u>Prayer:</u> Teach me oh Lord what you want me to learn today. Help me Holy Spirit to unfold today's daily scriptures. Amen!

<u>After reading question:</u> What is God saying to me today?

OT}—Israel's heart is divided and deceitful because of their material mindset and love for other gods, placing them to be found guilty and suffer punishment. Their exemplary life ends in Israel today. They are exiled in judgment!

Israel did not honor God on their appointed feast days, so God took them away. In their lands of exile, they will not be able to observe the lord's feast. God sends barrenness and bereavement as part of the judgment.

Hosea 9-10

Psalm 139:9-16

Proverbs 30:7-9

3 John

NT}—The Third Letter of John is another short letter written by John at about the same time as the first two. It is addressed to Gaius. Gaius is a popular Roman name, so it is hard to know exactly which one this is. We only know he must have been a leader in the church, and John loved him. John does not directly refer to himself. He only addressed it as the elder. Perhaps for the same reason, he does not directly refer to his readers in 2 John—the threat of persecution may be making direct reference unwise; and, of course, unnecessary.

Day 343—December 9

<u>Prayer:</u> Teach me oh Lord what you want me to learn today. Help me Holy Spirit to unfold today's daily scriptures. Amen!

<u>After reading question:</u> What is God saying to me today?

OT}—Just as we love our little children and chastise them as they get older, never throwing them out with the water, just loving them no matter what they do, is how God illustrates his love for Israel. This is the same love he has for us.

Often God does so much for us that we are unaware that often we attribute some blessing directly from the hand of God to some other source. For some, it is easy to blame God in a tragedy, but unheard of to thank him daily for the unseen blessings that are administered.

Hosea 11-12

Psalm 139:17-24

Proverbs 30:10-12

Jude

NT}—The Letter of Jude, written by Judas (Jude), brother of James and half-brother of Jesus (Matthew 13:55 and Mark 6:3) and was addressed to the Jewish Christians in Palestine. English translators have used the name Jude to avoid connection with Judas Iscariot, the man who betrayed Jesus. Because of the content similarity to the Second Letter of Peter, Jude may have been stimulated by Peter's message and felt to write his own letter to appeal to an apologetic approach to immoral men who pervert God's grace.

Day 344—December 10

<u>Prayer:</u> Teach me oh Lord what you want me to learn today. Help me Holy Spirit to unfold today's daily scriptures. Amen!

<u>After reading question:</u> What is God saying to me today?

OT}—A prophecy for Israel to return to the Lord. The same hope we get in our hearts when our child grows up and departs from the teachings of God.

Hosea 13-14

Psalm 140:1-8

Proverbs 30:13-15

Revelation 1

NT}—The Revelation to John, the last book of the Bible, written by Apostle John, stimulated by visions given to him by God. The Book of Revelation is often known as the Apocalypse of the New Testament.

Some Christians do not read the Book of Revelations because it is complicated to understand, and I agree. But as part of the Bible, we must read it with an open mind and try to understand it as best as we can. First, we ask Holy Spirit for his help, as well as other sources.[53]

Day 345—December 11

<u>Prayer:</u> Teach me oh Lord what you want me to learn today. Help me Holy Spirit to unfold today's daily scriptures. Amen!

<u>After reading question:</u> What is God saying to me today?

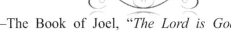

OT}—The Book of Joel, *"The Lord is God,"* is the only knowledge we have of this prophet. He was basing his prophecy on the illustration of the locust plague to use as a warning call.

Joel 1-3

Psalm 140:9-13

Proverbs 30:16-18

Revelation 2

NT}—Christ portrayed to the Seven Churches:

The seven stars are held in the hands of Jesus, indicating that they are essential and under his authority.

➢ The right hand is the sign of strength and control
➢ Messengers of the seven churches most likely mean angels, found as the means in other scriptures, but could be pastors or bishops since they are messengers of God
➢ Seven lampstands are the seven churches

Day 346—December 12

<u>Prayer:</u> Teach me oh Lord what you want me to learn today. Help me Holy Spirit to unfold today's daily scriptures. Amen!

<u>After reading question:</u> What is God saying to me today?

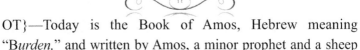

OT}—Today is the Book of Amos, Hebrew meaning "B*urden*," and written by Amos, a minor prophet and a sheep herder by trade.

Like Hosea, he began his ministry during the reign of King Jeroboam II.

The messages of Amos reflect the era of unprecedented economic and political prosperity in the Northern Kingdom of Israel. Not since the days of Solomon had times been so good.

Amos 1-2
Psalm 141:1-5
Proverbs 30:19-21
Revelation 3

NT}—Christ portrayed to the Seven Churches continued:

Sardis was a wealthy ancient city that was falling apart and started to decline.

Seven Spirits and Seven Stars: God has Holy Spirit in himself and Holy Spirit in fullness to give to the church.

Day 347—December 13

Prayer: Teach me oh Lord what you want me to learn today. Help me Holy Spirit to unfold today's daily scriptures. Amen!

After reading question: What is God saying to me today?

OT}—Israel's guilt is brought to light. And a word is spoken to the women of Basham who were not good examples for their husbands. God has always warned the world of coming judgments so that it may not bring them upon itself. In every case, the warnings were startlingly executed.

➢ Noah—was the flood
➢ Abraham and Lot—the destruction of Sodom
➢ Joseph—the seven-year famine
➢ Moses—the plaques on Egypt
➢ Amos—the downfall of Syria, Philistia, Tyre, Edom, Ammon, Moab, Judah, and Israel[54]

Amos 3-4

Psalm 141:6-10

Proverbs 30:22-24

Revelation 4

NT}—Christ as related to the world:

➢ The heavenly throne opens to John
➢ Twenty-four elders—represent the people of God
➢ A sea of glass—could be, washing in the Tabernacle
➢ Four living creatures—from comparison with Ezekiel 1:4-14 and 10:20-22, look like they are cherubim, Angelic Beings

Day 348—December 14

<u>Prayer:</u> Teach me oh Lord what you want me to learn today. Help me Holy Spirit to unfold today's daily scriptures. Amen!

<u>After reading question:</u> What is God saying to me today?

OT}—God expresses his deep grief and sorrow to the house of Israel.

On a positive note: The day is coming when the kingdom of David will be re-established, and God's people will dwell safely, living in the houses they have built and enjoying the fruit of their planted vineyards.

Amos 5-6

Psalm 142

Proverbs 30:25-27

Revelation 5

NT}—The heavenly throne continued:

The Scroll, The Lion, and The Lamb:

The Lord held a scroll on the throne. Written inside and on the back, it says that there is much information. Typically scrolls were only documented on one side.

➢ Seven Seals means it was tied with seven strings, sealed with wax. All seals must be broken first before the scroll can be read

➢ The Lion of the Tribe of Judah is the only one worthy to open the scroll. He is the Root of David, Messiah of Israel and Gentiles

➢ Lamb-is sacrificial love

Day 349—December 15

OT}—Today, in a series of five visions, Amos portrays the imminence of the day of doom, warning his people that they ought to prepare to meet God. For the God-fearing people, however, Amos has a word of hope and assurance.

Amos 7-9

Psalm 143:1-6

Proverbs 30:28-30

Revelation 6

NT}—The Seven Seals:

The first four seals bring four horsemen:

- ➢ White Horse—brings Jesus
- ➢ Flaming Red—brings war and conflict
- ➢ Black Horse—brings scarcity and inequity
- ➢ Pale Horse—brings death
- ➢ Fifth Seal—brings forth the cry of the Martyrs
- ➢ Sixth Seal—brings cosmic disruption

Day 350—December 16

<u>Prayer:</u> Teach me oh Lord what you want me to learn today. Help me Holy Spirit to unfold today's daily scriptures. Amen!

<u>After reading question:</u> What is God saying to me today?

OT}—Today is the Book of Obadiah, *"Servant of the Lord."* The only thing we know about him is what we read today. Obadiah predicts God's judgment in the destruction and extinction of the kingdom of Edom, who was the descendants of Esau. The Edomite invasion in the days of Jehoram, king of Judah, may have been the occasion for Obadiah's prophecy.

Obadiah
Psalm 143:7-12
Proverbs 30:31-33
Revelation 7

NT}—The Seven Seals continued:
After the six seals were opened, four angels were stationed at the earth's four corners, equivalent to the four points of the compass.

Who the 144,000 is controversial? We know they are identified as a group of Jewish believers who minister during the great tribulation and are given a seal of protection throughout that time.

The great multitude will be the gathering in the last days, and all present will worship God.

Day 351—December 17

<u>Prayer:</u> Teach me oh Lord what you want me to learn today. Help me Holy Spirit to unfold today's daily scriptures. Amen!

<u>After reading question:</u> What is God saying to me today?

OT}—The Book of Jonah is a little more known to us because of a story about him in the belly of the whale. He is a minor prophet, and his name means "*Dove.*" Jonah got a word from God to go to Nineveh to speak to the people about their wickedness, but Jonah did not feel the calling, so he tried to flee to Tarshish.

Jonah 1-2

Psalm 144:1-8

Proverbs 31:1-2

Revelation 8

NT}—The seventh seal is opened, and silence falls in heaven. Why? Most likely, it demonstrates an overwhelming silence at the judgments to come. Now that the seals have been opened, the scroll can be opened.

The Seven Trumpets:

➢ Trumpets were used in the Old Testament for war and the assembly of God's people

➢ Golden Censer represents the prayer of the faithful

All things will not be complete until Judgment Day, and when prayers come back to earth with a surge of judgment, verse 5 is powerful.

Day 352—December 18

<u>Prayer:</u> Teach me oh Lord what you want me to learn today. Help me Holy Spirit to unfold today's daily scriptures. Amen!

<u>After reading question:</u> What is God saying to me today?

OT}—After God got Jonah's attention for the second time, Jonah knew he better listen, so he went to Nineveh. But the outcome was not what Jonah expected.

Jonah's mission to Nineveh may be the latter part of King Jeroboam's reign.

Jonah 3-4

Psalm 144:9-15

Proverbs 31:3-4

Revelation 9

NT}—The Seven Trumpets continued:

The first four presented judgment:
 ➢ Fifth Trumpet—brings demonic locusts
 ➢ Sixth Trumpet—an army of destruction to complete the destruction of a third of mankind
 ➢ Star—refers to an angel

Day 353—December 19

<u>Prayer:</u> Teach me oh Lord what you want me to learn today. Help me Holy Spirit to unfold today's daily scriptures. Amen!

<u>After reading question:</u> What is God saying to me today?

OT}—*Mi-ka-yah,* meaning "W*ho is like the Lord,*" Hebrew for Micah.

Micah is a prophet from the Southern Kingdom of Judah during the reigns of Jotham, Ahaz, and Hezekiah. Micah brings a word concerning Samaria and Jerusalem.

Micah witnessed the Assyrian advance as Israel was reduced to an Assyrian province after the fall of Samaria in 722-721 BC, and Judah was repeatedly threatened under successive Assyrian kings.

His ministry was contemporary with the prophet Isaiah.

Micah 1-2

Psalm 145:1-7

Proverbs 31:5-6

Revelation 10

NT}—The Seven Trumpets continued:

Now before we get to the seventh trumpet, we have a pause with a mighty angel. Some believe Jesus is giving the last call before the seventh trumpet blows.

Day 354—December 20

<u>Prayer:</u> Teach me oh Lord what you want me to learn today. Help me Holy Spirit to unfold today's daily scriptures. Amen!

<u>After reading question:</u> What is God saying to me today?

OT}—Micah addresses the leadership, of the house of Israel, on the fate of Israel.

Note: Verse 12 of chapter 3 says Zion will be plowed like a field, which Jeremiah referenced in 26:18.

During the days of King Hezekiah, Micah spoke this prophecy. How, except by divine inspiration could Micah have foretold that this particular part of Jerusalem would be "plowed like a field?" In his book, *the Land and the Book*, Dr. William Thomson wrote about his first-hand knowledge that this had taken place.[55]

Micah 3-4

Psalm 145:8-14

Proverbs 31:7-8

Revelation 11

NT}—The Seven Trumpets continued:

This is where we see the two witnesses, whom some think to be Elijah and Enoch, because they were the only two, outside of Jesus, to be taken to heaven alive.

John is asked to measure the sanctuary of God, the altar, and worshippers. The idea of measuring communicates ownership, protection, and preservation. Then the seventh trumpet sounds in verse 15, and Jesus gets full reign.

Day 355—December 21

<u>Prayer:</u> Teach me oh Lord what you want me to learn today. Help me Holy Spirit to unfold today's daily scriptures. Amen!

<u>After reading question:</u> What is God saying to me today?

OT}—Micah speaks of a promise from God that he will show his mercy to the nations.

God reminds his people of his gracious acts on their behalf, how Balak sought to oppose Israel through pagan divination, sending for Balaam to put a curse on the Israelites, and how God saved Israel by causing Balaam to bless instead of curse. How God later led them across the Jordan River into the promised land, from Shittim to Gilgal.[56]

Micah 5-7

Psalm 145:15-21

Proverbs 31:9-10

Revelation 12

NT}—The Seven Figures:

The Women, The Child, and The Dragon:
- ➤ The Women—represents Israel
- ➤ The Child—represents Jesus
- ➤ The Dragon—represents Satan
- ➤ The angel Michael—the head of angelic beings
- ➤ Her descendants—which represents the Gentiles who come to faith in the tribulation

Day 356—December 22

<u>Prayer:</u> Teach me oh Lord what you want me to learn today. Help me Holy Spirit to unfold today's daily scriptures. Amen!

<u>After reading question:</u> What is God saying to me today?

OT}—The Book of Nahum, meaning *"Consolation"* or *"Comfort,"* is today's prophet. Uncertain about where he is from, he vividly describes the ruthless tyranny of the Assyrians as they victoriously advance and conquer nation after nation.

In his prediction, he graphically portrays the siege and fall of Nineveh, ending that great and mighty kingdom of Assyria.

Nahum 1-3
Psalm 146:1-5
Proverbs 31:11-12
Revelation 13

NT}—The Seven Figures continued:

The Two Beasts:
> Beast out of the sea—represents the antichrist
> Beast out of the earth—represents a false prophet who promotes the antichrist

Day 357—December 23

Prayer: Teach me oh Lord what you want me to learn today. Help me Holy Spirit to unfold today's daily scriptures. Amen!

After reading question: What is God saying to me today?

OT}—The Book of Habakkuk is another minor prophet. Habakkuk may have witnessed the Assyrian empire's decline and fall and the Babylonian Kingdom's rise. The book takes the form of a dialogue between God and the prophet because Habakkuk observes that leaders in Judah are oppressing the poor, so he raises the question of why God allows these wicked people to prosper.

Habakkuk 1-3

Psalm 146:6-10

Proverbs 31:13-14

Revelation 14

NT}—The Seven Figures continued:
Images of God's victory, and the beast's defeat fate of the 144,000; show that they emerge Victorians from the great tribulation.

➢ Angel Flying in Midair—preaches the gospel and announces judgment
➢ Second Angel—announces the fall of Babylon
➢ Third Angel—warns of coming judgment
➢ Fourth and Fifth Angels—are reapers of the harvest
➢ Sixth Angel—is acting in response to the prayers of the saint

Day 358—December 24

<u>Prayer:</u> Teach me oh Lord what you want me to learn today. Help me Holy Spirit to unfold today's daily scriptures. Amen!

<u>After reading question:</u> What is God saying to me today?

OT}—The Book of Zephaniah, "*He whom the Lord has hidden.*" His prophetic ministry is dated to the reign of King Josiah. Zephaniah warns that the day of the Lord will bring judgment on Judah and Jerusalem. It is believed that Zephaniah was referring to the Chaldeans, who accomplished this devotion of Judah in the years 605-586 BC.
Zephaniah calls Judah to repentance.

Zephaniah 1-3
Psalm 147:1-7
Proverbs 31:15-16
Revelation 15

NT}—Seven Angels with Seven Plagues:
These plaques are God's judgment on a disobedient world.
Their song of praise is sung as a perfect union between Law and Love, between the Old Testament and the New Testament.

The Bowls of Wrath:
Recorded as apocalyptic events and they will be the most severe judgments the world has ever seen

These bowls are literal bowls, or vials, containing God's wrath. They are flat and broad and can easily be poured out.

Day 359—December 25

<u>Prayer:</u> Teach me oh Lord what you want me to learn today. Help me Holy Spirit to unfold today's daily scriptures. Amen!

<u>After reading question:</u> What is God saying to me today?

OT}—The Book of Haggai, Hebrew meaning "*Festal,*" was a prophet who encouraged the returned exiles to rebuild the Temple. Haggai assures the people that they would prosper if they prioritized God's work. He points out that God has withdrawn his blessing because they are concerned with building comfortable mansions.

Haggai 1-2

Psalm 147:8-14

Proverbs 31:17-18

Revelation 16

NT}—The bowls are emptied on the earth:
- ➤ First Bowl—foul and loathsome sores: people who take the mark of the beast
- ➤ Second Bowl—sea turned to blood: all sea creatures die
- ➤ Third Bowl—fresh water polluted: putting a push on the destruction of mankind because time is short for Jesus's return
- ➤ Fourth Bowl—the sun scorches men: the failure of men to respond with repentance will lose out
- ➤ Fifth Bowl—a plague of darkness: a review of hell
- ➤ Sixth Bowl—armies gather for a great battle
- ➤ Seventh Bowl—is the final judgments

Day 360—December 26

<u>Prayer:</u> Teach me oh Lord what you want me to learn today. Help me Holy Spirit to unfold today's daily scriptures. Amen!

<u>After reading question:</u> What is God saying to me today?

OT}—The Book of Zechariah, in Hebrew, means *"The Lord has remembered."* It appears that he was a young man when he started his ministry. He begins with a call to obedience to listen to God's directions, maintain a vital relationship with God, or face God's judgment. Zechariah tried to encourage the builders when they started rebuilding the temple.

Zechariah 1-3

Psalm 147:15-20

Proverbs 31:19-20

Revelation 17

NT}—Christ the Victor:

Babylon the great harlot judged:

Babylon is associated with idolatry, blasphemy, and persecution of God's people. It is said that the antichrist will use this area for religious and commercial aspects. Through there, he will influence the earth as never before.

Day 361—December 27

<u>Prayer:</u> Teach me oh Lord what you want me to learn today. Help me Holy Spirit to unfold today's daily scriptures. Amen!

<u>After reading question:</u> What is God saying to me today?

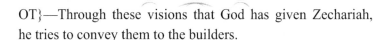

OT}—Through these visions that God has given Zechariah, he tries to convey them to the builders.

The total of these eight visions assures the builders that God has a long-range plan for Israel.

Zechariah 4-6
Psalm 148:1-7
Proverbs 31:21-22
Revelation 18

NT}—Babylon Judged continued:

Announcing the fall of Babylon: Babylon had a prominent commercial appearance, mainly because of its port access.

The problem I have with this is not knowing if this is a literal or symbolic city. If it is to be literal, then the area will need to be rebuilt. I believe the United States is using this area as a Military base.

Day 362—December 28

<u>Prayer:</u> Teach me oh Lord what you want me to learn today. Help me Holy Spirit to unfold today's daily scriptures. Amen!

<u>After reading question:</u> What is God saying to me today?

OT}—Zechariah once more points out that the key to a right relationship with God is obedience. Fasting for the sake of fasting is futile. Legalistic observance of the law could never serve as a substitute for reflecting God's love in daily living.

Zechariah 7-9

Psalm 148:8-14

Proverbs 31:23-24

Revelation 19

NT}—Beast and False Prophet judged:

> ➢ Jesus returns as conquering Lord on a white horse, eyes like a flame of fire, wearing a garment of glory. Jesus returns for a second time, calling all believers to himself with an invite to the Lamb's supper
> ➢ Then seven years of war begins
> ➢ The beast is then seized and thrown into the Lake of Fire, which is hell

Day 363—December 29

OT}—God is not pleased with the shepherds (kings) for how they handled the flock (God's people).

Zechariah prophesies the coming of Jesus.

Here the emphasis is on the long-range development, which portrays the establishment of the final kingdom and the introduction of Jesus coming humbly.

Zechariah 10-12

Psalm 149:1-5

Proverbs 31:25-26

Revelation 20

NT}—Satan, Sin, and Death are finally eliminated:

- ➢ Satan judged and bound for a thousand years
- ➢ Millennial reign—verses 20:4-6
- ➢ Rebellion and judgment—verses 20:7-15
- ➢ Jesus Christ expressed in the eternal kingdom

Day 364—December 30

Prayer: Teach me oh Lord what you want me to learn today. Help me Holy Spirit to unfold today's daily scriptures. Amen!

After reading question: What is God saying to me today?

OT}—All nations are called to worship the king, the Lord of Hosts, Jesus himself.

When the nations gather for battle against Jerusalem, the Israelites will recognize Jesus and emerge in victory. All nations will then come to Jerusalem to worship the king, the Lord of Hosts.

Zechariah 13-14

Psalm 149:6-9

Proverbs 31:27-28

Revelation 21

NT}—New Heaven, New Earth, New Jerusalem:

All Things Made New!

Using the Greek meaning for new, (*Kaine*), which means, "New in character, 'Fresh,'" the New Heaven and New Earth are refreshed, made better.

New Jerusalem descends from heaven sinless, pure, righteous, and holy.

Day 365—December 31

<u>Prayer:</u> Teach me oh Lord what you want me to learn today. Help me Holy Spirit to unfold today's daily scriptures. Amen!

<u>After reading question:</u> What is God saying to me today?

OT}—We end the Old Testament with the Book of Malachi, Hebrew *Malaki*, meaning *"my messenger."* The content of this book suggests that the second half of the fifth century, BC, was the time of Malachi's active ministry. I see three "F's":
- ➢ Chapter 1-Faith
- ➢ Chapter 2-Family
- ➢ Chapter 3-Finances
- ➢ Chapter 4-Salvation

Malachi 1-4

Psalm 150

Proverbs 31:29-31

Revelation 22

NT}—Conclusion: The interior of the New Jerusalem:
1. A River flowing from the throne of God
2. The Tree of Life

This is awesome; Bible begins with a tree of life in Genesis, where man was not allowed to eat, and we end the Bible with a tree of life that we are free to eat. Our future:
- ➢ No more curse (pain), and we never die
- ➢ See God face-to-face
- ➢ No more night; Jesus will be our sunlight 24/7

385 · My Daily Scriptures:

Last words:

I hope this guide was a blessing to you and you have learned some new things about the Word, God, Jesus, Holy Spirit, and yourself. Starting tomorrow, January 1, you will start it over again to increase your knowledge. God calls us to get into his Word every day and to spend time with him no matter what is going on in our lives.

Even though we live in a world of sin and devastation, we place our faith and hope on the end of the story. There is immense value in investing everything into Jesus!

Christ coming was foretold throughout the Old Testament, from Genesis to Malachi. Equally plain and inevitable of fulfillment are the warnings of Jesus and the prophets concerning the future that each day comes nearer to every nation on earth.[57]

Brothers and sisters, I do not consider that I have made it my own yet; but one thing I do: forgetting what lies behind and reaching forward to what lies ahead, I press on toward the goal to win the [heavenly] prize of the upward call of God in Christ Jesus. (Philippians 3:13-14)

Let's end the year with a prayer to God for your life:

I will give You thanks with all my heart;
I sing praises to You before the [pagan] gods.
I will bow down [in worship] toward Your holy temple
And give thanks to Your name for Your lovingkindness and
Your truth;
For You have magnified Your word together with Your name.
Amen! (Psalm 138:1-2)

Thank you for reading
My Daily Scriptures: A Day by Day
Bible Reading Guide.

Gaining exposure as an independent author relies
primarily on word-of-mouth, so if you have the time and
inclination, please consider leaving a short-written
review wherever you can."

It also helps others when considering the book.

Review Links: link.anthonyordille.com/ReviewChannel

Thank you

About the Author

Anthony Ordille was born in Hammonton, New Jersey, to a truck driver, a stay-at-home mom, and three brothers and two sisters. After attending Catholic school, he finished high school at a public school, where he graduated in 1976.

In Mr. Ordille's teen years, he walked away from serving God, became rebellious and hateful, and was on a destructive path doing things he is not proud of. Ordille lived a life filled with alcohol, drugs, lying, cheating, stealing, adulterous acts, rock-n-roll, basically a destructive lifestyle until he was thirty-two years old when he entered a rehab that introduced him to 12-step programs to help him with recovery. At forty-one, he struggled with alcohol again until he surrendered his life to Jesus Christ in the fall of 1998.

In 2013 Ordille published *An Injection of Faith: One Addicts Journey to Deliverance*, which is his testimony about his life.

Today he has been set free from addictive behaviors and wants the world to know that there is freedom when you allow God to take control. During the next couple of years, he was compelled to develop a 12-step program centered on the Bible's truths. In 2016 he released *12 Steps to an Addictive Free Life* and *12 Steps to an Addictive Free Life Workbook*, which is an introduction to the program AFL—Addiction-Free Life. In 2021 he released *My Daily Scriptures: A Day-by-Day Bible Reading Guide* to help Christians read through the Bible within a year. In 2022 he released *Breaking the Chains of Addiction: An Introduction to Addiction-Free Life.* In 2023 released *Overcome Addiction by God's Grace: 12-Steps to Freedom*, a revised title for the AFL program with added chapters.

Upon returning to God, he completed the Associate Degree Program of Christian Studies (ACS) and the Bachelor's Degree Program in Church Ministry (BCh.M). He completed all his certifications to be a License Minister from The Sure Foundation Theological Institute. On March 18, 2013, he was ordained in the Deacon Ministry with Gateway Church, Southlake, Texas. Anthony, father of two, and one adopted son, now resides in Dalzell, South Carolina, with his son, Jarred, and is actively involved at Christ Community Church.

He hopes that through his life experiences, those struggling with addictions will find the truth and follow his lead to a life of hope, peace, and forgiveness.

Other Books by this Author

Please visit your favorite book retailer to discover other books by Anthony Ordille:

-An Injection of Faith: One Addict's Journey to Deliverance
-Breaking the Chains of Addiction: An Introduction to Addiction-Free Life
-Overcome Addiction by God's Grace:12-Steps to Freedom
-Overcome Addiction by God's Grace:12-Steps to Freedom Workbook

Book locations all in one place:
link.anthonyordille.com/authorcentral

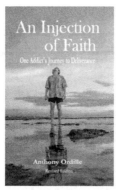
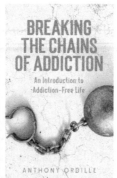
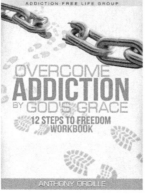

Connect with Anthony Ordille

Send all inquiries through the website at: anthonyordille.com
I appreciate you reading my book! Here are my social media
coordinates:
Friend me on Facebook:
facebook.com/anthonyordille

Like our pages:
facebook.com/aninjectionoffaithrevised
facebook.com/AFL12stepprogram

Follow me on Instagram:
www.instragram.com/anthonyordille_afl

Subscribe to my YouTube channel:
link.anthonyordille.com/youtubechannel

Favorite my Smashwords author page:
link.anthonyordille.com/smashwords

Favorite my Goodreads author page:
link.anthonyordille.com/Goodreads

Subscribe to my blog:
link.anthonyordille.com/Blog

Connect on Linkedin:
link.anthonyordille.com/linkedin

Visit my website:
anthonyordille.com

Join our Newsletter @:
link.anthonyordille.com/NewsletterSignup

[1] Roman Catholic Bible, Retrieved August 2, 2021, Bible.usccb.org/Bible,

[2] Jewish Bible, Retrieved August 2, 2021, www.myjewishlearning.com/article/Bible-101/,

[3] Bible Name, Retrieved August 2, 2021, www.worldhistory.org/Bible/,

[4] Hebrew Bible, Retrieved August 2, 2021, www.myjewishlearning.com/article/hebrew-Bible/,

[5] Deuterocanonical Books, Information from Simple English Wikipedia, the free encyclopedia, Retrieved online June 6, 2021, https://simple.wikipedia.org/wiki/Deuterocanonical_books#,

[6] AD and BC Become CE/BCE, Retrieved June 22, 2021, www.standard.co.uk/hp/front/ad-and-bc-become-ce-bce-6330342.html, By Indira Das-Gupta 12 April 2012,

[7] Priest Garments, Retrieved July 27, 2021, www.Bible-history.com/tabernacle/tab4the_priestly_garments.htm,

[8] Mustard Seed, Retrieved August 3, 2021, www.hunker.com/12310478/what-does-a-mustardplant-look-like,

[9] Definition of Church, Retrieved July 10, 2021, www.gotquestions.org/what-is-the-church.html,

[10] Definition of Tradition, Retrieved June 7, 2021, www.merriam-webster.com/dictionary/tradition,

[11] Jewish Festivals, Retrieved August 3, 2021, www.jewishvirtuallibrary.org/jewish-festivals-in-israel,

[12] Jewish Festivals, Retrieved August 3, 2021, www.jewishvirtuallibrary.org/jewish-festivals-in-israel,

[13] Abib, Retrieved August 3, 2021, www.abarim-publications.com/Meaning/Abib.html,

[14] Joanna, Retrieved July 6, 2021, www.gotquestions.org/Joanna-in-the-Bible.html,

[15] Jewish Festivals, Retrieved August 3, 2021, www.jewishvirtuallibrary.org/jewish-festivals-in-israel,

[16] Jewish Holiday Feast of Lights, Retrieved August 3, 2021, encyclopedia2.thefreedictionary.com/Feast+of+Lights,

[17] Jezebel Spirit, Retrieved July/10/2021,

[18] Stephen, Retrieved July 26, 2021, www.gotquestions.org/life-Stephen.html,

[19] 1 Chronicles 23, Retrieved July/29/2021, enduringword.com/Bible-commentary/1-chronicles-23/,

[20] Eunuch, Retrieved July 26,2021, www.newworldencyclopedia.org/entry/eunuch,

[21] Remark by Yoder, Mark, Lead Pastor, Christ Community Church Sumter, SC, Author of, "Garden to Garden",

[22] Definition of Coregency, Retrieved July 26, 2021, www.yourdictionary.com/coregency,

[23] Remark by Yoder, Mark, Lead Pastor, Christ Community Church Sumter, SC, Author of, "Garden to Garden",

[24] The Amplified Bible footnote page 740, Copyright 1987 by Lockman Foundation,

[25] Remark by Yoder, Mark, Lead Pastor, Christ Community Church Sumter, SC, Author of, "Garden to Garden",

[26] The Amplified Bible footnote page 746, Copyright 1987 by Lockman Foundation,

[27] City of Babylon, Retrieved August 11, 2021, www.history.com/topics/ancient-middle-east/babylonia

[28] Damascus, Retrieved July 26, 2021, www.gotquestions.org/Damascus-in-the-Bible.htm,

[29] The Amplified Bible footnote page 777/843, Copyright 1987 by LockmanFoundation,

[30] Definition of Faith, Retrieved August 2, 2021, www.dictionary.com/browse/faith,

[31] The Amplified Bible footnote page 797, Copyright 1987 by Lockman Foundation,

[32] The Amplified Bible footnote page 798, Copyright 1987 by Lockman Foundation,

[33] The Amplified Bible footnote page 802, Copyright 1987 by Lockman Foundation,

[34] The Amplified Bible footnote page 811, Copyright 1987 by Lockman Foundation,

[35] The Amplified Bible footnote page 823, Copyright 1987 by Lockman Foundation,

[36] Remark by Yoder, Mark, Lead Pastor, Christ Community Church Sumter, SC, Author of, "Garden to Garden",

[37] The Amplified Bible footnote page 898, Copyright 1987 by Lockman Foundation

[38] The Amplified Bible footnote page 909, Copyright 1987 by Lockman Foundation

[39] Hirsh G. Emil, Son of Man, Retrieved July 30, 2021, www.jewishencyclopedia.com/articles/13913-son-of-man,

[40] Commentary on Ammonite, Retrieved July 30, 2021, britannica.com,

[41] The Amplified Bible footnote page 945, Copyright 1987 by Lockman Foundation,

[42] The Amplified Bible footnote page 948, Copyright 1987 by Lockman Foundation, (Charles J. Elliott, A Bible Commentary),

[43] The Amplified Bible footnote page 950, Copyright 1987 by Lockman Foundation,

[44] Anointing Oil, Commentary description from *"The Power of the Anointing Oil"* book, by George Creppy,

[45] The Amplified Bible footnote page 970, Copyright 1987 by Lockman Foundation,

[46] Ezekiel Commentary, Retrieved July 31, 2021, enduringword.com/Bible-commentary/ezekiel-45/,

[47] Ezekiel Commentary, Retrieved July 31, 2021, enduringword.com/Bible-commentary/ezekiel-46/,

[48] Ezekiel Commentary, Retrieved July 31, 2021, enduringword.com/Bible-commentary/ezekiel-47/,

[49] Ezekiel Commentary, Retrieved July 31, 2021, enduringword.com/Bible-commentary/ezekiel-48/,

[50] Nebuchadnezzar's Lineage, Retrieved July 31, 2021, chronologicalbiblestudies.com/clndrdte_Sep6_more.htm,

[51] The Amplified Bible footnote page 1461, Copyright 1987 by Lockman Foundation, Webster's New International Dictionary *"peace"*,

[52] Seventy-Sevens of Daniel 9:24-27, Retrieved Jul 31, 2021, Chronologicalbiblestudies.com,

[53] Revelation Commentary, Retrieved July 1, 2021, enduringword.com/Bible-commentary/revelation-1/,

[54] The Amplified Bible footnote page 1019, Copyright 1987 by Lockman Foundation,

[55] The Amplified Bible footnote page 1034, Copyright 1987 by Lockman Foundation,

[56] The Amplified Bible footnote page 1036, Copyright 1987 by Lockman Foundation,

[57] The Amplified Bible footnote page 1019, Copyright 1987 by Lockman Foundation,

Printed in Great Britain
by Amazon

25573162R00218